How to Write, Illustrate, and Design Children's Books

How to Write, Illustrate, and Design Children's Books

by Frieda Gates

LLOYD-SIMONE PUBLISHING COMPANY

First published 1986 in the United States by
Lloyd-Simone Publishing Company
32 Hillside Avenue, Monsey, New York 10952
Tel. 914-356-7273

Distributed by Library Research Associates, Inc.
Dunderberg Road RD 5, Box 41
Monroe, New York 10950
Tel. 914-783-1144

Library of Congress Catalog Card Number 86-81279
ISBN 0-938249-25-8

Manufactured in U.S.A.

First printing, 1986

Dedicated to
Jeanne Gardner

Contents

Acknowledgments

I would like to thank the many children's book writers and illustrators who provided me with information and advice, and who graciously gave permission to reproduce their work. I am also indebted to the numerous teachers, child psychologists, and librarians who took the time to answer my questions and comment on my ideas; and to my students of many years at the Parsons School of Design and Rockland Community College, who eagerly offered the use of their work and furnished me with direction and inspiration.

I especially want to thank Jeanne Gardner and Nanette Carey for their invaluable assistance, advice, and encouragement; Carol and Murray Tinkelman for their referrals; Barbara Bernstein of Finkelstein Memorial Library and Lois Hink of Margetts Elementary School for their masterly aid in children's literature research; and in memory, Lucille Corcos-Levy, who was my mentor for many years.

I also wish to express my appreciation to the many publishers of children's books who permitted me to reprint illustrations, and particularly to Louise Bates of Putnam Publishing Group and Alix Harper of Walker Publishing Company.

Above all, I would like to thank my husband, David, for his encouragement, guidance, and invaluable assistance.

Introduction

In our culture, we believe that writing is a noble pursuit and that writing for children is supremely noble. This belief, coupled with an awareness of the many excellent children's books produced every year, can be a formidable deterrent to aspiring authors. With such thoughts as "who am I to write a book?," and "nothing less than a masterpiece will do," many books never get started and many never get finished.

The chapters ahead endeavor to overcome such barriers. In addition to serving the needs of professionals who wish to expand their expertise from writing or illustration to the total package, it provides beginners with the inspiration and step-by-step guidance necessary for creative success.

Although great numbers of children's books are produced by highly-trained and experienced writers and illustrators, even more are produced by novices. Young and old, rich and poor, college-educated and self-educated, their only common attributes are productivity, creativity, and an interest in effectively communicating to children.

Creativity cannot be learned from a book or a teacher. Rather, it is an innate faculty that merely needs to be given the opportunity to flourish, which is largely accomplished by believing that your values, judgments, abilities, and ideas are as good as anyone else's. Of course, while you must have a strong belief in yourself in order to be creative and productive, you must also be receptive to advice and criticism. It is important to remember that it is not what *you* think of your project that ultimately matters, it is what others think.

While this book cannot teach creativity, it provides the information and guidance needed to apply it. In addition to thoroughly describing the methods for developing story ideas, it provides complete how-to information for every procedure involved in producing a children's book, including story structure and writing methods, illustration styles and techniques, book design, and mechanical preparation. It also provides complete information on getting your book published, including submissions, contracts, and other publishing industry procedures. It even includes information on how to publish your book yourself.

You will find that producing a book for children is a highly enjoyable and rewarding experience. Besides the satisfaction of providing pleasure, entertainment, and education to children, it offers a wide range of expressive possibilities. Your story can be new and different or it can be old and familiar, and your approach to it can be silly or serious, verbal or visual, playful or pedantic. With so much to choose from and with so many publishers constantly seeking new material, your opportunities for creative expression are virtually unlimited.

The History of Children's Books

BEFORE CHILDREN'S BOOKS
Childhood had to be recognized as a distinct social structure and psychological condition before books would be written expressly for children, and such recognition did not occur until the 16th century. Prior to that time, children were regarded as not having any special needs or interests; they were simply miniature beings who had to learn to act like adults as soon as possible. At the age of seven, in fact, by which time they would have learned to communicate through speech, children were considered to be mature enough to assume adult responsibilities.

Throughout the Middle Ages, literacy remained limited to the clergy and select members of the privileged classes. Even then, formal schooling for children, which was in the hands of the clergy, did not begin until the age of ten or older, and the books they used were not specifically designed for children. Before the introduction of printing, all religious, lesson, and even secular books were hand-lettered by monastic scribes. Being so rare and precious, they had to be strictly utilitarian and instructional. Books for the amusement of children were therefore not only economically impossible, but, as mentioned earlier, the special needs and interests of children had yet to be recognized.

One of two important innovations in medieval lesson books was a text from the 8th century by Aldhelm, Abbot of Malmesbury, who designed lessons set to rhyme as well as in the form of questions and answers, methods which remained in use until the end of the 16th century. The other innovation was an encyclopedia dealing with such topics as natural science, religion, morals, and customs, which was written in the 11th century by Anselm, Archibishop of Canterbury.

BLOCK-PRINTED BOOKS
Various methods of producing books more rapidly were being explored during the early 15th century when woodblock printing, previously used to print patterns on cloth and playing cards, was introduced into the production of books. Block printing made it possible to produce more than one book at a time, but due to the difficulty in cutting small, intricate letters, block-printed books consisted almost entirely of pictures.

A popular block-printed book was *Biblia Pauperum* (Poor Man's Bible), which was made up of a series of pictures describing well-known Bible stories. Labels identified the people pictured, and balloons coming from their mouths enclosed the words they were saying. Usually a short explanation accompanied each picture. These pictures were not unlike our contemporary comic strips or children's picture books. Since so few people knew how to read, block-printed books remained popular well into the 16th century, even after the invention of printing from movable type.

THE INVENTION OF MOVABLE TYPE
Johann Gutenberg's invention of movable type, around 1450, marked the beginning of modern printing, and indirectly resulted in the acknowledgment of childhood. A number of German printers learned the technique and traveled to other countries to set up their presses, and consequently the craft spread rapidly. Woodcuts like those used in block-printed books illustrated many of the early printed books. To save work, a woodcut was frequently used for more than one illustration. For instance, a picture of a city might first appear as Rome, and a few pages later appear again as Paris or some other city mentioned in the text.

The invention of movable type created literate man. The availability of printed matter enabled more people to learn to read, to develop ideas, and to spread knowledge. Whereas previously the child had only to learn to speak to become an adult, he was now required to also learn to read. An intervening stage in human growth between infancy and adulthood, called childhood, was therefore acknowledged. This development did not occur overnight; it required at least 200 years for recognition and another 250 years for complete acceptance.

PRINTING IN ENGLAND
In 1477, William Caxton set up the first printing press in England. During his career as scholar, author, translator, and editor, as well as printer, publisher, and bookseller, Caxton printed almost one hundred works. Among these were Chaucer's *Canterbury Tales,* Malory's *Tales of King Arthur,* and *Aesop's Fables.* Caxton's books were originally intended for adults, but over the centuries many of these classics have periodically been revised and rewritten for children.

The earliest known illustration of a printing press, 1499.

England's high regard for literacy led to the creation of schools and ultimately to the transformation of English society. In 1480, there were 34 schools: by 1660 there were 444. Designed for the preparation of literate adults, schools served to identify childhood as the natural period for learning.

In the mid-1500's, the hornbook was a popular means for school children to learn language, prayers, and some aspects of religious instruction. Not really a book, it was a printed lesson sheet tacked onto a wooden paddle that measured about 2¾ by 5 inches. The lesson sheets were covered with transparent horn (hence the name) and bound along the edges by strips of brass. During the period from approximately 1746 to 1770, the hornbook was replaced by a folded piece of cardboard, called a *battledore,* which was often illustrated with woodcuts.

Orbis Pictus (The World Illustrated) is considered to be the first picture book created expressly for children. It was written in 1637 by a Moravian bishop and educator, John Amos Comenius, and was translated into English in 1658. "I will show you everything, I will name all things to you," Comenius promised his students and readers.

William Caxton's "Easop" (Aesop's Fables), published in 1484.

Hornbook, 16th century (courtesy American Antiquarian Society).

Battledore, 18th century (courtesy American Antiquarian Society).

CHILDREN'S LITERATURE— 16TH AND 17TH CENTURIES

In the early 16th century, by which time childhood had come to be recognized, schoolmasters and parents began to impose stringent discipline on children. The natural inclinations of children were looked upon not only as evil, but also as an impediment to learning. The only legitimate books printed for children were intended either for instruction or for instilling the edifying principles of conduct. It is understandable, then, that the so-called chapbooks which emerged in England around 1641 were frowned upon. These chapbooks were small, crudely-printed paper books consisting of 16 to 64 unbound pages that were sold for a penny or two by street peddlers called chapmen. Poorly written and crudely illustrated, they contained condensed versions of traditional legends, fables, and fairy tales. Among the first of these books were

Illustrations from 17th century chapbooks. (Clockwise from top left) *Tom Thumb; Jack the Giant Killer; Robin Hood; Dick Whittington.*

The New England Primer, c. 1685.

such classics as *Tom Thumb, Jack the Giant Killer, Dick Whittington,* and *Robin Hood.*

The Puritans, who would not allow their children to read chapbooks, brought hornbooks to America. Books for Puritan children dealt with religion and morals, and children were instructed to emulate martyrs who went proudly through life and joyously to death. One such book, published in 1671, was James Janeway's *A Token for Children, being an Exact Account of*

the Conversion, Holy and Exemplary Lives, and Joyful Deaths of Several Young Children. A great work, however, did emerge from Puritan literature, this being John Bunyan's *The Pilgrim's Progress.* Published in 1678 as a book for adults, it has since become a children's classic.

The first book printed in America for children is believed to have been John Cotton's *Spiritual Milk for Boston Babes in either England: Drawn out of the Breasts of both Testaments for their Souls' Nourishment, but may be of like Use to any Children,* published in 1656.

For many generations in colonial America, the dominant book for children was the *New England Primer,* also known as "the little Bible." It was compiled and published by Benjamin Harris sometime between 1685 and 1690.

SECULAR LITERATURE FOR CHILDREN— 17TH AND 18TH CENTURIES

A lighthearted movement came to children's books with the 1697 publication in France of *Contes de ma Mère l'Oye* (Tales of Mother Goose), by Charles Perrault or his son, Pierre (there is some question as to which one). This collection of fairy tales, which Perrault developed from folklore, was translated into English in 1729 and in time became the recommended classic for young children. Some of the best-known fairy tales—"Red Riding Hood," "Puss-in-

Boots," "The Sleeping Beauty," and "Cinderella"—come from Perrault's collection.

John Newbery, an Englishman, is remembered as a man whose love for children led him to publish some of the first books specifically designed for them. His books were meant to delight his young readers rather than instill in

Frontispiece of the first French edition of Perrault's *Fairy Tales* (1697).

A 1729 woodcut for "Red Riding Hood," believed to have been copied from the first edition of Perrault's *Fairy Tales* (1697).

A 1742 engraving for "Red Riding Hood" based upon the 1729 woodcut illustration shown at left.

them a fear of the wrath and vengeance of God. Newbery was influenced by the philosophy of John Locke, whose writings, which included *Some Thoughts Concerning Education* (1693), advocated milder ways of child rearing. *A Little Pretty Pocketbook,* subtitled *Intended for the Instruction and Amusement of Little Master Tommy and Pretty Miss Polly,* was the first of more than forty children's books that Newbery published between 1744 and 1767. Two of his most famous books were *Mother Goose's Melody* or *Sonnets for the Cradle,* based on Perrault, and *The History of Goody Two Shoes,* supposedly written by Oliver Goldsmith. Newbery even launched the first periodical for children, entitled *The Lilliputian Magazine.*

The advent of secular literature for children did not mean that religious teaching ceased to be of prime importance in children's books. It would be more than a century before religion was no longer a strong influence and an integral part of children's literature.

Two children's classics (although written for adults) that managed to emerge from Puritan England are Daniel Defoe's *Robinson Crusoe,* published in 1719, and Jonathan Swift's *Gulliver's Travels,* published in 1726.

For most of the 18th century, writings for American children came from England and were Americanized by American printers: London became Boston Town, and the Lord Mayor became the Governor. Isaiah Thomas, a Massachusetts printer who pirated many of Newbery's books, is credited for making available the first appealing books for American children.

SOME ACCOUNT OF THE AUTHOR TOMMY TRIP, AND OF HIS DOG JOULER.

TOMMY TRIP, the author of the following sheets, is the only son of Mr. William Trip, of Spittle Fields, London. He is but short in stature, and not much bigger than Tom Thumb but a great deal better, for he is a great scholar, and whenever you see him you will always find him with a book in his

I

A page from *A Pretty Book of Pictures for Little Masters and Misses: or, Tommy Trip's History of Beasts and Birds. With a familiar description of each in verse and prose. To which is prefixed The History of Little Tom himself, of his dog Jouler, and of Woglog the Great Giant.* Ninth Edition. London: Printed for J. Newbery, in St. Paul's Churchyard, 1767.

A chapbook illustration for *Robinson Crusoe,* from Daniel Defoe's original edition of three volumes published in 1719. Because the story was so well known, this chapbook version contained only illustrations.

A NEW DIDACTICISM

In 1762, Jean-Jacques Rousseau proclaimed his theory of a new approach to training and educating children through his book, *Emile.* Rousseau's belief in a free and happy childhood effected a revolutionary change in the attitude towards children. It would seem that Rousseau's philosophy would have resulted in a pleasant change from the morbid didacticism of Puritan children's literature, but unfortunately, his followers merely developed a new style of didactic writing. Instead of the terrifying theological didacticism of the Puritans, the new style was intellectual and moralistic didacticism: a lesson had to be learned from everything a child read and did. A classic example is Thomas Day's, *The History of Sandford and Merton,* published in four volumes from 1748 to 1789, which is a moralistic novel dealing with a poor, honest boy's endeavor to reform a rich, spoiled boy.

By the late 18th and early 19th centuries, the writing of children's books had become an approved occupation for English gentlewomen, many of whom were exponents of the new style of didactic writing. In 1788, Mary Wollstonecraft, the mother of Mary Shelley (who was the author of *Frankenstein* and the wife of the poet, Percy Shelley), published what was probably the most repellent piece of English Rousseauism, this being her book, *Original Stories from Real Life, with Conversations calculated to regulate the Affections and form the Mind to Truth and Goodness.* Another didactic author was Mary Edgeworth, whose first volume of short stories, *The Parent's Assistant* (1796), contains her famous story, "The Purple Jar."

Exceptions to this trend were Charles Lamb and his sister, Mary, who deplored the pedantic stories written for children. They published two volumes of *Tales from Shakespeare* in 1807, thus providing children with reading to be enjoyed for its own literary charm. These tales were immediately successful, and are still regarded as among the best retellings of great literature for young people.

THE INDUSTRIAL REVOLUTION—LATE 18TH AND 19TH CENTURIES

The industrial revolution greatly changed the adult and juvenile book industry in the 19th century. As a result of new inventions, it became possible to produce large numbers of books cheaply. The Fourdrinier machine, named after the French inventor who patented it in 1799, could make paper ten times as quickly as the old methods. Frederich König's steam-powered press, invented in 1814 and first used in Germany, increased the speed of printing. Two American inventions, Otto Mergenthaler's Linotype machine (1886), and Tolbert Lanston's Monotype machine (1887), increased the speed of setting type. By 1820, machines had been invented to cloth-bind books, and in 1890 the dust jacket was introduced. In 1796, an Austrian, Aloysius Senefelder, invented the lithographic method of printing, and the first successful color printing using this method was introduced in the 1830s. This invention was particularly important in the printing of picture books for children.

Other forces in the expansion of juvenile publishing were the growth of the population and the development of schools and libraries. Towards the middle of the 19th century, publishers also became aware that children were not all alike; that sex, age, and interests varied. As a result, a wide range of books appeared, including books for boys, books for girls, books for young children, and books for older children.

THE
RENOWNED HISTORY
OF
PRIMROSE PRETTYFACE,
WHO
BY HER SWEETNESS OF TEMPER AND LOVE OF LEARNING
WAS RAISED FROM BEING THE
Daughter of a Poor Cottager
TO
Great Riches
AND
TO THE DIGNITY OF THE
Lady of the Manor.
SET FORTH
FOR THE BENEFIT AND IMITATION OF THOSE PRETTY LITTLE
Boys & Girls
Who by learning their Books and obliging Mankind,
Would to Beauty of Body add Beauty of Mind.

Adorned with Cuts by BEWICK

YORK:
Printed for T. WILSON & R. SPENCE
1804
(Price Sixpence)

This book, typical of 18th century didactic literature, proclaimed that being good would bring a just reward.

Poetry.

Although poetry books for children had been published in the 18th century, such as Isaac Watts's *His Divine and Moral Songs for Children* (1715), and William Blake's epoch-making book, *Songs of Innocence* (1789), the 19th century brought lighthearted verse. William Roscoe's *The Butterfly's Ball,* published in 1807, was a milestone in the shift from moral and didactic literature to sheer nonsense for its own sake. Other early 19th century books which contained such poems were Ann and Jane Taylor's *Original Poems for Infant Minds by Several Young Persons* (1804), which included the poem, "Twinkle, Twinkle, Little Star;" Clement Moore's *A Visit From St. Nicholas* (1822); and Edward Lear's *Book of Nonsense* (1846).

AND the Snail with his horns,
  Peeping out of a shell.
Came fatigued with the distance,
  The length of an ell.

A Mushroom the table,
  And on it was spread,
A water-dock leaf,
  Which their table-cloth made.

The Butterfly's Ball (1807), by William Roscoe.

There was an old person of Cromer,
Who stood on one leg to read Homer;
When he found he grew stiff, he jumped over the cliff,
Which concluded that person of Cromer.

Book of Nonsense (1846), by Edward Lear.

Songs of Innocence (1789), by William Blake.

Der Struwwelpeter or *Slovenly Peter* (1844), by Dr. Heinrich Hoffmann.

Perhaps the most bizarre poetry book of this period was *Der Struwwelpeter* (Slovenly Peter), published in Germany in 1844 by Dr. Heinrich Hoffmann, a physician at a lunatic asylum. Complaining that picture books for young children were "long tales, stupid collections of pictures, moralizing stories…," he wrote and illustrated a book for his three-year-old son which described the dreadful consequences that befell nasty, cruel, and disobedient children, such as the thumb-sucking boy whose thumbs were cut off by the scissor-man (see illustration). Subtitled *Pretty Stories and Funny Pictures for Little Children,* this book was probably the first example of sick humor in children's literature. Because such humor is easily misconstrued, *Slovenly Peter* appealed to parents of all types, stern as well as fun-loving, and thus was very popular. It went into at least 500 German editions and 100 English editions.

Punch and Judy (1828), by George Cruikshank. The engravings were hand-colored.

Jack and Jill went up the hill
To draw a pail of water;

"Jack and Jill," from *Mother Goose's Melodies* (1833).

"The Tame Stag—a Fable," from *The First Book of Poetry* (1825) by W.F. Mylius. Silhouette illustrations cut from black paper were commonly used to illustrate children's books in the 19th century.

Under the Window (1878), by Kate Greenaway.

Picture Books.

The example set by Comenius, who created the first picture book for children in 1637, was not followed for many years. Only in the late 18th century did pictures begin to play an essential role in children's books, and even then they were generally of poor quality. By the middle of the 19th century, however, alphabet books, nursery rhyme books, books of games and riddles, and simple storybooks, all employing large type and many pictures, had become very popular. Crude woodcuts had given way to the finer wood engravings (see Printmaking, page 80), and while black & white illustrations remained predominant throughout the 19th century, color illustrations were being used more and more frequently. The hand coloring of black & white prints was the most common technique, but by mid-century, hand-coloring began to give way to color printing, which was constantly improving in quality and speed of production. The first color-printed children's books of real excellence started to appear in 1865, when Edmund Evans, a highly-skilled English printer, began his collaboration with the three great picture-book artists of the time, Walter Crane, Randolph Caldecott, and Kate Greenaway. Working with Evans, Crane illustrated over thirty nursery-age books between 1867 and 1876. Caldecott's first books illustrated in collaboration with Evans were *The House that Jack Built* and *John Gilpin* (1878), and Greenaway's first book was *Under the Window* (1878).

The House that Jack Built (1878), illustrated by Randolph Caldecott.

Fairy and Folk Tales.

Fairy and folk tales had been kept out of respectable print during the 18th century. The literate of the Tudor and Stuart eras regarded them as peasant crudities; the Puritans objected to them as untrue, frivolous, and of dubious morality; and Rousseau rejected them as useless. By the middle of the 19th century, however, fairy and folk tales had become more generally acceptable, and thus were being published more frequently. Among the popular English-language works were translations of Perrault's tales from French, the Grimm brothers' tales from German, Hans Christian Andersen's tales from Danish, and Peter Christen Asbjörnsen's and Jörgen E. Moe's tales from Norwegian. *Uncle Remus* stories, collected by Joel Chandler Harris from plantation slaves of African origin, appeared in America in the early 1880s. American writers who created their own fairy and folk tales were Washington Irving, who produced *Rip Van Winkle* in 1819; Frank Stockton, who produced *The Castle Bim* in 1881; and L. Frank Baum, who produced *The Wonderful Wizard of Oz* in 1900. In England, Joseph Jacobs compiled English, Celtic, and Indian folk tales between 1890 and 1894, and Andrew Lang, who did extensive research into the origins of fairy tales from various countries, compiled numerous volumes of them, and also wrote some of his own invention.

German Popular Stories by the Brothers Grimm. Translation by Edgar Taylor with illustrations by George Cruikshank, 1823.

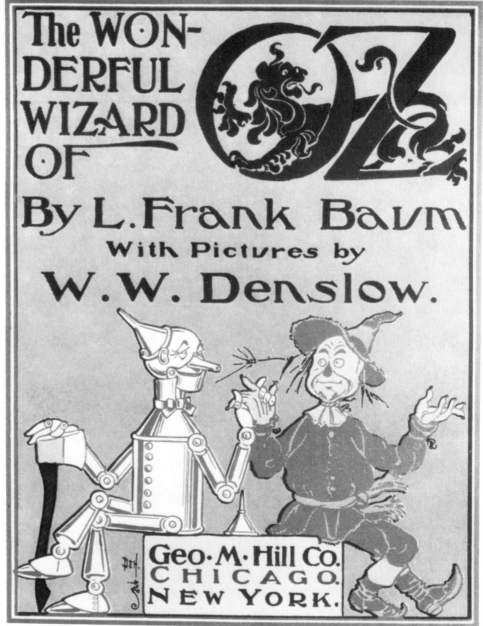

Book cover, 1900.

"Merry's Museum," from *Peter Parley's New Stories* (1842), by Samuel Griswold Goodrich.

THE BEGINNING OF MODERN CHILDREN'S LITERATURE

Despite the continuing controversy regarding the nature and function of children's literature, and despite the abundance of second-rate books, the 19th century was the beginning of the golden age of imaginative writing for children. While didactic literature prevailed throughout the century, the movement away from it began as early as 1839 with the publication, in England, of Catherine Sinclair's *Holiday House.* This book, which portrays children in all their naturalness—naughty as well as nice—is regarded as the forerunner of such later 19th century classics in the modern idiom as Charles Dickens's *A Christmas Carol* (1843), Lewis Carroll's *Alice's Adventures in Wonderland* (1865), Louisa M. Alcott's *Little Women* (1868), Robert Louis Stevenson's *Treasure Island* (1883), Mark Twain's *The Adventures of Huckleberry Finn* (1884), and C. Collodi's *Pinocchio* (1891).

Purposeful and Moral Books.

Since there continued to be some resistance to fairy and folk tales in the 19th century, religious and moral tales were still the prevailing reading material for children.

Samuel Griswold Goodrich, the first American author to write purposeful juvenile literature, claimed to be horrified by such tales as *Little Red Riding Hood* and *Jack the Giant Killer.* Beginning in 1827, he produced and published about 120 pedantically-written books in the fields of science, history, and geography. His *Tales of Peter Parley* series was imitated by many authors in America and England.

The Religious Tract Society, established in England in 1799, was the first of many such organizations to publish inexpensive, religion-based storybooks designed to further the education of children. The American Tract Society enlisted Jacob Abbott, among others, to write books that were "clearly and absolutely of moral and religious character," as well as "American and for American children." Abbott produced 180 volumes between 1834 and 1879, including a "Rollo" series for boys and a "Lucy" series for girls.

Another leading American moralistic author was Martha Farquharson, who wrote under the pseudonym of Martha Finley. Her *Elsie Dinsmore* series, which she began in 1868, totaled 26 volumes.

Alice's Adventures in Wonderland (1865), by Lewis Carroll, with illustrations by Sir John Tenniel.

THE GOLDEN AGE OF THE 20TH CENTURY

Over the past century, the ever-strengthening belief that education and literacy are essential to the well-being of civilization has resulted in important advancements in all aspects of children's book creation, production, and utilization. By 1920, special training courses for children's librarians had been established, and libraries were becoming increasingly involved with facilities and programs specifically designed for children. The first children's book editor was appointed by Macmillan in 1918, and other publishers soon followed suit. Children's book sales flourished with the addition of children's sections in bookstores and department stores. The annual Children's Book Week began in 1919, and in 1922 the American Library Association presented the first John Newbery Medal for the most distinguished contribution to American literature for children. In 1924, the first weekly page devoted to the review of children's books was established in *The New York Herald Tribune*.

Brooklyn's Pratt Institute Library, built in the late 19th century, was the first free public library in Brooklyn and New York (then separate cities), and also the first in the world to provide for a children's room in its original plans. Now serving solely as a college library, it has been designated a landmark by New York City because of its Tiffany-designed interior.

The first Children's Book Week poster, done in 1919 by Jessie Willcox Smith.

Throughout history, most children's books were poorly designed and printed, type was often difficult to read, and covers were of shoddy materials. By 1920, however, much more attention was being paid to design and illustration. Also, technical advances made it possible to produce books of ever-improving quality at ever-increasing speed and volume, making them less and less expensive. During the 1920s and 1930s, new developments in offset lithography made it possible to economically reproduce pictures in both black & white and color, which resulted in a surge of large, handsomely-illustrated picture books.

Paper and labor shortages during the war years of the 1940s curtailed the output of books, but the postwar years have more than made up for this hiatus.

From 1950 to the present, printing technology has been advancing at a mind-boggling pace, and publishing activities seem to be constantly on the increase. In spite of the distraction of television, or perhaps to make up for it, the public is on a book-buying spree that shows no signs of abating.

At no time in the history of publishing have there been such opportunities for writers and illustrators of children's books as there are now. In addition to the benefit of high-quality yet inexpensive printing and binding, there is an even bigger benefit to be derived from a buying public that has a keenly-developed and ever-increasing awareness of the important role that books play in cultivating the ideas, values, and knowledge of children.

Markets, Categories, and Trends

MARKETS

Books. The children's book departments of American publishers have grown steadily since the 1950's, and currently publish more than 3,000 titles annually. These include library, trade, mass-market, and textbook editions.

Library editions are durably-bound hardcover books that may be sold only to libraries or may also be sold to the bookstore trade. School and public libraries account for approximately 80 to 90 percent of library edition sales.

Trade editions include both hardcover and paperback books, and are sold primarily to bookstores, although libraries may also buy them. If the binding isn't sufficiently durable, libraries usually re-bind them.

Mass-market books are produced in hardcover and paperback and are sold at newsstands, drugstores, variety stores, and supermarkets, as well as at bookstores. Because of large printings, they are relatively less expensive than trade books.

Textbooks are designed for classroom use and their sales are usually restricted to schools. While considerable effort is made to make textbooks entertaining, their main function is to teach. Trade book publishers, therefore, are on a constant lookout for curriculum-related books that can be read for pleasure as well as for information. Whether fiction or nonfiction, of course, such trade books must be accurate if they are to be adopted by schools for supplementary reading.

Merchandise Books. Sometimes referred to as "publishing stepchildren" because they are part book and part toy, merchandise books are a unique and increasingly-important mass-market product. They may be made of cloth, cardboard, or plastic; they may contain smells, textures, or movable parts; and they may include buttons, zippers, and bows to help teach a child to dress. Included in this category is a wide assortment of mini-books and odd-shaped books. Merchandise books are more visual then literary, and generally cater to the younger age groups.

The first book of this type was produced in 1965 by Random House as a promotional premium for Maxwell House Coffee, with both companies sharing the production costs. The book was Bennett Cerf's *Pop-up Riddles,* and an optimistic printing of 50,000 copies sold out quickly. By the fall of 1969, Random House had issued eleven new pop-up titles on its own.

The normal first printing of a trade book usually runs between 3,000 and 30,000 copies, whereas the minimum printing of a merchandise book is rarely less than 20,000 and sometimes as high as 250,000 copies. Because of the cost advantages in printing large quantities, publishers can afford to use full-color printing and expensive binding methods and materials, and still sell their products for less than the price of trade editions. To cut costs further, manufacturing is often done in places like Japan, Hong Kong, or Taiwan, where labor is relatively cheap.

Merchandise book publishers tailor their product to reach a well-calculated market. Marketing people determine what appeals to the parents of young children, and make the books available where they shop. Bookstores are of limited importance; it is the supermarkets and the department and discount stores that account for the largest sales. Often it is the price or size of a book, rather than its content, that makes it sell. Also, sales of a book may vary in different parts of the country. A best-seller in the south and midwest might not even be available in New York City. A unique function of merchandise books (as well as general mass-market books) is that they serve an audience whose only exposure to reading may be school texts and comic books.

The writing and illustrating of merchandise books is usually not very lucrative. Authors are often in-house editors working on salary, and freelance writers and illustrators are generally paid a flat rate rather than royalties.

Magazines. Approximately forty juvenile magazines are published in the United States, and their categories and criteria are generally the same as for library, trade, and mass-market books, the major difference being the length of submissions and perhaps a greater emphasis on topical subject matters. Further information on juvenile magazines is provided on page 107.

Two views of a page from *Who Lives Inside?* (1976), a merchandise book that has liftable flaps to reveal the hiding places of various animals. Written by Lynda Graham Barber and illustrated by Ray Barber.

CHILDREN'S BOOK CATEGORIES

Children's books are categorized by age group, literature class, or genre, and subject matter, usually in that order of importance. Age group is the most basic categorization because it relates to the reading ability, comprehension, and interests of the child, and thus determines the genre and subject matter as well as the way it is presented. There are various methods of dividing children into age groups, perhaps the most common being young childhood (ages two to seven), middle childhood (ages seven to eleven), and older childhood (ages eleven and over). Young childhood can be further divided into pre-readers (ages two to four) and beginning readers (ages four to seven).

Books for Young Childhood.

Because pictures play such an important role in books for pre-readers and beginning readers, all books for this age group can be broadly described as picture books. To more accurately define the function of pictures and text, however, publishers divide them into the categories of picture books, easy-to-read picture books, and picture storybooks.

Picture books are the pre-reader's first encounter with art and literature. They include nursery rhyme and Mother Goose books, which the parent reads while the child looks at the pictures, and alphabet, counting, and simple concept books, which introduce the child to the basic sounds, symbols, and meanings of language through pictures that require little or no text.

A young child's interests change rapidly, and identifying objects and repeating words and rhymes are soon outgrown. Having learned to recognize individual letters and words in picture books, the child is eager to begin reading stories. This desire is fulfilled with the easy-to-read picture book and the picture storybook. While both types of books involve simple stories illustrated in such a way that the young child can virtually read the stories from the pictures, their difference is that easy-to-read books are designed for beginning readers to read on their own, whereas picture storybooks usually need to be

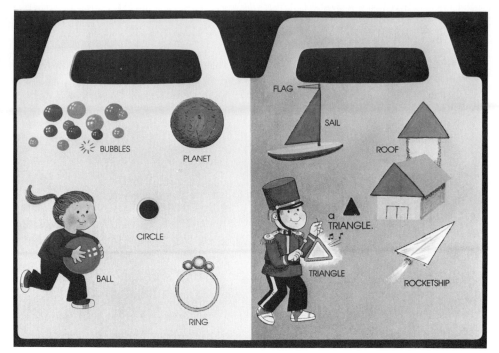

Shapes (1985). A picture book written and illustrated by Tony Tallarico. This is a "board book" (printed on stiff board) that has die-cut geometric shapes and a die-cut handle.

The Walking Coat (1980). A picture storybook written by Pauline Watson and illustrated by Tomie DePaola.

read to the child until a certain level of reading competency has been attained.

Easy-to-read picture books are a comparatively recent innovation, having been introduced in the 1950s. Employing simple plots, controlled vocabulary derived from suggested word lists, large type, and delightful illustrations that graphically describe the text, easy-to-read picture books serve to fill the gap between picture books and picture storybooks. One of the most famous earlier books in this genre is *The Cat in the Hat* by Dr. Seuss. Other excellent examples are the four "Little Bear" books, written by Else Homelund Minarik and illustrated by Maurice Sendak, and the series about a dog named Harry, written by Gene Zion and illustrated by Margaret Bloy Graham.

The picture storybook has a much longer history than easy-to-read books. Perhaps the most famous book in this genre is *The Tale of Peter Rabbit* by Beatrix Potter, who initially wrote and illustrated the story in a letter to a friend's sick child. Published in 1901 and filled with Miss Potter's charming drawings, this story is regarded as a milestone in children's literature, marking the beginning of the modern picture storybook.

Edgar Allen Poe's *The Gold Bug and Other Tales* is an illustrated book for older children. Published in 1953, the illustrations are by Jacob Landau.

"We look brave," said Frog.

"Yes, but are we?"

asked Toad.

43

Frog and Toad (1972). One of a series of easy-to-read picture books written and illustrated by Arnold Lobel.

Books for Middle and Older Childhood.

Whereas reading level is the most important classification factor in books for young children, literature class and subject matter take precedence in books for the middle and older age groups. Pictures continue to play an important role in books for these age groups, but rather than serving as an aid to reading and comprehension, they serve to amplify or further explain the text. This difference in picture function is the distinction between a picture book and an illustrated book.

There *is* one category of books for middle and older age groups, however, that continues to stress reading ability. Called "hi/lo" books (high interest/low reading level), this category was recently introduced to acknowledge the increasing number of poor readers in intermediate and high school grades. Much like easy-to-read picture books, hi/lo books employ short and simple texts, with illustrations (frequently photographs) that serve to carry the reader along.

Genre and Subject Matter.

Because of the reading-level factor, it is impossible to categorize children's books by one strict set of criteria. For example, nursery and Mother Goose rhymes could also be classified as poetry and verse, and counting books could also be classified in the informational book genre under the subject of mathematics. And since they additionally fall into the category of picture books, that too, could be their classification. For this reason, the following categories are based on the dominant characteristics of children's books, which may be reading level, literature class, or subject matter, or any combination of the three. This inexact method of classification may be somewhat confusing, but it does have the advantage of freeing the author from stereotyped thinking and rigid preconceptions during the creative process. The first categories listed describe the various types of picture books, and the later categories describe the literature classes and subject matters that apply, in most cases, to all age groups.

Nursery and Mother Goose Rhymes.
Nursery rhymes have a long tradition, and until the invention of printing were largely transmitted from one generation to another by word of mouth. Since then, they have been published in dozens of compilations, and continue to be a favorite subject for writers and illustrators today.

One of the earliest known nursery rhyme collections in English was *Tommy Thumb's Song Book,* published in 1744 by Mrs. Cooper of Paternoster Row. It contains such familiar rhymes as "Sing a Song of Sixpence," "Baa Baa Black Sheep," and "Hickory Dickory Dock."

The name *Mother Goose* seems to have originated with Perrault's *Contes de ma Mère l'Oye* (Tales of Mother Goose), published in France in 1697. This collection of tales, which may have been written for adults, included such classics as "Little Red Riding Hood," "Cinderella," and "Puss in Boots." Perrault's book was translated into English in 1729, and sometime between 1760 and 1781 the English publishing firm of John Newbery published a compilation of nursery rhymes entitled *Mother Goose's Melody,* which was reprinted in America by Isaiah Thomas around 1785.

It is important to note that Perrault's book contained only tales, whereas

A mid-19th century illustration portraying Mother Goose as a woman.

Newbery's book contained only rhymes. Newbery's influence obviously prevailed, for since his time the name *Mother Goose* has been reserved as a classification for traditional nursery rhymes, while traditional nursery tales are classified as folk tales. Non-traditional rhymes for young children are usually classified as nursery rhymes or as poetry and verse, not as Mother Goose rhymes.

Many Mother Goose verses are non-sensical jingles, while others reveal bits of history, customs, manners, and beliefs. There have been numerous attempts to link specific social and political events as well as specific historical

figures with some verses, but such speculations have never been taken seriously, for they are not a factor in a verse's appeal to children.

There have been many approaches to Mother Goose compilations through the years. Since they all employ the traditional wording of verses, the variations in approach involve the particular selection of verses as well as the content, style, and technique of the illustrations. In some books, the illustrations are literal depictions of the text in regard to period and situation, their uniqueness being the individual style and technique of the illustrator. In other books, the period, situation, style, and/or technique are altered in such a way that new meanings and nuances are introduced. A marvelous Mother Goose book, published in 1882 and still popular, is Randolph Caldecott's *Hey Diddle Diddle.*

Compilations of non-traditional nursery rhymes, which may be newly-created rhymes, variants of Mother Goose rhymes, or rhymes from other cultures, are at least as numerous as Mother Goose books. There is an extremely wide variety of books in this category because both verbal and visual creativity is involved, as is superbly exemplified in Arnold Lobel's *Gregory Griggs and Other Nursery Rhyme People,* published in 1978.

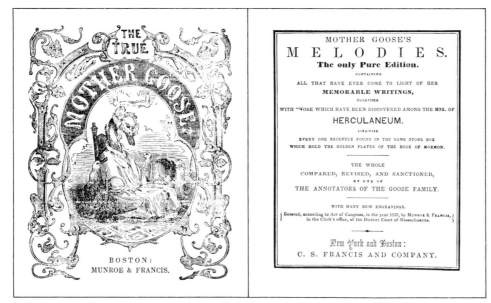

Pages from the Munroe & Francis edition of *Mother Goose's Melodies* (1833). Note that Mother Goose is portrayed as a goose.

This edition of Mother Goose has remained in print since 1916.

ABC Books. Also called *alphabet books* or *picture-alphabet books,* ABC books help young children to learn the alphabet, both verbally and visually, plus helping them to identify objects. Some books, such as the *New England Primer* (c.1685), even provide moral instruction.

The first ABC book printed in England is believed to be *A Method or comfortable beginning for all unlearned, whereby they may be taught to read English, in a very short time with Pleasure,* issued in 1570 by John Hart. Illustrated with small wood cut depictions of objects for each letter, this book set a precedent for teaching the alphabet to young children through the use of pictures.

In addition to their educational value, ABC books are delightful entertainment for children as well as a delightful endeavor for authors, especially writer-illustrators. They have been created in a multitude of themes including comic, animal, object, rhyme, and story-telling alphabets, and in a multitude of styles, techniques, sizes, and shapes. Kate Greenaway's 1886 book, *A Apple Pie,* is probably the most famous ABC book, and Walter Crane (1845-1915) produced a large number of outstanding nursery picture books based on alphabets.

The origin of the famous alphabet-picture story, *The Adventures of A, Apple Pie,* is unknown. It has been illustrated by numerous artists over the last two centuries, and this 1886 version by Kate Greenaway is probably the most famous.

39

"D" is for Rover (1970), is a humourous alphabet teaching book written by Leonore Klein and illustrated by Robert Quackenbush.

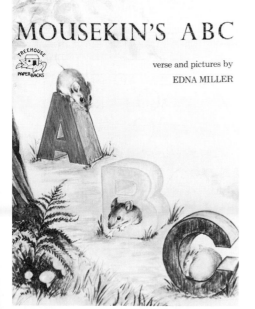

Mousekin learns his ABC's while exploring the woods. Written and illustrated by Edna Miller (1972).

Counting Books. The simplest counting books merely illustrate the basic numbers (figures and spelled-out) with well-known objects of matching quantity, the aim being to help young children recognize numbers, understand their numerical value, and name them in correct sequence. More advanced books involve higher numbers, simple addition and subtraction, and other more complex concepts. While there is a limit to the mathematical concepts that can be employed in counting books for young children, thematic and pictorial possibilities are virtually unlimited. Among the more popular themes are animals, birds, fish, insects, flowers, fruit, toys, transportation vehicles, and musical instruments. Single numbers are also popular themes, such as James Krüss's book, *Three by Three,* in which all pictures and verses relate to the number three. For added interest, some books use rhymes, while others tell a story.

Books that teach counting through pictures are a fairly recent development. There are, however, a number of Mother Goose rhymes in which counting is involved, such as "One, Two, Buckle My Shoe," "One, He Loves; Two, He Loves," and "One to Ten." Books for learning mathematics in an entertaining way began to appear in the early 19th century, a famous example being *Marmaduke Multiply's Merry Method of Making Minor Mathematicians,* which teaches the multiplication table by means of catchy rhymes and engaging woodcuts.

The Rooster Who Set Out to See the World (1972), written and illustrated by Eric Carle, is a counting book dealing with addition and subtraction: as different animals meet they are added, and as they part company they are subtracted. This illustration is from the German edition (1982), which is entitled *Gute Reise, bunter Hahn!*

From Ungskak 7 to Oyaylee 10 (1965), written and illustrated by Lucille Corcos, is a counting book in the American Indian language.

A page from the Munroe and Francis version of *Marmaduke Multiply's Merry Method of Making Minor Mathematicians,* published in Boston in 1841.

Concept Books. Concept books are an even more recent innovation than counting books. They deal with the various dimensions of abstract ideas, such as size, shape, weight, growth, distance, speed, time, love, friendship, and death. Some concepts, such as size, shape, growth, and distance, can largely be described in pictures, whereas concepts such as weight, speed, time, love, friendship, and death require more verbal description in order to be understood. Concepts involving feelings, such as love, friendship, and death, are particularly difficult for young children to understand, and are best explained through a story.

There are two methods of teaching concepts: by analogy, or similarity, and by contrast, or difference. Some books use one or the other method, and some books use both. The concept of roundness, for example, might be described by depicting all round objects that the child is familiar with, or it might be described by comparing round objects with square and triangular objects.

The abstract elements of color and design, as well as book size, shape, and construction, can serve as factors in teaching concepts, especially those that are difficult to explain through literal graphic images alone. Weight, for ex-

ample, can be described by the page-position of objects: the lightest objects at the top and the heaviest objects at the bottom. Similarly, size can be described by using the page size, rather than another graphic image, as a basis for comparison: a small image on a vast expanse of white denotes tinyness, and an image so large that it runs off the four sides of the page denotes hugeness. The same idea can be used to denote loud and soft sounds as well as near and distant objects.

The effectiveness of the above examples can be enhanced with color. Light values and weak colors generally

Nonna (1975), by Jennifer Bartoli, deals with the death of a grandmother. Illustrations are by Joan Drescher.

denote light weights, soft sounds, and distant objects, whereas dark values and intense colors generally denote heavy weights, loud sounds, and near objects. Color is also useful for describing states of mind. Hot red, for example, suggests emotional moods such as love, anger, and excitement, while cool blue suggests unemotional moods such as melancholy, serenity, and contemplation.

Concepts dealing with shape might involve the shape of the book. A square book would help to describe the concept of squareness, and a tall, narrow book would help to describe the concept of width: when held vertically, the book would depict narrow objects, and when held horizontally, it would depict wide objects. Fold-outs, die-cuts, pop-ups, and other unusual book-construction methods are useful for describing concepts that involve sequence, time, growth, and action.

Small as a Raisin Big as the World (1961), written by Carolyn Ramirez and illustrated by Carl Ramirez, uses contrast to demonstrate the concept of size.

Inside: Seeing Beneath the Surface (1975), written and illustrated by Jan Adkins, leads the child from the concept of sight to that of insight.

Folk Literature. Folk literature reflects and preserves the traditional customs and beliefs of simple peoples throughout the world. In nonliterate cultures of the past it was transmitted orally and meant for people of all ages, and this continues to be true in primitive societies today. In cultures with a widespread reading population, however, the primary audience for folk literature is children.

The categories of folk literature are folk tales, fairy tales, and fables, myths, and epics. All distinctive art forms in their own right, they share the common purpose of serving to teach or convey standards of what is right or good.

Folk Tales. The folk tale is usually a short, brisk, action-filled story with clearly-defined characterizations and a simple plot: very good is pitted against very bad, and very good always wins out. Popular themes are the reversal-of-fortune tale, in which a dire situation is overcome; the superhero tale, in which the protagonist displays super-human capabilities; the droll tale, in which human fallibilities and foibles are made fun of; the talking-animal tale, in which animals talk to each other or to humans; and the explanatory tale, in which facts or events are explained either realistically or fantastically.

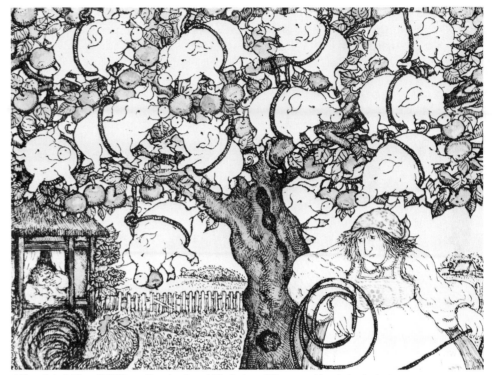

A Treeful of Pigs (1979), written by Arnold Lobel and illustrated by Anita Lobel, is an original story in the folklore tradition.

Little One Inch (1977), by Barbara and Fred Brenner, is an adaptation of a Japanese folk tale.

The Terrible Nung Gwama (1978), a folk tale from southern China, was adapted and illustrated by Ed Young.

"The Five Little Elves" is a 19th century fairy tale from the book, *Sunny Stories*. It was written by Grace C. Floyd and illustrated by T. Noyes Lewis.

Fairy Tales. The fairy tale is like the folk tale in all respects except that it involves supernatural creatures and happenings. In addition to fairies, there are hobgoblins, brownies, elves, witches, wizards, giants and ogres, fairy animals, and magic objects. Belief in such creatures was once common among both children and adults, and even today there are many uneducated (and even some educated) adult individuals and groups that continue to believe in them.

Unlike other forms of folk literature, which are both traditional and of unknown authorship, there are many modern fairy tales that are contemporary in theme and wholly the creation of a known individual.

Fables, Myths, and Epics. Whereas folk and fairy tales are more for enjoyment than for edification and appeal to even the youngest of children, fables, myths, and epics are higher orders of literature which, while eminently entertaining, are primarily intended to instruct. The fable is a simple, brief narrative that teaches a moral lesson, much like a proverb in dramatic form. Most fables involve animals or objects which have human behavioral traits. This is as compared to parables, in which the characters are generally human beings.

Myths are far more complicated than fables and employ highly complex symbolism to attempt to explain natural phenomena; the origins and history of civilization; social and religious customs, beliefs, and meanings; and the hardships and realities of existence. Because of a lack of scientific knowledge in early cultures, the explanations are closely associated with supernatural beings and powers.

The Beasts of Never (1968) describes mythical monsters. It was written by Georgess McHargue and illustrated by Frank Bozzo.

How the Hibernators Came to Bethlehem (1980) is an original Christmas myth written by Norma Farber and illustrated by Barbara Cooney.

Epics are lengthy narratives, often in verse, that have a human hero as protagonist. Heroic in action and scale, written in elevated style, and seemingly authentic historically, the epic embodies the highest ideals and aspirations of a nation and era. The terms *epic, legend,* and *saga* are often used interchangeably, but to be more precise, an epic is long narrative poetry, a legend is long narrative prose, and a saga is a long prose narration of a medieval Icelandic or Norse hero or family, or a modern story of that type.

Star Ka'ats and the Plant People (1979) is a science fiction story written by Andre Norton and Dorothy Madlee. Illustrations are by Jean Jenkins.

Gassire's Lute (1971) is a West African epic translated by Alta Jablow and illustrated by Leo and Diane Dillon.

Fantasy. Since fantasy is an element in all folk literature, as well as in almost all other types of literature for very young children, there would not be much value, from a classification standpoint, to lump all literature employing fantasy into that category. Consequently, the category of fantasy is usually reserved for books for middle and older age groups that involve objects, beings, and/or situations from beyond the world of reality.

Surrealism is generally classified as fantasy, its only difference being that it is more closely related to reality. In its purest form, it presents images that are true-to-life as individual entities, but fantastic in their juxtaposition.

While science fiction may also be classified as fantasy, it has become so popular that it is really a category in itself. Like surrealism, it is usually more closely related to reality than fantasy in general. As its name suggests, it takes the facts and theories of the social and physical sciences into the realm of pure imagination.

Poetry and Verse. As with fantasy, poetry pervades so much of the literature for younger children that it is a subordinate classification factor for books for that age group. Thus, it is usually used as a primary classification only for books for middle and older age groups.

There are three basic forms of poetry in children's literature: lyrical, narrative, and humorous. Lyrical poetry stresses the abstract qualities of the sounds and rhythms of words, and is often set to music. Narrative poetry tells a story in rhythmic verse, and includes epics, romances, ballads, and story poems. Humorous poetry stresses situations that are amusingly possible but not probable, whereas nonsense verse stresses the absurdly impossible. While absurdity in itself is humorous, its chief purpose in nonsense verse is to create delightful abstract sounds and rhythms, much as in lyrical poetry.

The Pirate of New Orleans (1975), a historical story written in verse, describes the part that John Lafitte and his buccaneers played in the New Orleans battle of the War of 1812. It was written by Carl Carmer and illustrated by Marilyn Hirsh.

The Remarkable Ride of Israel Bissell as Related by Molly the Crow (1976) is a humorous historical account of Bissell's ride to spread the news of the American Revolution. Written by Alice Schick and Marjorie N. Allen. Illustrated by Joel Schick.

Historical Stories. There are two categories of historical stories: historical realism and historical fiction. Historical realism denotes a story written more than seventy-five years ago that realistically depicts the life of the times, such as *The Adventures of Tom Sawyer* and *Little Women*. At the time such stories were written they would have been classified as contemporary realism, but the passage of time has given them a historical designation.

Historical fiction is the category for recently-written stories that weave fictional elements into an accurate depiction of a historical period. Their purpose is not to teach the cold facts of history, but rather to provide the reader with a sense of the spirit of a period, and of what it would be like to live in it.

Contemporary Realism. Also called modern fiction, this is an extremely broad and rich category that encompasses every aspect of contemporary life. It includes animal, family life, sports, adventure, mystery, and romantic stories, as well as stories about minority groups and children of other countries. While the primary consideration in realistic stories is entertainment, they frequently provide the reader with guidance. In stories where the reader can identify with the characters, he may gain insight into his own problems and aspirations; and in stories about other peoples and cultures, he may gain an understanding and respect for attitudes, beliefs, and ways of life that differ from his own.

Bug Scanner and the Computer Mystery (1983) is a contemporary mystery story written by Walter Oleksy and illustrated by Anthony Accardo.

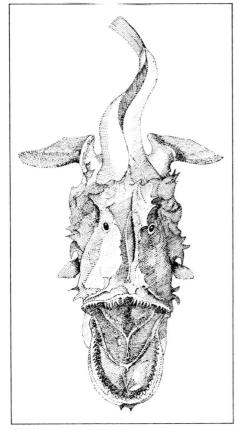

Nature's Light: The Story of Bioluminescence (1974) is a science book written by Francine Jacobs and illustrated by Pamela Carroll.

Informational Literature (Nonfiction).

The major subject divisions in this category are science, mathematics, social studies, history, biography, art, games and hobbies, crafts and how-to, language skills, and reference books. While factual accuracy and clarity of presentation are the most important criteria for all informational books, trade books designed to supplement texts and other curricular materials may have as much entertainment value as they have instructional value.

Suitability for specific age groups is also an important criterion. Books for the very young, such as concept books, must use vocabulary that the child is familiar with, whereas books for older age groups are more appreciated if they challenge the child with some new terminology that expands his vocabulary and understanding.

Informational literature is described in greater detail in the chapter on *Writing,* page 38.

The Big Dipper (1962), from the science book series, "Let's Read and Find Out," was written by Franklyn M. Branley and illustrated by Ed Emberley.

Armor (1963), a historical description of the making and wearing of armor, was written and illustrated by Sean Morrison.

TRENDS

Editors, teachers, librarians, and parents used to believe that children's books should reflect only the niceties of life. Over the past thirty years, however, this belief has largely been discarded. Although many traditional standards still endure, today's books are expected to realistically depict all aspects of our rapidly-changing, often unfair, and sometimes cruel world.

American publishers have developed a sensitivity to the diversity of children in our country. Such diversity is not new, but only recently has it begun to be acknowledged in children's literature. In place of the stereotyped images that were projected for so many years, children can now find their unique counterparts regarding intelligence, abilities, aptitudes, ethnic backgrounds, and environments.

An ongoing effort is being made to give minorities their share of heroes. In the 1960s, the paucity of books featuring Black children induced editors to start to fill that void. Beginning in the 1970s, other ethnic groups pressed for recognition: Spanish-speaking Americans urging that their stories be published in dual-language; Asian-Americans seeking mainstream recognition; and Native Americans desirous of preserving their customs and beliefs.

The women's movement has made us aware of the rigid role models in traditional children's books. This awareness has not only resulted in a move away from sexual stereotyping, it has engendered other changes in social attitudes, such as the recognition of the elderly and the handicapped.

Newsworthy current events, newly-prominent personalities, and other topical subjects of popular interest are all acceptable themes for current juvenile books, providing that the treatment is in good taste and at a level of understanding that is appropriate for the intended age group. When a subject comes into vogue, a flurry of books on or related to

Do I mind not having a real hand on my left arm? Yes, I do. Having a hook is a pain in the neck. My mother has to help me with it every morning. The straps and buckles have to be fastened just right or the hook won't work.

Captain Hook, That's Me (1982), a story about being handicapped, was written by Ada B. Litchfield and illustrated by Sonia O. Lisker.

I am Freedom's Child (1970), which concerns people living in harmony, was written by Bill Martin, Jr., illustrated by Symeon Shimin, and hand-lettered by Ray Barber.

that subject will appear almost simultaneously. For example, when the King Tut exhibition came to the United States, so many King Tut books surfaced for both adults and children that the situation was referred to as "Tut glut." Similarly, the recent spread of computers into all areas of life has made them a popular subject matter for children's books, fictional as well as nonfictional.

Trends swing back and forth. In the 1970s, editors were looking for realistic stories about children solving their personal problems, and containing the message that life is a struggle for everyone. Fantasy, almost ignored in the 1970s, was brought back in the 1980s by the success of Kit Williams's *Masquerade,* and the book, *E.T.,* which was made from the motion picture.

Sports books continue to be popular, and humorous books are always in demand. For years, poetry books were not especially sought after, but a recent revival of interest in poetry, both in and out of schools, has created a demand for them in all age groups. Informational books almost outnumber all other types of books put together. Social studies, science, and biographies designed for specific reading and comprehension levels serve to supplement the increasing complexity of school curriculums. The how-to books that are most popular nowadays are those that have a storyline or provide background information regarding the origin and history of the subject.

The recognition that children are not reading as much or as well as they did in pre-television times has created a heightened interest in picture books

and easy-to-read picture books as a means of luring young children into the world of literature. Books in series are also being increasingly sought by publishers, especially for the seven to eleven age group. Children in that age group are interested in stories that broaden their horizons, and are able to handle lengthy and/or complex subject matter if it is presented in easily-assimilated segments. If the first book in a series becomes popular, sales of subsequent titles are usually guaranteed.

To keep abreast of current trends, it is wise to study books published within the last three or four years, particularly those by new authors; they often reflect the most current interests of editors. However, although it may be profitable to write a book that is "in," it is risky to pick a subject just because it is currently popular. While some trends represent important new directions in publishing, others are mere fads that will have disappeared by the time your manuscript is ready to submit.

Jumping onto the bandwagon requires more speed and agility than it does creativity. Thus, while current trends may influence you, it is ultimately more important to follow your own dictates and write what appeals to you personally. Your book may not be trendy today, but if it is truly creative it may be the trend of tomorrow.

I, Tut (1979), a historical story about King Tutankhamen and his reign, was written by Miriam Schlein and illustrated by Erik Hilgerdt.

Creativity Resources

In her book, *Writing Books for Children,* Jane Yolen says that "Your mind is a scrap heap," and that "Everything you have ever seen, heard, read, felt is stored away in bits and pieces there." When these bits and pieces suddenly float up to the surface, Ms. Yolen explains, it is called *inspiration.* But while this is a good description of inspiration, the beginner should not take it to mean that creativity involves nothing more than waiting for the Muse to strike. In order to express your innate creativity in a particular endeavor, you must acquire a good knowledge of that endeavor, and you must also develop methods of organizing and storing new "bits and pieces" of information that have creative potential.

Following are the practices that writers and illustrators employ as an aid to achieving their creative goals. These practices might pertain to a specific book, but they also serve as a general source of ideas for future books. For this reason, professionals regard them as an important and ongoing aspect of their career activities.

LITERATURE RESEARCH

An idea is two or more previously-unrelated elements that your mind joins together to form a new and meaningful entity. You don't invent the elements; rather, you invent their unique juxtaposition. Sometimes the elements are contained in your mind, and an external influence suggests their juxtaposition. Equally often, one or more of the elements are externally derived, and your mind suggests their juxtaposition.

In either case, your mind needs external data and stimulation in order to create new ideas, and one of the most important sources for a children's book creator is existent children's literature. Read as many diverse books as possible, as well as reviews and descriptions of children's books in publishing journals and catalogues. *The Horn Book,*

School Library Journal, Publishers Weekly, Booklist, Kirkus Reviews, and the *Bulletin of the Center for Children's Books* contain current book reviews, and are available at most libraries. Publishers' catalogues are free, and are obtainable by writing directly to them. Their addresses can be found in *Writer's Market* and *Literary Market Place.* If you wish to research extant literature on a particular subject for the purpose of developing new ideas, refer to the annual *Subject Guide to Children's Books in Print.* Available at most libraries, it lists over 40,000 books indexed under some 7,100 subject headings. It is so minutely categorized that you can find, for example, all books in which mice are featured.

The Lion and the Unicorn is an international critical journal that explores one genre or one other aspect of children's literature in each yearly or biyearly issue. Articles include book reviews, critical pieces, and interviews. If your library doesn't have them, current and back issues may be obtained for a small fee from: The Lion and the Unicorn, Department of English, Brooklyn College, Brooklyn, N.Y. 11210.

The Children's Book Council, 67 Irving Place, New York, N.Y. 10003, offers a variety of information, including a list of their publisher-members with the names of current editors, and a members' program list which describes the types and numbers of books that each publisher issues annually. Send a stamped, self-addressed envelope with your request.

Following are other sources of information that may have inspirational as well as informational value:

Books and Magazines on Writing. There are dozens of books on writing, and many of them are specifically for children's literature. Monthly magazines that are especially helpful for beginning authors are *The Writer* and *Writer's Digest.* Even publications that are primarily for adult literature contain suggestions that can be adapted to children's literature.

Books on Child Development. Behavioral traits and abilities of the various age groups may suggest unique ways of structuring and presenting stories and information.

Recommended Word Lists. Word lists for vocabulary guidance for different reading levels are available from some publishers, and can also be obtained from school and public libraries. While meant as a practical aid in writing, they may suggest story and presentation ideas.

Children's Librarians. Become acquainted with children's librarians at your local school and public library. In addition to helping with your research, they know what kinds of books children are most interested in. Ask their opinions of your ideas and plans, and whether a book such as you propose would be a desirable acquisition.

Children. Make a point of talking to children whenever possible. Find out what their personal interests are, what appeals to them in literature, and what they think of your ideas. If your book is for the younger age group, it is also important to solicit the opinions of parents of young children, for they are the ones who choose the child's reading matter.

IDEA FILE

Save anything and everything that has even the remotest possibility of serving as a source of inspiration, such as photographs, illustrations, magazine articles, newspaper stories, and even advertisements. A news item about a newly-prominent person may suggest a biography; a new development in science may suggest an informational book, a science fiction story, or even a fairy tale; and a human interest item may suggest a story in the contemporary realism category. Any ideas that occur to you should be immediately jotted down and filed along with the item.

JOURNAL

A large looseleaf binder makes a good journal for jotting down ideas, incidents, conversations, memories, etc. You don't have to write in it daily, but you should record your thoughts while they are still fresh in your mind. Descriptions of places, events, and characters not only serve as possible story ideas, they also serve to improve your writing ability. A small notebook is useful for recording ideas and impressions when you are away from home.

SKETCHBOOK

Illustrators and writer-illustrators should keep a sketchbook for recording visual ideas and impressions. Not only is it an excellent source of inspiration and information, but it is an ideal way to develop drawing ability and style. Sketch anything and everything; outdoors, indoors, anywhere, and any time. Even mindless doodling can inspire a story.

PICTURE REFERENCE FILE

If you are an illustrator or writer-illustrator, make a habit of saving all printed pictorial material that might have value for future reference. If the material is in book, booklet, or magazine form it can be stored in a bookcase, but if it is in single-sheet form you must categorize and file it in folders. In the beginning you might make do with only a few broad categories, such as humans, animals, birds, dwellings, vehicles, and landscapes. When the material in a category becomes excessive it can be further divided. Humans, for example, can be divided into babies, young children, teenagers, adults, and old people.

In addition to saving materials that have value as drawing aids, it is also helpful to save the work of other illustrators. If the work is in a book that you don't own, make a xerographic copy of it.

The ideal cabinet for a picture reference file is a legal-size office file. The legal size is desirable because many printed pieces are wider than 11 inches, and folding would make them difficult to thumb through.

EDUCATIONAL COURSES

Writing and art courses are offered in most continuing education programs at colleges and high schools, and some programs offer courses in children's book writing and/or illustration. Even if you are fully proficient in all aspects of your publishing endeavor, such courses may provide you with inspiration, guidance, and discipline.

WRITERS' ORGANIZATIONS

Although being a published writer is sometimes a requirement for membership, many writers' organizations offer information and services to help beginning writers. Group-sponsored meetings, conferences, workshops, and newsletters can provide both practical and inspirational assistance. An associate membership in the Society of Children's Book Writers, P.O. Box 296, Mar Vista Station, Los Angeles, CA 90066, is open to anyone with an interest in children's literature, whether or not he or she has been published. Other groups are listed in the *Directory of Writing Organizations.* Containing the names and addresses of over 400 writing organizations in the United States and Canada, it is published by North Louisiana Publishing Company, P.O. Box 37649, Shreveport, LA 71133. *Literary Market Place* also contains such a listing.

ASPIRATIONS AND GOALS

Your primary reason for wanting to write and/or illustrate a children's book is probably to satisfy your own creative ambitions and abilities, but to be successful at it you must not permit your ego gratification to take precedence over your reader's gratification. There are numerous examples of children's books that were failures for this reason, especially in regard to illustration. Conceived as personal showcases for talent, they failed to attract the interest of children.

An excellent and still-appropriate list of reader-oriented goals for writers and illustrators of children's books was set forth in the very first issue of *St. Nicholas Magazine for Children* in 1873 by Mary Mapes Dodge, author of *Hans Brinker* or *The Silver Skates,* and the magazine's first editor. Following is her credo:

(1) To give clean, genuine fun to children of all ages. (2) To give them examples of the finest types of boyhood and girlhood. (3) To inspire them with an appreciation of pictorial art. (4) To cultivate the imagination in profitable directions. (5) To foster a love of country, home, nature, truth, beauty, and sincerity. (6) To prepare boys and girls for life as it is. (7) To stimulate their ambitions —but along normally progressive lines. (8) To keep pace with a fast-moving world in all its activities. (9) To give reading matter which every parent may pass to his children unhesitatingly.

DEVELOPING OBJECTIVE JUDGMENT

In Zen, it is said that you have achieved *sartori,* or enlightenment, when you can observe yourself walking along a road. Such an achievement, which suggests utter objectivity, is also the ultimate goal in creative endeavors, for it permits the creator to judge his own work in the same way that an observer would.

The best way to develop objective judgment is in classroom critiques, where you evaluate the work of your classmates, and they evaluate your work. In evaluating the work of others you learn the skill of critical analysis, and you also learn that your judgment of a piece generally coincides with that of everyone except the person who created it. This knowledge not only makes you more receptive to the criticism of others, but it encourages you to learn to avoid personal bias when evaluating your own work.

Another aid in developing objective judgment is to evaluate a number of children's books, applying the same criteria employed by teachers and librarians. The NW/SW/SC/NE/SE Branch Library Media Examination Center distributes a *Media Evaluation Form* for the use of reviewers. The evaluation form shown here includes much of the same assessment criteria.

BOOK EVALUATION

TITLE _____

AUTHOR _____ ILLUSTRATOR_____

PUBLISHER_____

Circle one number in each category. 1–very poor; 2–poor; 3–good or average; 4–above average; 5–high, excellent, outstanding.

		LOW				HIGH
1.	Objectivity (free from bias, misleading emphasis, and sex, race, ethnic and religious stereotypes)	1	2	3	4	5
2.	Accuracy	1	2	3	4	5
3.	Up-to-date	1	2	3	4	5
4.	Appropriateness of vocabulary, concepts, and treatment for levels suggested	1	2	3	4	5
5.	Scope (does it cover the subject well? Is too much material covered? Not enough?)	1	2	3	4	5
6.	User interest (motivating, attention-getting, attention-keeping for intended audience?)	1	2	3	4	5
7.	Organization	1	2	3	4	5
8.	Writing quality	1	2	3	4	5
9.	Illustration quality	1	2	3	4	5
10.	Layout design quality	1	2	3	4	5
11.	Explanatory materials and directions (clear? adequate?)	1	2	3	4	5
12.	Physical features (binding, paper, size, durability, ease of use)	1	2	3	4	5
13.	Overall estimate	1	2	3	4	5

COMMENTS:

CREATIVE PARTNERSHIPS

It is very difficult to share creativity. There are numerous cases where two people were successful in producing a book together, but there are many more where they were not. I have seen many students try to work in collaboration, either both writing, or one writing and the other illustrating, and I have worked in the same situations myself. I have illustrated another person's writing, and I have shared in the writing. It has never been easy.

Joint writing ventures are especially difficult, but even writing-illustration partnerships can create problems. The writer usually has a mental picture of how the illustrations should look, and what the illustrator ultimately produces is often entirely different from what the writer had in mind. This can lead to disappointment and occasionally to unpleasantness. There are also problems of arranging schedules to work together, sharing costs (paper, art supplies, mailing fees, etc.), and how much each person has contributed in time and effort. Before embarking on collaborations, therefore, it is important to agree on working arrangements and responsibilities, and to put the agreement in writing. Try not to let a potentially rewarding venture damage a friendship.

It is true, of course, that children's books are frequently illustrated by someone other than the writer, but such arrangements are carefully controlled by the publisher. The writer may have a certain input regarding illustrations, and the illustrator may have a certain amount of artistic and interpretive freedom, but it is the editor who has the first and last word in all decisions.

Writing

IDEAS

A great amount of research has been done on the human brain in recent years, and perhaps the most useful information to emerge is a better understanding of the functions of the brain's two hemispheres. Scientists have determined that the left hemisphere, among other functions, controls verbal communication and logical thought, and operates in a step-by-step, sequential, or linear, fashion. The right hemisphere, conversely, controls visuo-spatial understanding as well as creative thought, and operates in a random, or non-linear, fashion.

Having learned that the right brain is the seat of creativity, many creative hopefuls have deduced that the left brain should not be permitted to play a part in their creative endeavors because it will stifle creativity. This is an erroneous deduction. While the left brain is not in itself creative, it provides the right brain with much of the data necessary for creativity.

An ideal method for including your left brain in creative endeavors is to list all the related factors of a subject in a column on the left side of a sheet of paper. Some of this data may already reside in your left brain, and you can find additional data in a dictionary, word thesaurus, encyclopedia and other research sources. This column of information represents all the similar, or analogous, factors of a subject that are probably known by most people. For example, under the subject *lion* you might list *animal, large, cat, tan or brown, shaggy mane, tufted tail, sharp teeth, sharp claws, carnivorous, Africa, southern Asia, zoo, courageous, cruel, ravenous, social lion, lionheart (brave and magnanimous), king of beasts, roars, leaps,* etc.

After you have made a substantial list of analogous factors in the left column, then list their opposites in the right column, such as *small* next to *large, cowardly* next to *courageous, herbivorous* next to *carnivorous, squeeks* next to *roars,* and *kind* next to *cruel.* If an opposite feature doesn't come to mind, just write "not" before the analogous word, such as *not animal* next to *animal, not Africa* next to *Africa,* and *not*

ravenous next to *ravenous.* While your left brain and external research sources provide much of the right-column data, you will find that your right brain soon comes into play. For example, if the lion is not ravenous, perhaps it is on a diet or anorexic; perhaps it is a vegetarian and just not ravenous for meat; or perhaps it is too small (like a mouse?) to qualify as rapacious.

The more extensive your left-brain list of analogous and opposite factors, the easier it is for your right brain to create new permutations. Once your right brain becomes active, you will find that it is no longer hindered by the logic of the left brain, and "far out" thoughts

come easily to mind, either while you are compiling your list, or at some later time when a mindless task permits your right brain to wander freely.

This method of developing ideas is similar to "free association" and "brainstorming," the major difference being that it makes use of the left brain as a tool for gathering and organizing data in a way that is conducive to creative thought. Brainstorming is a creative technique that originated in advertising agencies, and involves a group of people freely expressing their random thoughts and ideas on a subject. Each person's "brainstorm," however frivolous it may be, serves to lead the group

---

LION

animal	not animal
large	small
cat	not cat
tan or brown	not tan or brown
shaggy mane	bald
tufted tail	untufted tail
sharp teeth	toothless
sharp claws	chewed nails
carnivorous	herbivorous
Africa	not Africa
Southern Asia	not Southern Asia
zoo	free
courageous	timid
cruel	kind
ravenous	not ravenous
social lion	anti-social
lion-hearted	cowardly
king of beasts	not king of beasts
roars	squeeks
leaps	limps

An "analogous/opposite" word-list method of developing ideas.

toward a creative solution. You might try this technique with one or more friends, either during or after compiling your list.

In her book, *Writing the Natural Way,* Dr. Gabriele Rico describes a similar method of developing ideas, but rather than using a columnar listing of data, she uses a "clustering" technique in which individual encircled words radiate in all directions from a nucleus word (see illustration). While this technique graphically suggests the randomness of right-brain thinking, it does not easily permit the juxtaposition of opposites, which is essential to creativity.

Many people tend to believe that a creative work can be constructed entirely of analogous elements, but an analysis of any successful work, whether it be writing, visual art, or music, will demonstrate that its dynamics are due to a stress of opposites. As Johannes Itten of Bauhaus fame has said, "all artistic effects are based on the creation of contrasts." There is, in fact, a field of philosophy called *dialectics* in which the major premise is that everything in the universe, art included, involves a constant confrontation of opposites. In Plato's Academy, dialectics was regarded as "the supreme philosophical method, indeed the highest of human arts," and it continues to occupy the interests of many recent philosophers, most notably Georg Wilhelm Hegel (the father of modern thought) and Jean Paul Sartre.

The Wonderful Wizard of Oz (1900), written by L. Frank Baum and illustrated by W.W. Denslow.

Not only must your ideas be based on the interplay of opposites, but, to achieve maximum dynamic or dramatic effect, the opposites must be as polarized as possible, which more often than not involves exaggeration. It has been said that the creative writer's goal is not to depict a person accurately, but to exaggerate a person accurately.

As your ideas begin to take form, you will probably need to make supplementary lists for the various aspects of your story. For example, if L. Frank Baum had used such a method for creating his book, *The Wonderful Wizard of Oz,* he might have made separate lists for the lion that wants courage (courageous/cowardly), the tin woodman that wants a heart (inorganic/organic), the scarecrow that wants a brain (straw-filled head/human brain), and the girl (Dorothy) who wants to go home (at home/lost).

Don't be swayed by those successful professionals who claim that their ideas are pure inspiration and require no preliminary planning or other left-brain activity. Some people are so innately creative that they have never had to consciously think about their methods; they just do it and it works. This doesn't

A "clustering" word-list method of developing ideas, as described in *Writing the Natural Way* by Dr. Gabriele Rico.

mean, however, that their left brains are inactive. Most likely, their left brains are constantly compiling internalized lists of analogies and oppositions of which they are not consciously aware. The best advice for the creative hopeful comes from Thomas Edison, who said that "genius is 2% inspiration and 98% perspiration." Perspiration implies effort, and successful effort implies a goodly amount of left brain activity, whether it be consciously willed or not.

OUTLINES

Some fiction writers never outline their stories, claiming that an outline is too restrictive. They believe that as soon as you have the creative impulse to write, you should put it down on paper right away, not dwelling over the best way to begin, nor worrying about how the story will end.

Most writers, however, and especially non-fiction writers, believe that an outline is necessary. Some use a "slap-dash" system of outlining, vaguely describing the direction of the story or perhaps only the next few chapters, while others prepare detailed outlines with chapter by chapter breakdowns and character sketches and dialogue.

As with ideas, some experienced writers have an innate sense of story structure and dramatic presentation, and don't need an externalized outline to guide them. Such a sense, however, usually comes only with substantial writing experience. If you are a beginning writer, therefore, you will find an outline greatly beneficial, even though you may not adhere to it completely. In addition to showing where to begin and how to end, it will keep you from meandering or straying from the plot with unrelated incidents—a sure way to lose a child's interest.

Sometimes a story outline is so well resolved in your mind that you need only commit it to paper for minor refinements. More often than not, however, you have nothing more than a vague idea in mind, and an outline is needed to help develop it. In fact, the procedure for developing ideas, as described in the preceding section, is often incorporated into the outlining procedure. Suppose, for example, that

(Above and opposite page) Illustrations from *Beauty and the Beast and Other Stories,* published by Henry Altemus Company in the late 19th century.

the unknown original author of the fairy tale, *Beauty and the Beast,* had started out with the simple objective of creating a story based on good/bad oppositions. A list of things analogous with good, plus a list of their opposites, would produce such word pairs as beautiful/ugly, kind/cruel, selfless/selfish, generous/greedy, and love/hate. In assigning these characteristics to people, the author employs exaggeration and also creates new oppositions, often by juxtaposing contradictory characteristics in the same person. For example, ugliness is personified by a beast (exag-

geration), and the ugly beast lives with a beautiful girl (three oppositions; male/female, ugly/beautiful, and animal/human). Further oppositions in the beast characterization are that he is kind (beastly/kind), and in reality a handsome prince (handsome/ugly and animal/human).

Did the author of *Beauty and the Beast* develop such complex characterizations and interrelationships during the idea stage, or did they begin to emerge during the outlining stage? Perhaps the idea stage resulted in nothing more than a one-sentence theme description, such as, "Beauty, in payment for her father's debt, goes to live with a beast." Using this as a basic guide, the author might then have prepared a rough outline to flesh out the story further, such as:

1. Beauty, who is as good as she is beautiful, does all the household chores, including waiting on her two sisters, who are jealous of her because they are not quite as beautiful.

2. Beauty's father, returning from a trip, brings Beauty a rose which he has taken from a Beast's garden. The angered Beast has demanded the father's life in exchange for the flower.

3. Beauty goes to the Beast and offers herself in place of her father.

4. The Beast proves to be as kind as he is ugly, and Beauty learns to love him for himself. Her love transforms the enchanted Beast into a handsome prince.

Perhaps such an outline was sufficient for the author to proceed with writing the story, or perhaps it was used as a guide for more-detailed outlines. In any event, it can be seen that such a progressive procedure, if pursued far enough, would ultimately result in a full-blown story, including all the *ifs, ands,* and *buts.*

Analyzing someone else's work of art, of course, is a lot easier than creating your own. Because the right brain operates in a random fashion, ideas arise in no particular sequence and for no particular purpose. It is just for these reasons, therefore, that you should make use of the foregoing left-brain methods of structuring your creative output. If you are unable to state the theme of your story in a single sentence, and further unable to describe the plot in a brief, coherent outline, it means that your story is confused. And nothing turns off a reader faster than confusion.

USING INDEX CARDS FOR RESEARCH AND OUTLINES

One of the best ways to record and store all the data you collect and create is a file system using 3 x 5 index cards. This system is used by many writers, adult as well as juvenile, and fiction as well as nonfiction. The cards are convenient to carry when doing research away from home, and are easy to file and refer to. Make an index-card record of every reference book you use, recording the title, author, publisher, and library code number. Be sure to note which library each book came from so you can easily find it if you need it again. These cards represent your bibliography.

Record information taken from these reference books onto other cards, using a code of your own to indicate which book the data came from. The code should be a number or letter that refers to a corresponding number or letter on your bibliography cards. Be sure to note whether you are paraphrasing, quoting, or expressing an opinion, and also note the page number of the reference book. Take the time to write clearly. Too often, notes written hastily can't later be deciphered and are wasted.

Index cards are also ideal for creating outlines. They make it easy to add, delete, or rearrange data, and when all laid out in proper order, they provide you with a graphic picture of your thought process. Write boldly and clearly, and lay out the cards as you write them, either pinning them onto a large panel (Homosote or cork works well), taping them onto a wall (use drafting tape or Scotch Magic Plus Removable Transparent Tape so it won't pull off the paint or wallpaper), or arranging them on a large table. Major topics (such as chapter heads) are arranged horizontally along the top edge of the layout area, and minor topics (such as subheads within chapters) are arranged vertically under the appropriate major topic. After you have created your outline, file each grouping of cards in the same sequence so they can be used for reference in writing your book.

Try this procedure, even if your story is quite short. You will be amazed at how easy it is to structure your thoughts when they are graphically externalized and readily rearrangeable. An out-of-order card is so obvious, in fact, that even the casual observer can spot it.

LITERARY ELEMENTS IN FICTION

Before you begin to write your story, and even before you prepare your outline, you should become familiar with the six traditional literary elements: theme, plot, characterization, setting, viewpoint, and style.

Theme—The Main Idea or Concept.

The theme is the subject or central core of a story. In writing for children, it is preferable to have a single theme that they can easily understand and relate to through their own experiences. This means that their limited reading ability, comprehension, interests, and emotional growth must be given careful consideration. Some of the most popular themes for children's books have been based on love, reassurance, independent achievement, and overcoming personal difficulties and problems.

Plot—What Happens.

A plot is a series of interrelated actions that progress to a climax. There must be a beginning, a middle, and an end. In order to be convincing, events should be designed to unfold in a lifelike way. Unlike some books for adults, where very little may happen, stories that appeal to children are usually filled with lively action and satisfying results.

It is generally believed that there are only ten basic plots in the world, and that only four of these (listed below) are commonly used in books for children under fourteen.

Plot #1—Incident. An event takes place on an excursion, where the main character is in a familiar situation and/or surroundings; or it takes place on an adventure, where the situation and/or surroundings are unfamiliar.

Plot #2—Achievement. A main character struggles to reach a goal, using courage, ingenuity, a special ability, or any combination of these attributes.

Plot #3—Wish Fulfillment. A seemingly impossible desire is gratified, usually as a result of an unwitting act by the main character.

Plot #4—Misunderstanding, Discovery, and Reversal. The main character's actions are based on the misunderstanding of an action, motive, or situation. He discovers his mistake and reverses his belief.

Your plot should begin with a stress of opposites, such as a conflict, contradiction, paradox, or problem. It should then go on to explain and expand the oppositional situation as simply as possible, and conclude with its resolution, or climax. After the climax, be careful not to drag out your ending, or to introduce new elements or ideas, particularly oppositional ones. Just briefly describe the benefits of having resolved the conflict, and end your story on a note of tranquility and harmony ("and they lived happily ever after").

Characterization—How the Characters are Revealed and Understood.

Whether a story is realistic or fantastic, its characters must be believable and consistent. They must behave, in all situations, in accordance with who and what they are, and they must be composed of sufficient traits so as not to appear wooden or one-dimensional. As in real life, some of a character's traits may be mildly paradoxical, such as a man who loves dogs but hates people, or even bizarrely paradoxical, such as a thief who cannot tell a lie. The major character in a story is known as the *protagonist,* which implies that a struggle against adversity (an *antagonist)* is an essential aspect of that role.

While theme and plot are undoubtedly the most important literary elements in a story, it is the characters and their actions that serve to transport the reader through the story.

Setting—Where and When the Story Happens.

The setting in time and place can be vague and broad, or it can be minutely detailed. The emotional and social atmosphere is also an aspect of setting to be considered. Settings may be of major or minor importance, but in either case they must be handled well for the story to be convincing.

Viewpoint—Through Whose Eyes and Mind the Story is Told, and Who is the Storyteller.

Following is a list of the methods for handling viewpoint. Some of these methods are commonly believed to be unsuitable for children's literature, but this does not mean that they must be rigorously avoided. The only way to determine viewpoint is to try various methods to find which best suits your story and your writing style. If an unusual viewpoint seems to be called for, show a sample of your writing to a few astute people to see if they think it is appropriate for your story and for your intended audience.

Single Viewpoint. Almost all writers believe that children's stories should be told from the viewpoint of the main character, although the viewpoint of a minor character is occasionally used. The storyteller can be the viewpoint character (first-person narration), or it can be the author seeing through the eyes and mind of the viewpoint character (third-person narration). Some authors believe that children don't relate well to first-person narration, and others believe that it is too limiting. This is as compared with third-person, or author, narration. While the author-narrator cannot know what any character other than the viewpoint character sees, thinks, and feels, he *can* objectively describe the viewpoint character, as well as other characters and situations, in a way that would be impossible for the viewpoint character to do himself.

The advantage to the single-viewpoint method, whether it be first-person or third-person, is that the reader closely identifies with the viewpoint character. Rather than being a spectator, the reader becomes a participant, seeing, hearing, feeling, and experiencing events just as the viewpoint character does.

Minor-character viewpoint, incidentally, is always narrated in first person. This is because if the author were to narrate a story through the eyes of a minor character, it would automatically transform the minor character into the main character. Minor-character viewpoint is used where the author wants first-person narration, but not by the main character. In a hero story, for example, first-person narration by the hero would sound like bragging. On the other hand, first-person narration by an inept main character could be humorous and/or appealing, whereas narration by a minor character (or the author) might make him seem pathetic.

Omniscient Viewpoint. Also called *multiple viewpoint,* omniscient viewpoint is where the author, as narrator, knows and describes what every character is seeing, thinking, and feeling. This method, which tends to make the reader a spectator rather than a participant, requires more skill than the single viewpoint, and was popular in children's literature until the late 19th century.

Since then, its use has been largely restricted to adult literature, where being an all-seeing and all-knowing spectator is often the best way to deal with subjectivity and other complexities of life.

Shifting Viewpoint. This method is similar to single viewpoint, the difference being that the viewpoint shifts from one character to another at certain times. For example, chapter one might be from the viewpoint of Character A, chapter two might be from the viewpoint of Character B, chapter three might return to the viewpoint of Character A, etc. Only one viewpoint at a time can be used (otherwise it would be omniscient viewpoint), and the viewpoints should not shift so frequently that the story becomes jerky or confusing. Shifting viewpoint is generally difficult for young children to relate to, and thus is primarily used for teenage and adult literature.

Objective Viewpoint. This is where the author, acting as reporter, simply describes what is seen or heard from the viewpoint of a bystander. Usually expressing no opinions, and not knowing what any of the characters see, think, or feel, the author can offer the reader only the straight facts. Many writers believe that a story that doesn't describe feelings and emotions is no story at all. However, if the factual elements are handled well, it is possible to use them to produce powerful feelings and emotions in the reader. By not revealing the characters' motives or intended actions beforehand, the author is able to create mystery, suspense, and surprise. Alfred Hitchcock was a master of this technique.

Style—How the Idea is Expressed. Style is the distinctive or characteristic mode of expression of an individual, and since no two individuals are alike, there is no satisfactory explanation or infallible guide for developing it. Self-expression is a mysterious thing. Paraphrasing from Zen writings, if you attempt to grasp it, it will elude you. This means that if you consciously impose a style on your writing, it will intrude on your subject matter, and it will also not be you expressing yourself. Rather, it will be what you think you *ought* to be,

what you admire in the work of others, or what is the latest fad.

The best approach to style can be found in *The Elements of Style* by William B. Strunk, Jr. and E. B. White. As slim as it is, this gem of a book seems to contain everything you need to know about the use of words and punctuation, as well as the development of style. Among their "gentle reminders," the authors recommend that you place yourself in the background, not be concerned with style, and simply do a careful, honest, and solid job of writing. They also say you shouldn't worry about being an imitator, but on the other hand you shouldn't imitate consciously. As you become proficient at writing, your style will emerge, and when this happens you will find it increasingly easy to successfully express yourself in your own inimitable way.

THE FIRST DRAFT
Don't expect to sit down and write a perfect story from beginning to end. To write is to write, rewrite, and rewrite again. A blank sheet of paper is both a threat and a challenge. The best way to start is to be unconcerned with whether your story will be successful or not. Relax and write for the pure enjoyment and satisfaction of expressing yourself.

Gather together some sharpened pencils, a pad or pack of lined paper, your everyday dictionary plus an elementary level dictionary (for children of 4th to 6th grade reading levels), and *Roget's Thesaurus of Words and Phrases.* Sit at a comfortable desk and have your files, notes, and outline handy. Your initial writing, called a first draft, can be freely written without concern for spelling, grammar, punctuation, overwording, or too many details. In this first draft, you may minutely describe characters and their surroundings if it helps you to get the feeling of the story. You can always delete in subsequent drafts if you later feel that your descriptions are overdone, or if they will be adequately depicted in illustrations. In writing a picture book it is important to think visually, being mindful that what you write must be graphically depictable. Remember that thoughts and conversation arc not easily illustrated. Short scenes, different settings, and minor characters (possibly even some not mentioned in the text), keep a picture book moving and make it easier to blend text and illustrations.

While the title of your book is of great importance, it needn't be determined beforehand. Professional writers usually use a "working title" just to identify the book they're working on, and make a list of title ideas as they come to mind. This list of proposed titles is later passed around among editors and friends for their opinions and suggestions, and as often as not it is one of their title suggestions that is ultimately adopted. Keep in mind that the title should be as short and as provocative

as possible. Try to capture the mood of the story, but don't reveal its resolution. Although titles can't be copyrighted, it would be unwise to use an existent one. Check the *Subject Guide to Children's Books in Print* (see page 35) to insure against duplication.

At the outset of writing your story, you will probably want to experiment with viewpoint (see page 42). Try writing the first page or two from different viewpoints to see which best suits your style, your story, and your reader level.

Opening lines are called *grabbers,* and many writers consider them the most important part of a story. If a good grabber doesn't come to you immediately, proceed without it. Later, either in the same or in a subsequent draft, one

will probably spring to mind.

A device to use when writing fantasy is to include the word "once" in your opening line. "Once upon a time…," "There was once…", or "It happened once, long, long, ago…", are all familiar openers. "Once" becomes a magic word and usually sets the mood for an imaginary tale.

To capture the reader's attention, your opening lines should contain a suggestion of suspense, apprehension, or conflict. A few of the more common ways of doing this are a description of the main character and his problem; a conversation that piques the reader's curiosity; or a provocative anecdote, quotation, or statement that sets the mood of the story.

76

on their feet and hands, to make the arches.

The chief difficulty which Alice found at first was to manage her ostrich : she got its body tucked away, comfortably enough, under her arm, with its legs hanging down, but generally, just as she had got its neck straightened out nicely, and was going to give a blow with its head, it *would* twist itself round, and look up into her face, with such a puzzled expression that she could not help bursting out laughing : and when she had got its head down, and was going to begin again, it was very confusing to find that the hedgehog had unrolled itself, and was in the act of crawling away : besides all this, there was generally a ridge or a furrow in her way, wherever she wanted to send the hedgehog to, and as the doubled-up soldiers were always getting up and walking off to other

A page from a facsimile of Lewis Carroll's manuscript (with his own illustration) for *Alice's adventures Under ground.*

Alice's Adventures in Wonderland

Alice thought she had never seen such a curious croquet-ground in her life: it was all ridges and furrows; the croquet-balls were live hedgehogs, and the mallets live flamingoes, and the soldiers had to double themselves up and stand on their hands and feet, to make the arches.

The chief difficulty Alice found at first was in managing her flamingo: she succeeded in getting its body tucked away, comfortably enough, under her arm, with its legs hanging down, but generally, just as she had got its neck nicely straightened out, and was going to give the hedgehog a blow with its head, it *would* twist itself round and look up into her face, with such a puzzled expression that she could not help bursting out laughing: and when she had got its head down, and was going to begin again, it was very provoking to find that the hedgehog had unrolled itself, and was in the act of crawling away: besides all this, there was generally a ridge or a furrow in the way wherever she wanted to send the hedgehog to, and, as the doubled-up soldiers were always getting up and walking off to other parts of the ground, Alice soon came to the conclusion that it was a very difficult game indeed.

78

A page from Lewis Carroll's book, *Alice's Adventures in Wonderland.* Illustrations are by Sir John Tenniel. Note that this page is the final version of the manuscript copy shown at left.

Many writers like to write the first draft in longhand because they believe it puts them in closer touch with their thoughts. At the end of each working session, however, it is a good idea to type what you have written. A handwritten first draft is so filled with scribbled words, crossed-out words, added words, and other graphic confusions that it is not easy to read, and easy reading is important for three reasons. One is that at the beginning of each work session it is necessary to scan your previous writing to get the story back in mind; another is that you frequently have to check back in your writing to avoid inconsistencies, duplications, etc.; and a third is that you must be able to read your story rapidly and without hesitation in order to gain a sense of the abstract sounds and rhythms of words, which are as important to the story as their meanings.

THE SECOND AND LATER DRAFTS

After you have written and typed your first draft (using double spacing), the next step is to make handwritten corrections on it, just as an editor would do. If added material is too extensive to fit between the typed lines, write it on a separate sheet, note where it is to be inserted (on that sheet and at the point of insertion), and make it the following page in the manuscript. For example, if it follows page 10, make it page 10A.

If you are going to do the illustrations yourself, you should make thumbnail sketches (and perhaps thumbnail page layouts as well) at the same time that you edit the first draft. Planning the illustrations will suggest many changes in the text. For example, there may be no need to verbally describe minute external aspects of characters and situations if they are to be illustrated.

Making rough sketches is a good idea even if you are not going to do your own illustrations. A sketch helps you see if your major scenes and situations provide the right elements for dynamic graphic depiction. Because it is generally believed that the beginning of a story must be illustrated (a picture can be at least as much enticement as words), rough sketches serve the writer

as well as the illustrator. If your opening sketch is not provacative, it probably means that your opening lines do not adequately describe the story's thematic conflict. And if you go for pages without finding anything new and interesting to illustrate, it probably means that a situation is either being dragged out or is lacking in physical action.

In addition to improving the action and verbal depiction of characters and situations, you must correct grammar, spelling, and punctuation; eliminate repetition; and generally tighten up your story. Wordy and involved first-draft sentences need to be pruned of extraneous words and awkward or complex constructions. For easiest reading, experts recommend that there be no more than ten words per sentence and preferably fewer than eight. Eleven to fourteen words is considered fairly easy reading, and the maximum length for 6th, 7th, and 8th grade students is seventeen to twenty words. Picture books vary from 100 to 1,000 words, with most ranging between 500 and 1,000. Picture storybooks can have as many as 8,000 words.

Pay particular attention to your vocabulary. If necessary, a difficult word may occasionally be used, but first try to express yourself in a simpler way. It is ultimately the editor's job to decide on the reading level of your audience, but you should have some idea of it and write accordingly. If you are writing an easy-to-read picture book, you should use a word list recommended for that age group (see page 35).

After you have finished editing your first draft, retype it carefully in its entirety. By this time, your story will be well-enough written to be read as a finished work, and you don't want to confuse or distract the reader (either you or others) with a messy graphic presentation.

There are a number of ways of testing the second draft of your story. One is to read it aloud to yourself, trying to hear it as if for the first time. It may be hard for you, as author, to judge the story's content, but you should be able to judge its abstract sounds, rhythm, and flow. If you hear a discordant sound or pas-

sage, don't hesitate to change, rearrange, or eliminate it. It may be precious in itself, but if it doesn't fit the overall scheme it must be dealt with ruthlessly.

Let other people read your story or read it to them. And *do* consider their comments. You might tend to believe that children are your best sources for criticism, but they are not able to be objective. On the opinions of children, J. R. R. Tolkien said: "They like or try to like what is given to them; if they do not like it, they cannot well express their dislike or give reasons for it." Of course, everyone likes to be a critic, and you must learn to accept or reject comments with astuteness and objectivity.

Another way to test your story is to ask yourself (as well as others) the following questions:

1. Is there a clearly-defined theme?
2. Is the plot simple, dealing with one concept? Does it wander?
3. Have I been aware of the limitations of my audience?
4. Does the text suggest good picture possibilities?
5. How does it sound when read aloud? Is it rhythmic and flowing?
6. Did I accomplish what I intended to?
7. Are there boring spots?
8. Would I enjoy the story if I hadn't written it?
9. Does it have a professional quality?

Edit your second draft in the same way you edited the first draft, and be particularly careful when you retype it. A third draft is frequently the final one, and should be prepared as a finished manuscript (see *Submitting the Manuscript,* page 102).

NONFICTION OR INFORMATIONAL BOOKS

Attractive and well-written informational books for all reading levels are currently in abundance, and publishers are constantly seeking more. The sixth edition of *Children & Books,* by Zena Sutherland, Dianne L. Monson, and Mary Hill Arbuthnott, states that "their numbers and variety are so staggering that they are more than a trend; they are practically inundation."

While the major challenge in writing nonfiction is to make factual information interesting and understandable, your most important initial job is to thoroughly research your subject. To do this, you must be familiar with the reference department of your library. You will find two categories of reference books there: those that supply information directly, such as encyclopedias, dictionaries, directories, and almanacs; and those that point to where the information can be found, such as book and periodical indexes. Book and periodical indexes list consecutive-reading books, newspaper articles, and magazine stories by subject category. Since this "end-product" literature is not reference data in the technical sense, it may be located in other departments of the library (such as the circulation department). Your reference department librarian can guide you to the reference books you need, but you can also refer to *The Guide to Reference Books,* revised by Eugene P. Sheehy, which most libraries have. For greatest convenience and efficiency, you can acquire, at a small fee, *Reference Books: A Brief Guide,* published by the Enoch Pratt Free Library, 400 Cathedral Street, Baltimore, MD 21201. Following is a list of some of the most commonly-used reference books that are available at the majority of libraries.

Direct-reference Books.

Oxford English Dictionary (13 volumes). J.A. Murray, et al. Oxford University Press, New York, NY. Contains information about the history of words. You may use it to find when a word was first used and to authenticate dialogue.

Chronology of the Modern World. Neville Williams. McKay Company, Inc., New York, NY. Lists events, discoveries, and statistics from 1763 to 1965.

The Encyclopedia of American Facts and Dates. Edited by Gorton Carruth. Thomas Y. Crowell Company, New York, NY. Lists facts, events, and dates pertinent to America.

Reference Guides.

The Subject Guide to Books in Print. R.R. Bowker Company, New York, NY. Lists U.S. books in print arranged by subject, author, and title. Bowker also publishes *The Subject Guide to Children's Books in Print.* Both are updated annually.

Cumulative Book Index (CBI). H.W. Wilson Company, New York, NY. Lists all books published worldwide in English, in and out of print.

The Readers' Guide to Periodical Literature. H.W. Wilson Company, New York, NY. Lists magazine articles, by subject and author, in over 150 periodicals from 1900 to the present.

Poole's Index to Periodical Literature. Houghton, Mifflin Company, Boston, MA. Lists the subject content of British and American magazines published between 1802 and 1908.

National Geographic Magazine Cumulative Index. National Geographic Society, Washington, DC. Lists articles from 1899 to the present. Most libraries stock back issues.

The New York Times Index. Lists articles from 1851 to the present in book and microfilm form.

The London Times Index (Palmer's Index to the Times Newspaper). Lists articles from 1790 to the present in microfilm form.

The American Library Directory. R.R.Bowker Company, New York, NY. Lists locations of U.S. libraries.

Subject Collection: A Guide to Special Book Collections in Libraries. Compiled by Lee Ash. R.R. Bowker Company, New York, NY. Lists information on the special book collections in U.S. libraries.

History and Biography.

Studying history is no longer simply the memorization of names, dates, places, and related facts. Today's educational emphasis is on understanding the period and the conditions that led to important events and circumstances. The same is true with biographies. Many recently-written biographies, particularly those that are historical, read like novels based on the lives of famous persons. Whether you are writing history or biography, it is important to be factually accurate. It is equally important to give life to the people and events being described. (Also see *Historical Stories,* page 31.)

History. *This Time, Tempe Wick?* (1974) is a humorous tale that takes place during the American Revolution. Written by Patricia Lee Gauch and illustrated by Margot Tomes.

Biography. *Sky Pioneers: The Story of Wilbur and Orville Wright* (1963) is a story about the constant experimentation and inventiveness of the Wright brothers. Written by Jeanne LeMonnier Gardner and illustrated by Douglas Gorsline.

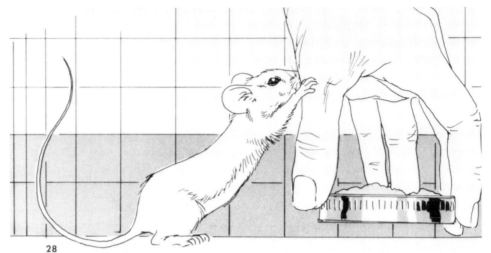

Science. *Whitey and Whiskers and Food* (1964) is the story of a controlled scientific experiment in nutrition. Written by Constantine Georgiou and illustrated by Taylor Oughton.

Science.

As with books on history and biography, the emphasis in books on science is no longer the mere issuing of facts. Today's science books for children show rather than just tell, and strive to elicit the child's participation. Simple, illustrated explanations, as well as instructions for conducting experiments, must be geared to particular age groups. Metaphors in the text and illustrations are frequently used to make difficult concepts, procedures, and operations easier to understand.

Social Studies.

Books in this category have to do with people and their association with other people. Under the heading of social studies in primary and secondary education are (in addition to history) such subjects as geography, economics, sociology, psychology, anthropology, politics, religion, and philosophy. In children's books today, some of these subjects may overlap, and the major objective is to provide "real experience" as opposed to passive description. This is often done by dealing with a particular child in a particular location, and by giving specific instances rather than collective generalizations.

Social Studies. *The Wineglass: A Passover Story* (1978) concerns the conflict of two different generations of religious thought between a boy's old-fashioned grandfather and his modern parents. Although this story is about Judaism, it has a universal appeal. Written by Norman Rosten and illustrated by Kaethe Zemach.

How-to Books.

Some publishing companies do not publish how-to books, some publish them occasionally, and others publish them in large numbers, often in series. After you get an idea for a how-to book, your next step should be to look in *The Subject Guide to Books in Print* (see page 46) to find out how many books on that subject have already been published. If there are a substantial number, it would probably be unwise to produce another unless you have a unique approach.

To be successful, a how-to book must be well-designed, well-illustrated, and written with the utmost clarity. Instructions must be concise, precise, and easy to follow. Include every detail, no matter how insignificant it may seem, and don't take anything for granted on the part of the reader. The failure to explain a procedure, or to include every step in it, can mean failure for the project, which makes the book worthless.

To be absolutely sure that your how-to project will work, you must actually create it yourself, writing down each step as you perform it. The cost factor is an important consideration. Keep supplies at a minimum, and try to make use of tools and materials commonly found in the home.

A storyline or related information can make a how-to book more attractive to some publishers and book buyers. For example, a book on how to make bird houses and feeders could include a story or information about birds, and a book on how to make simulated colonial American artifacts could explain their original purpose and method of crafting. If sufficiently curriculum related, such books are sometimes adopted by schools as supplements to textbooks.

Following is an outline for my book, *Easy to Make North American Indian Crafts,* which was published in 1981 by Harvey House, New York, NY. This book explains how North American Indians made and used their artifacts for daily living, and provides directions for simulating these artifacts with the use of easily-found materials. An "extra-easy" method is included for younger children.

Shelters. The types of houses built by tribes in different parts of the country. Directions for building an outdoor tepee using sheets, and an extra-easy indoor tepee using paper. Authentic design symbols are shown.

Costumes. The clothing worn by tribes in different parts of the country, including seasonal dress. Directions for making outfits for a male and female, including felt moccasins, bags, and pouches. Extra-easy outfits are made of paper.

Headdress. The meaning of feather headdresses. Directions for making headdresses and war bonnets using real and fake feathers. Extra-easy war bonnet is made of paper.

Ornaments and Jewelry. Indian sources of materials. Directions for making ornaments and jewelry, using foodstuff, paper, plastic, aluminum, and other found materials.

Bead Weaving. Indian uses and sources. Directions for making a wooden loom and an extra-easy cardboard loom. Methods of weaving are described.

Cloth Weaving. The methods used by Indians. Directions for making a wooden loom and an extra-easy cardboard loom, and for weaving a small mat.

Basketry. The styles used by different tribes. Directions for making a "lazy squaw" shallow basket and an extra-easy basket made of paper.

Pottery. Indian methods. Homemade clay recipes, and directions for making a bowl.

Musical Instruments. Indian music; its use and sounds. Directions for making a drum, rattle, and bells.

Games. The types of games played by different tribes. Directions for making a bowl game and toss ball, and playing instructions for them.

Owner Sticks. Their meaning and use, and directions for making them.

Masks. The various tribal beliefs in spirits, and the use of ceremonial masks. Directions for making a Kachina mask and an Iroquois Corn Husk mask.

Shields. Indian uses and materials. Directions for making a cardboard shield.

Totem Poles. Their original use and meaning. Directions for constructing a large pole using cartons, and for carving a small pole from wood.

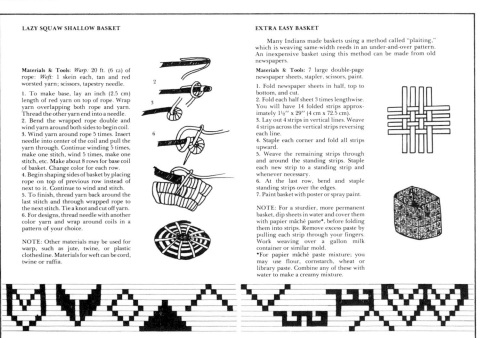

This spread from *Easy to Make North American Indian Crafts* (1981), written and illustrated by Frieda Gates, shows the methods of making Indian baskets.

INDEXING

An index is required for most informational or factual books, particularly where the text is lengthy. Indexing can be done only after it has been determined on which page the copy will appear. This is usually after the type has been set in galley, or rough, proofs. Sometimes the type is set as it will appear on each page (page proofs). If not, the proofs must be cut up and pasted onto the paged dummy.

To compile an index, read through the copy and record each word or subject to be indexed, plus page number, on individual 3 x 5 index cards. Don't alphabetize the cards at this time; just throw them in a pile. Also, if the same word or subject appears on more than one page, don't try to find the previous card on which it was recorded; just make out a new card. After all the entries have been recorded, then alphabetize the cards. If there is more than one card for a word or subject, record all the page numbers on one card and eliminate the others. Finally, type the entries on 8½" x 11" white bond paper, with one entry per double-spaced line. (Nowadays, indexing is often done on a word processor.)

PRACTICE EXERCISES

Following are some of the practice exercises that I give to my students. Over the years, many of these student exercises have resulted in stories that were successful enough to submit to publishers.

It is important to be aware that the method of developing ideas, as described at the beginning of this chapter, can be applied to at least some of these exercises. With an "altered tale," for example, your left column would list all of the existent factors of a traditional folk or fairy tale, and your right column would list their opposites.

It was the first day of school in a quiet wooded knoll at the edge of a mountain lake. Terrance Timothy Thorton Turtle the third (III) was kissing his mother goodbye.

"It's getting late, Timothy! You know you need extra time to walk to school," said his mother. "And remember dear," she added, "do your best. It would make your late father and me very proud . . . especially since you are named after him."

"Oh yes, Mother, I will," Timothy nodded, and off he went, down the path toward school.

As Timothy passed each marker, Mr. Owl told him the name of each number. Timothy passed four, five, and six. As he was nearing seven, he saw Weeza sound asleep. His heart started thumping and he whispered when he asked Mr. Owl what number was on the sign. "Seven" Mr. Owl whispered back.

7 seven

Exercise #1—Altered Tale. *The Tortoise and the Hare,* rewritten by Peg Sterling as *Terrance Timothy Thorton Turtle the Third,* is a story and counting book. Illustrations are from her dummy.

1. Altered Tale.

Rewrite a fairy tale, folk tale, or fable. Alter the story by changing the ending; by presenting it in a present-day setting; or by telling it from another viewpoint. These tales and fables are usually in the public domain and can be used without fear of copyright infringement. Following are brief descriptions of some altered tales written by students:

Red Riding Hood is a young, street-smart Black girl who lives in a ghetto. She sets out to deliver a welfare check to her grandmother, when Wolf, a local hooligan, tries to trick her into giving him the check.

Cinderella, a modern feminist, doesn't depend on a handsome prince for fulfillment. Rather, she uses her own abilities to start a cleaning business.

Three pigs inadvertently steal building supplies from Mr. Wolf's lumber yard. The eldest pig helps to save Mr. Wolf's failing business and marries Mr. Wolf's daughter.

A boy borrows a computer from a mysterious librarian, and it spews out so much continuous-fold paper that the entire town becomes covered with it.

Exercise #2—What If. "What if I could do anything I wanted to?" was the question that inspired Helena Willenbrink to write *Mess,* which is about a boy who, in doing anything he wants to, messes up his life. This illustration is her finished art.

2. What if.

Think of a question beginning with "What if" that can be used as an idea for a story. A serious question might be, "What if the world ran out of oil resources?", and a whimsical question might be, "What if people could fly by flapping their arms?" To create a provocative question, browse through books and magazines with "What if" in mind. It is not necessary to alter more than one element in a found situation, but that one altered element should be a unique and dramatic reversal of reality.

3. Why, What, Where, How, and Who.

Think of a question beginning with one of the above words that a child might ask. Provide an answer that is factual, fictionally realistic, or fantastic. Following are some examples:

Q—*Why* do I have to eat my vegetables? A—An informational story on health, or a story about a child or animal who wouldn't eat any nutritious food.

Q—*What* makes it rain? A—A fantasy involving crying angels, or an explanation of weather and seasons.

Q—*Where* did Daddy (or Mommy) go? A—A story about death or divorce, or a story about the various occupations of working parents.

Q—*How* do you make a pie? A—A silly story about mud pies or other preposterous pies, or a cook book written especially for children (also see Exercise 8).

Q—*Who* is the sandman? A—A fantasy about the sandman, information on why we need sleep, or sleeping habits and conditions of humans and/or animals in different parts of the world.

Exercise #3—Why. "Why do I have to eat my vegetables?" inspired Carolyn Louche to write *Sir Dudley,* a story about a dragon who would only eat junk food. This illustration is her finished art.

Exercise #3—What. "What makes it rain?" inspired Cynthia Mauro Reisenauer to create *Weather Forecast,* a concept book about a young rabbit who learns about the seasons from a wise owl. This illustration is her finished art.

Exercise #3—Who. "Who is the sandman?" resulted in *A Grain of Sand* by Frances Vernieri, a collection of short stories involving dreams. This illustration is from the cover of her dummy.

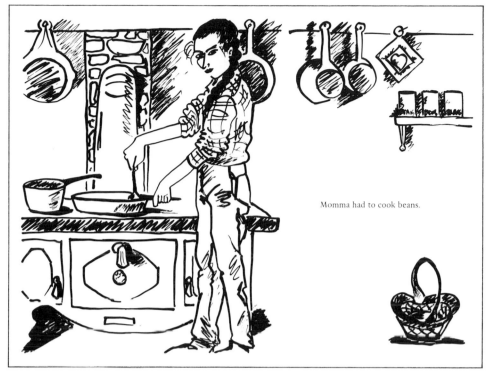

Momma had to cook beans.

Exercise #3—Where. "Where did Daddy Go?" led Mary Altobelli Murphy to write *A Fish Story* (Daddy went fishing). This illustration is from her dummy.

4. A Title in Search of a Story.

In a classroom situation, each student submits two or three made-up story titles written on separate pieces of paper. Each student then draws a title from the collected papers and, in an hour or so, creates a story idea to fit the title that was drawn. If a title isn't inspiring, the student may draw another, but two is the maximum. The short time limit forces the student to pay attention to the overall scheme rather than the details of writing. This makes it a good exercise for beginners, who tend to rush into finished writing without having adequately resolved the story idea. If you are not in a class, you can practice this exercise with one or more friends. Be sure to set a strict time limit for yourself, however, for this is an important aspect of the exercise. Of course, if a good story idea results from it, you can pursue it further at any pace you find suitable.

How to eat an orange . . .

The orange is a round fruit.

It has a tough skin which you do not eat. You take it off.

Hold the orange. Insert finger under skin. Pull off skin.

Continue until all skin is removed.

Exercise #3—How. "How to eat an orange" is one of ten how-to descriptions in Grace Mitchell's book, *Ten Things to Learn How to Do.* These illustrations are from her dummy.

Exercise #4—A Title in Search of a Story. Sandra Willemsen's title, *Juanita's Unicorn,* was developed into a story about a little girl's friendship with an imaginary unicorn. This illustration is from her dummy.

5. A Picture In Search of a Story.

This is similar to the previous exercise, the difference being that instead of story titles, each student contributes a few provocative photographs, either personal or taken from publications. The challenge is to create a story idea to go with the picture.

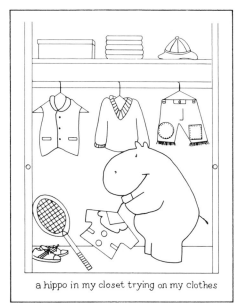

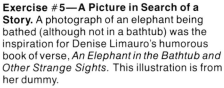

a hippo in my closet trying on my clothes

Exercise #5—A Picture in Search of a Story. A photograph of an elephant being bathed (although not in a bathtub) was the inspiration for Denise Limauro's humorous book of verse, *An Elephant in the Bathtub and Other Strange Sights.* This illustration is from her dummy.

6. Create a Character.

Describe a character in minute detail—height, weight, coloring, sex, likes, dislikes, abilities, habits, etc. Be able to envision this character and predict the reactions he or she would have in any given situation. In a group or class, questions and situations involving the imaginary character are presented to the creator for an immediate response. Such characterizations can often suggest a story idea. The character, incidentally, does not have to be human, and might even be fantastic.

Exercise #6—Create a Character. Maury Haykin created a nasty/nice *Jennifer Bunny.* These illustrations are from the front and back covers of his dummy.

Exercise #7—Memories. The recollection of a childhood experience involving the learning of the value of money inspired Frances Wetmore to create the story, *Nicholas Needed a Nickel.* This illustration is from her dummy.

7. Memories.

Recall an interesting experience from your childhood. If possible, get details from relatives or friends to help you reconstruct it and perhaps provide further elaboration. It may have been your first day at school, the birth of a sibling, the death of a pet, or a visit to the dentist. You may fabricate some of the story to make it more interesting or to fill in unremembered details.

8. How-to.

Explain in detailed steps how to lace and tie a shoelace, play a game, do a simple craft project, or perform any other activity requiring instructions. An important part of this exercise is that the instructions must be arranged in proper sequence.

Baboons making banana bread.

Exercise #8—How-to. Grace Mitchell's how-to book incorporates animals, the alphabet, and cooking. Entitled *Baboons Bake Banana Bread,* there is an animal-food illustration, plus the food recipe, for every letter of the alphabet. This illustration is from her dummy.

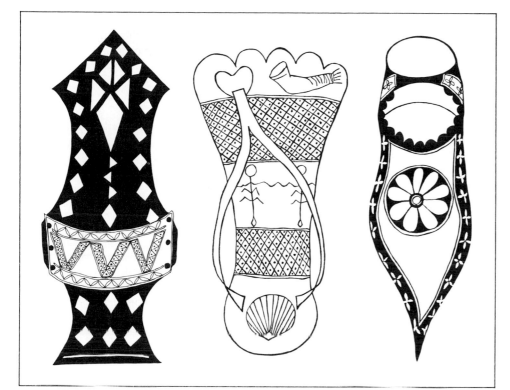

Exercise #9—Non-fiction. An article about shoe-related foot problems was developed into *A Footwear Book* by Mako Sakita. The book is a study of footwear from various countries and eras. This illustration is from her dummy.

Exercise #11—ABC/Counting/Concept Story. *Aunt Agatha's Halloween ABCs* is a story about a Halloween party attended by monsters. The names of the monsters, as well as other words in the verses, concentrate on specific letters of the alphabet. The story is by Nanette Cary and the illustrations for the dummy are by Cynthia Mauro Reisenauer.

9. Non-fiction.
Rewrite a magazine or newspaper article to the level of a beginning reader. Be sure to choose an article that would be of interest to a young child.

10. Biography.
Write a biography for a beginning reader, using a recommended word list for that age group (see page 35). Your subject need not be dead or famous. It might even be an acquaintance you admire.

11. ABC/Counting/Concept Story.
Using a special occasion that a young child would be familiar with, such as a holiday, public event, or birthday, create a story that involves the teaching of letters, numbers, or an abstract idea. For example, the names of the various things associated with Halloween could be the basis for an ABC book; the numbers of candles, guests, presents, etc. at a birthday party could be the basis for a counting book; and the various types of races at an outing could be the basis for a concept book dealing with speed and/or distance. The story may be either fiction or nonfiction.

Exercise #10—Biography. An admired family friend was the subject for Helena Willenbrink's story, *Chores All Done*. This illustration is her finished art.

Illustration

For her book, *Six Impossible Things Before Breakfast,* Norma Farber was portrayed by six different illustrators as Lewis Carroll's "White Queen at Breakfast." This is an example of how uniquely different each artist's interpretation of the same subject can be.

(Clockwise from top left)
Illustrations are by Tomie DePaola, Charles Mikolaycak, Friso Henstra, Hilary Knight, Lydia Dabcovich, Trina Schart Hyman.

ILLUSTRATION 55

Although children's books have budget restrictions regarding color, size, technique, etc., they offer an artist more freedom of expression than most other commercial art forms. Carried too far, however, such freedom can result in illustrations that function more as a vehicle for the artist's talents than as an enhancement of the story. Pictures should serve to explain and enlarge upon the text, set an appropriate mood, and provide an enjoyable art experience. Good illustrations can help to sell a so-so story, and poor illustrations can hinder the sales of a great story.

There are two basic working arrangements in children's book illustration. In one, the illustrator is also the designer of the book. Using the specifications provided by the publisher (such as book size, number of pages, and number of colors) the illustrator makes a layout of every two-page spread, roughly indicating the type and illustrations. After this has been approved by the publisher, the illustrator refines the layouts and assembles them in actual book form. This is called a *dummy*. After the dummy has been approved, the finished art is executed, with each illustration placed on a separate board. The illustrator/designer may also prepare the artwork for printing, which involves specifying the type as well as pasting up the type and illustrations on specially ruled boards called *mechanicals*. Since this is a highly technical procedure, however, many publishers prefer that it be done by their own trained personnel.

In the other arrangement, the illustrator, working closely with the publisher, merely provides the finished illustrations for a book. The publisher's designer then makes page layouts, deciding where the type and illustrations should be placed.

This chapter deals only with the procedure of making finished-art illustrations, whereas the chapter on *The Dummy* deals with book designing, and the chapter on *Preparation for Printing* deals with mechanicals. Even if you are planning to do only the finished-art illustrations for a book, it is important to read all three chapters first. There are many technical requirements that have to be taken into consideration when doing illustrations for reproduction, and a knowledge of them beforehand will avoid later grief.

STYLE AND TECHNIQUE
The style of an illustration refers to the distinctive or characteristic mode of expression of the individual artist, as well as to the various categories of art, such as representational, impressionistic, expressionistic, surrealistic, fantastic,

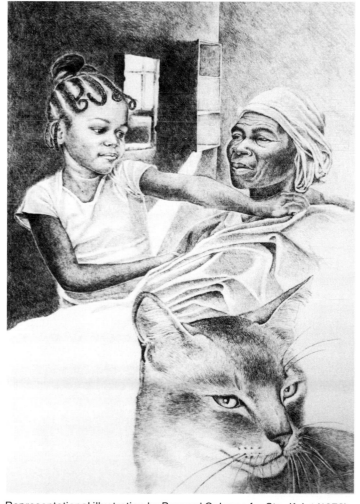

Representational illustration by Bernard Colonna for *Star Ka'at* (1976), written by Andre Norton and Dorothy Madlee.

Cartoon illustration by Dennis Kendrick for *Scarlet Monster Lives Here* (1979), written by Marjorie Weinman Sharmat.

Expressionistic illustration by Jacob Landau for *Our Eddie* (1969), written by Sulamith Ish-Kishor.

Fantasy illustration by Sofia Pelkey for *Holidays of Legend* (1971), written by Mildred H. Arthur.

folk art, cartoon art, and naive art.

Representational illustrations are more or less realistic, to the point of simulating photography (photo-realism). *Impressionistic* illustrations are usually spontaneous-looking and devoid of details, their purpose being to capture the fleeting visual impression of objects or situations. *Expressionistic* illustrations are meant to express the underlying emotional or psychological meaning of a situation, and thus the imagery is usually distorted in color and/or in form. *Surrealistic* illustrations make use of real-life images and are usually realistically executed, but the juxtaposition of images is unreal (such as a wishing-well in the middle of an ocean). *Fantastic* illustrations employ images and situations that are largely the product of the artist's imagination. Unlike surrealism, fantasy art has little relation to reality. *Folk art* usually employs the traditional motifs, symbols, and methods that are representative of a specific folk culture. *Cartoon art* employs distortion, exaggeration, absurdity, and incongruity, and is frequently used as a means of creating humor. *Naive art* is often meant to convey the impression that it was created by an inept or untrained artist, which may or may not be true.

Technique refers to the tools, materials, and methods used in the execution of illustrations. As the remainder of this chapter indicates, there are a great variety of techniques commonly used in illustration, and it is desirable for the artist to be familiar with as many as possible. Choosing the right technique is just as important as choosing the right style, for both play a big part in the ultimate success of an illustrated book.

SUPPLIES

Specific tools and materials are suggested for use with the techniques described in this chapter, but this doesn't preclude other possibilities. Experiment with the tools and materials you already have, and also investigate the vast selection available at art supply stores. Free catalogs can be acquired at most stores and are an invaluable source of information.

ILLUSTRATION 57

And, oh, what they saw there! Across from the sheep and stalls, tents spread over the field like giant umbrellas, and under them and between them were people—rosy-cheeked people—singing and shouting and dancing and laughing and eating and drinking....

Impressionistic illustration by Trina Schart Hyman for *On To Widecombe Fair* (1978), written by Patricia Lee Gauch.

Surrealistic illustration by James Barkley for *Winds* (1970), written by Mary O'Neill.

Naive illustration by Jay Ells for *Spoiled Tomatoes* (1970), written by Bill Martin, Jr. Hand lettering by Ray Barber.

Folk-art illustration by Ed Young for *The Emperor and the Kite* (1967), written by Jane Yolen. Mr. Young employed a cut-paper technique similar to that used in traditional Chinese folk art.

PRELIMINARY SKETCHES

Illustrations always begin with a series of preliminary sketches. The earliest sketches are usually not much more than doodles, their purpose being to see what your ideas look like in graphic form. These are called *thumbnail sketches,* or *thumbnails,* because they are usually quite small. After you have made some thumbnail sketches that seem to be good graphic solutions, enlarge them to your final working size and proceed to develop them, from rough to tight, in a series of sketches. Good materials for sketching are a soft graphite pencil, a kneaded eraser, and a pad of layout (also called visualizer) paper. Work directly on the pad, and after you have finished a sketch, tear it off and place it under the next clean sheet for use as a guide for the following sketch (layout paper is transparent enough to permit this). If the finished illustration is to be in color, your final sketches should also be in color. Good color mediums for sketching are color markers, pastels, and colored pencils.

Style and technique are usually determined in the sketch stage, and should be influenced by the book's content, age level, and writing style. The art for a humorous book would certainly be handled differently than that for a tragic story. Guesswork is permissible in thumbnails and rough sketches, but when it comes time to do the tight sketches, it is important to have carefully researched the story to be certain

Photograph of models posed for use in illustration.

Pencil tracing of photograph.

Thumbnail sketch.

ILLUSTRATION 59

that the pictorial details are in keeping with the written descriptions. Even highly-stylized illustration requires accuracy in regard to content.

PICTURE REFERENCE SOURCES

A personal clipping file is a handy picture reference source, but it may be necessary to look further. Some libraries have picture collections which are categorized into a wide variety of subjects. Mail order catalogs are a helpful source for furnishings, clothing, and various kinds of equipment; check the index for the item you need to draw.

Trace photographs or illustrations for information, and then enlarge, reduce, and otherwise modify elements so the end result will be your own creation. Don't consider this cheating. Professional illustrators use all kinds of reference material. Some even set up models and photograph a situation to use in an illustration.

WORKING SIZE AND BLEED

The working size for an illustration need not be the same as the reproduction size. Most illustrators prefer to work 20% to 50% larger than reproduction size. This not only makes execution easier, but the later reduction tends to clean up imperfections and improve sharpness. When working larger than reproduction size, keep in mind that later reduction will also reduce the thickness of shapes as well as the space between shapes. This is especially important with pen and ink work involving fine lines and dots, which may disappear or fill in when reduced.

If an illustration is designed to run off the edge of a page, it is necessary to extend the drawing 1/8″ or more beyond the edge. This extended portion is referred to as a *bleed*. The reason for this is that the trimming of pages is seldom exact, and the bleed is to insure that the picture doesn't end short of the trimmed edge. If your working size is larger than your reproduction size, the bleed must be proportionately wider than 1/8″.

Credits: Thumbnail sketch, photograph, tracing, and tight pencil drawing are by Sukey Remensperger. Finished pen and ink illustration is by Grace Mitchell.

Tight pencil drawing incorporating elements taken from the photograph with elements created by the illustrator.

Finished pen and ink illustration with crop marks indicating the portion of the illustration that will be reproduced. Note that the illustration bleeds well beyond the crop marks. The original art is 200% (or twice the size) of the reproduction shown here.

ENLARGING AND REDUCING ARTWORK

During the sketching stage, it is frequently necessary to enlarge or reduce picture elements taken from reference sources. Also, if the rough sketches are done at reproduction size, they will need to be enlarged to the working size of the finished illustrations. There are a number of methods for enlarging and reducing, the most common of which are described below.

Diagonal-line Scaling. To determine the outer dimensions of an enlargement or reduction, tape a piece of tracing paper over the original art, draw a rectangle at the outside dimensions of the area to be enlarged or reduced (using a T-square, triangle, and sharp pencil), and draw a line through diagonal corners. Any new-size rectangle, then, whose horizontal and vertical lines intersect the diagonal line, will be in exact proportion to the original rectangle.

Grid Scaling. If the details of the original art need to be accurately enlarged or reduced, first determine the outer dimensions by the diagonal-line method described previously. Then, on separate pieces of tracing paper draw two grids, one at the original size and one at the scaled size. To make propor-

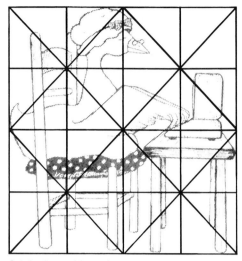

Original art with tracing-paper grid taped over it.

tionately scaled grids without measuring, draw a diagonal line opposite the one that already exists, and then draw horizontal and vertical lines at their intersection, thus dividing the rectangle into 4 boxes. Repeat this process in each of the 4 boxes, thus dividing the rectangle into 16 boxes. Finally, tape the appropriate grid onto the original art and copy the content of each grid segment, by eye, onto the scaled grid drawing. A 16-box grid is usually adequate, but for greater accuracy it may be further divided by the same process.

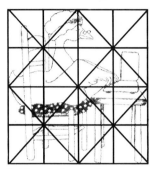

Grid-scaled reduction.

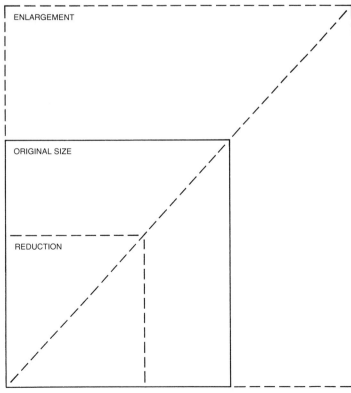

Diagonal-line scaling method.

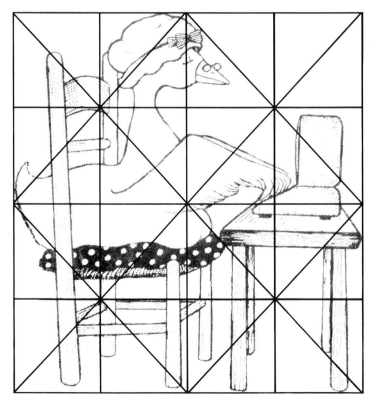

Grid-scaled enlargement.

ILLUSTRATION 61

Art Projector Scaling. There are numerous projectors on the market that enlarge and reduce opaque original copy. While some of these projectors cost many hundreds of dollars, there are others that are inexpensive enough for the home studio. The use of these projectors is both simple and accurate: tape the original copy onto the wall or copyboard, adjust the projector so that the desired-size image is projected onto the working surface, and copy what is seen.

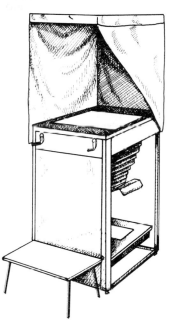

This Goodkin Model A art projector has an enlargement-reduction range of 4X to ¼X (400% to 25%). The image is projected up through and upon the drawing surface, and the unit can be used in a brightly-lit room. This type of art projector is commonly referred to as a "luci" or "luci camera", which derives from its scientific Latin name, "camera lucida."

This relatively inexpensive opaque projector will enlarge 6″ x 6″ copy up to 7′ x 7′ (larger copy can be projected in sections). It cannot reduce, and it must be used in a darkened room.

Photostats. For utmost accuracy in enlarging and reducing artwork, it may be desirable to use photostats, or stats, which are black & white paper photographic prints made directly from opaque original copy. In addition to their use as a guide for sketches, photostats may also be used as finished art for reproduction. For example, if the working size of a line-copy illustration is larger than reproduction size, a reproduction-size photostat is made of it for use in the mechanical.

For further information on photostats, including how to order them, see *Photostats,* page 134.

The above line illustration was executed larger than reproduction size. Below is the reproduction-size photostat that was made of it for use in the mechanical.

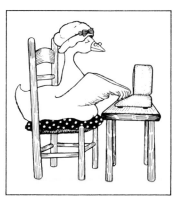

Circular proportional scale.

Circular Proportional Scale. This inexpensive plastic device, which is comprised of two rotary scales, provides a fast and extremely accurate method for obtaining enlargement and reduction proportions. Its use is described on page 135.

Office Copier Scaling. A number of brands of office copiers will enlarge and reduce to one or two sizes, and there are others which will enlarge and reduce to any percentage of size from 50% to 200%. This process is both inexpensive and fast, and while not usually sharp enough for finished art, is of great benefit in developing sketches. Look into this process at your local copying and duplicating service.

TRANSFERRING DRAWINGS

After the final preliminary drawing has been made on layout, tracing, or bond paper, it must be transferred onto another surface for finished rendering. The graphite transfer method is most commonly used to transfer drawings onto illustration board, and the tracing box transfer method is most commonly used to transfer drawings onto bristol or other fairly thin board.

Graphite Transfer Method. Apply graphite to the back of the drawing by rubbing it with a large 2B pencil, or by sanding the pencil on a sandpaper pad, allowing the graphite powder to fall onto the back of the drawing. In both methods, spread the graphite evenly with a facial tissue. Then attach the drawing to the illustration board, using tape at all four corners, and trace the outlines of the shapes with a sharp, hard pencil, such as 7H, 8H, or 9H. Use sufficient pressure when tracing, but be careful not to cut through the paper. After tracing a few lines, lift the lower tapes to check the darkness of the transferred lines. After the entire drawing has been traced, again lift the lower tapes to check that the drawing is completely transferred. Don't remove all four tapes until you have made this check, since accurate repositioning is extremely difficult.

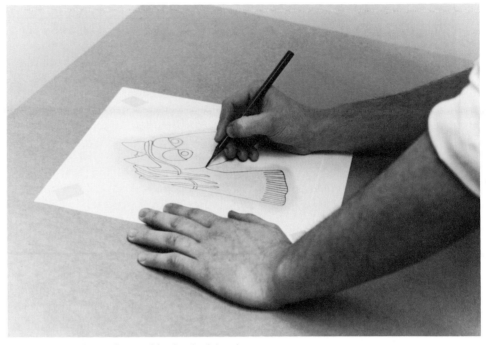

Tracing the outlines of a graphite-backed drawing.

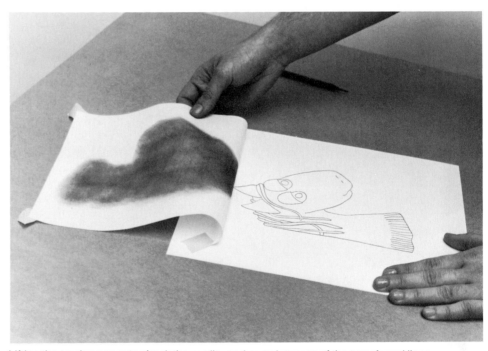

Lifting the tracing paper to check the quality and completeness of the transferred lines.

ILLUSTRATION 63

Using a tracing box.

Tracing Box Transfer Method. A tracing box (also called a light box) is a wood or metal box having a frosted glass or translucent plastic top and an interior light source. The artwork to be traced is placed on the lighted surface, and a sheet of paper or bristol board is placed over it for tracing. Since the light must pass through both materials, neither can be extremely opaque. A serviceable substitute for a tracing box is simply a translucent plastic sheet propped in such a way that a light can be placed beneath it. A daylit window is another alternative, the drawback being that it is very tiring to work on a vertical surface.

Most illustrators prefer to use the tracing box transfer method whenever possible because it is fast, and also because it permits drawing changes to be made during the transfer procedure.

A translucent plastic sheet placed over an inverted drawing table lamp is an inexpensive alternative to a tracing box.

TECHNIQUES

Illustration techniques can be divided into two categories: line and continuous-tone. Line copy is any original art composed of solid blacks and whites with no intermediate gray tones, such as pen and ink illustrations. Continuous-tone copy is any original art containing gradated or blended tones, such as photographs and pencil, pastel, oil, acrylic, watercolor, and gouache illustrations.

To reproduce line copy, the printer simply makes a photographic line negative, which is then used to image the printing plate. To reproduce continuous-tone copy, the printer must photograph it through a halftone screen. This converts the tones into minute dots of varying sizes which, when printed, optically mix with the white of the paper to simulate the tones of the original art.

Halftone reproduction of a photograph, made with an 85-line screen (85 lines per inch). A 133- or 150-line screen is normally used in book printing.

Detail of the above halftone, enlarged to show the dot pattern.

Since line copy is less expensive to reproduce than continuous-tone copy, the choice of technique may be limited by the publisher's budget. Similarly, since one-color printing is less expensive than two-, three-, or four-color printing, the number of colors may also be limited. For these reasons, it is essential for the illustrator to discuss the printing budget with the publisher before deciding on the technique and number of colors to be employed.

The following techniques in this chapter are grouped into line and continuous-tone categories. Also, color requirements and limitations are discussed in this chapter as well as in the chapter, *Preparation for Printing.* Read these sections, select the technique and number of colors that fall within the printing budget, and then confirm the appropriateness of your selection with the publisher before proceeding with your illustrations.

LINE COPY TECHNIQUES

Pen and Ink.

Artists have been drawing with pen and ink for centuries, and many effects are possible with this simple technique. The line and the dot are the two basic elements, and their variations are virtually unlimited. Many different kinds of pens can be used. Some must be dipped while others are self-feeding. A variety of nib styles is available, producing anything from hairline thins to heavy, bold lines. Waterproof black ink is best for this technique because its density makes it easier to reproduce. Also, being waterproof when dry, it will not mix with white retouch paint applied over it. The board most commonly used for pen and ink work is two-ply bristol. Kid or vellum finish is preferable to plate finish. If a rag-content bristol board is used (such as Strathmore), ink corrections may be made by erasing with a single-edge industrial razor blade. The blade must be very sharp and the pressure on it must be very light so as not to gouge the surface. Done properly, this is a better method than using retouch white, for it permits further inking on the smooth surface of the board itself.

Retouch white, of course, is useful for small corrections. Use zinc or Chinese white gouache, thin it with water in a small palette so that it flows well, and apply with a small, red sable watercolor brush.

Household ammonia will dissolve dried waterproof ink. Keep a small bottle on hand for cleaning pens.

Gillott split-nib freehand drawing pens are popular with many artists. The #170 pen has a medium-fine point, and the #290 pen has a super-fine point.

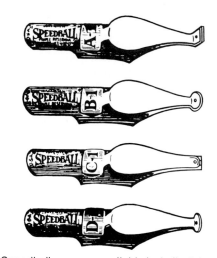

Speedball pens are available in 4 nib styles, with 6 to 9 sizes in each style. The round "B" style and the chisel-shaped "C" style are particularly useful for illustration and lettering.

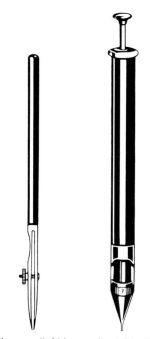

The ruling pen (left) is an adjustable-thickness pen for ruling mechanically-perfect lines. The scriber lettering pen (right) operates like a tube-feed technical pen such as the Rapidograph, the difference being that it is not a fountain pen; it is filled with an ink dropper and must be cleaned after use (which is easy because of its simple mechanism).

ILLUSTRATION 65

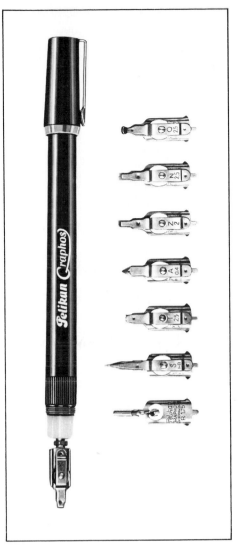

The Pelikan Graphos is a self-feeding pen that has an assortment of nib points in various styles: tube-feed (like the Rapidograph); split-nib (like freehand drawing pens); ruling-nib (like ruling pens); and round- and chisel-nib (like B- and C-style Speedball pens). Each style is available in many sizes.

Contour-line drawing. Contour-line, or outline, drawing, devoid of shading, is the purest, simplest, and most direct pen and ink technique. Because of the lack of shading, the line itself must serve to suggest three-dimensional form. Lines can be continuous or broken, as well as constant or variable in weight. Flowing, unmodulated lines can best be achieved with a tube-feed technical fountain pen, whereas variable-weight lines can best be achieved with a flexible-nib drawing pen. This pure line technique is commonly used for instructional drawings.

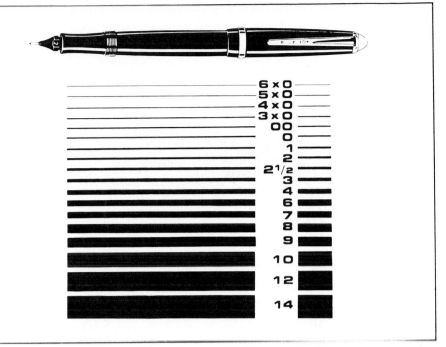

The Koh-I-Noor No. 3060 Rapidograph is a tube-feed technical fountain pen. Points are available for various line widths, as shown above. The tube-feed pen is very versatile, and can be used for freehand drawing, line-ruling, and template work. It also has a compass attachment.

Contour-line drawing. This illustration was done with a B-style Speedball pen for *Easy to Make Puppets* (1976), written and illustrated by Frieda Gates.

Crosshatching—tightly executed. *Backyard Bestiary* (1979), by Rhoda Blumberg. Illustrated by Murray Tinkelman.

Crosshatching. Crosshatching is the criss-crossing of lines, and there are two main reasons for its use. One is to model forms to suggest their three-dimensionality, and the other is to create an effect of light and shade, or *chiaroscuro.* It is also sometimes used to create surface texture or decorative patterns. Crosshatching may be used in conjunction with contour-line drawing, or it may, in itself, serve to define the contours of forms. There are infinite variations in crosshatching techniques. Lines may be mechanically-straight, irregular, wavy, slanted, continuous, or broken. To achieve a modulation from light to dark, lines may be made progressively thicker, or constant-weight lines may be spaced progressively closer. Every artist develops his own approach and technique. As with contour-line drawing, a technical fountain pen is best for constant-weight lines, and a flexible-nib drawing pen is best for variable-weight lines.

Pen Stippling. Pen stippling serves the same purposes as crosshatching, the main difference being that dots rather than lines are used to create areas of tone. The dots may be regular or irregular in size and shape, and tones are darkened by decreasing the interval between dots and/or increasing the size of the dots. Stippling may be used in conjunction with contour-line drawing or other techniques, and is especially effective in suggesting distant or indistinct imagery. Every type of pen produces a distinctive dot shape, and it is therefore desirable to experiment with many types during the process of developing this technique. (Also see *Brush Stippling,* page 78.)

Spattering. This technique is used to create textural effects, and is usually employed in conjunction with other techniques, such as contour-line drawing. It is achieved by running a stick across the bristles of a toothbrush that has been wetted with ink. Use frisket paper, (see *Air Brush,* page 77) to mask areas that are not to be spattered. A good amount of experimentation is necessary to learn how to control the spatter. Keep in mind that the dots must be large enough to reproduce well as line copy.

ILLUSTRATION 67

A Bird That Imprisons Itself

Pen Stippling. *Strange Creatures* (1981), by Seymour Simon. Illustrated by Pamela Carroll.

Crosshatching—loosely executed. *Holidays of Legend* (1971), by Mildred H. Arthur. Illustrated by Sofia Pelkey.

A lot of witches had a party. They invited nobody but themselves. That's just what you would expect of witches.

For the party, they changed themselves into all kinds of pretty things like butterflies and birds and rabbits. Even so, it was a mean party. The witch-butterflies and witch-birds and witch-rabbits spent the whole time grabbing, growling and grumbling loudly. No one in the neighborhood could sleep a wink.

Finally the mayor himself put on his bathrobe and marched up to the door. He knocked loudly. A rabbit looked out.

"I know all you rabbits and butterflies and birds are really witches. And if this party doesn't quiet down right now, there will be absolutely no celebration of HALLOWEEN this year!" His voice sounded like an angry father's.

A few minutes later, the only sound was the soft swish of many brooms flying home through the night.

Spattering. *The Mean Mouse and Other Mean Stories* (1962), by Janice May Udry. Illustrated by Ed Young. This illustration had to be reproduced here entirely in halftone because the witches are black continuous-tone copy. In the book itself, however, the spattering and town scene are brown line copy. A paper mask was used to create the moon shape.

Brush Drawing.

A red sable watercolor brush dipped in ink, dye, watercolor, or gouache produces a variety of lines that differ substantially from pen lines. These pointed brushes come in 16 sizes ranging from #000 to #14. A #3 brush is recommended for general line work, as smaller brushes tend to require too-frequent dipping. Many illustrators avoid waterproof ink because it eventually damages brushes.

Brush drawing produces a loose, free style. The dry-brush technique is executed by wiping the brush on scrap paper, after dipping, to remove some of the ink. When used with textured board or paper, this technique produces graduated tones that will reproduce as line copy.

Coquille Board.

This textured board offers an inexpensive way to achieve accurately-controlled tonal effects for line copy reproduction. Ink can be used for solid areas, and a lithographic crayon or pencil is used for tones. The pressure on the tool determines the lightness or darkness of the tones. Both fine and coarse finishes are available in this board.

Coquille Board. *North American Indian Masks: Craft and Legend* (1982), written and illustrated by Frieda Gates.

Brush drawing. *Grimm's Fairy Tales* (1962), edited by Louis and Bryna Untermeyer. Illustrated by Lucille Corcos. This illustration is for "The Six Servants."

ILLUSTRATION 69

Scratchboard.

Scratchboard is cardboard with a white clay working surface. After coating this surface with ink, a pencil drawing is traced onto it using the graphite transfer method (page 62). Various scratchboard tools are then used to scratch away the ink coating, exposing the underlying white surface. This technique produces extremely precise, sharp, and contrasty lines and shapes that reproduce particularly well. Corrections are made by smoothing the clay surface with a knife or razor blade and then recoating it with ink. If care is taken to not scratch too deeply, several reworkings are possible.

Shading and Pattern Film.

Screen tints and patterns printed on self-adhesive film offer an alternative to crosshatching and stippling. In using this film, cut a piece larger than required from the sheet, but do not cut through the protective backing paper. Peel off the film (using a knife to lift a corner) and apply to the artwork. Press firmly on the artwork, cut to the desired shape with a frisket or X-acto knife, and remove the surplus film. Finally, place a sheet of paper over the film for protection, and burnish evenly and firmly. Highlights may be achieved by scraping the film with a sharp knife, but be careful not to gouge the surface. An enormous selection of tints and patterns is available, providing an inexpensive alternative to halftone reproduction.

Scratchboard. *A Jungle Jumble* (1966), by Anico Surany. Illustrated by Leonard Everett Fisher.

Shading film. Shading film being applied to a line drawing (Formatt).

A few of the hundreds of screen tints and patterns available in shading and pattern film (Zipatone).

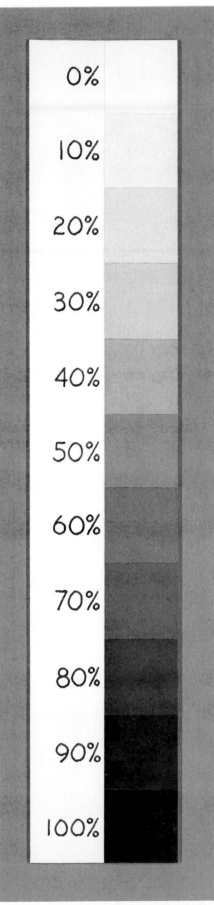

A hand-made gray scale made by intermixing black and white gouache.

CONTINUOUS-TONE COPY TECHNIQUES (HALFTONE REPRODUCTION)

As mentioned previously, continuous-tone copy is any original art containing gradated or blended tones, such as pencil, pastel, oil, acrylic, watercolor, and gouache illustrations. All of these mediums can be used for one-color reproduction by using black, white, and grays. If more than one color is used, the art must be reproduced by four-color process (see page 84), which is the most expensive form of reproduction.

Because of the screening process, some loss of contrast occurs in reproduction. It is therefore advisable to overemphasize the contrast between values in the original art. If there is not at least a 10% value difference between a form and its background, the form may not be discernible when reproduced. A gray, or value, scale with 10% increments from black to white is useful for this purpose. It can be purchased from a photo or art supply store, or it can be made using black and white gouache.

The variety of surfaces and mediums employed in continuous-tone illustration is extremely wide. It is wise to investigate and experiment to find which you prefer and which are most suitable for your story. Combinations of mediums (mixed media) are also possible and should be explored.

Pencils.

Graphite drawing pencils are available in 17 degrees of hardness from 6B (very soft) to 9H (very hard). *Layout* and *sketching pencils* are large, soft, intense-black graphite pencils. *Colored pencils,* with either thick, soft leads or thin, hard leads, are waterproof, non-fading, and do not easily smudge. *Water-soluble colored pencils* are also useful. They can be used in combination with a wetted brush to create color washes. Soft, medium, and hard *carbon* and *charcoal pencils* produce a flat, intense black that resembles the qualities of printing ink (graphite produces a shiny gray-black). Black *lithographic pencils* are waxy, and come in many degrees of hardness. They are also available in crayon form.

Pencil drawings can consist of lines, crosshatching, and stippling in any variety of stroke weights and lengths. Strokes can be smudged if desired, but to avoid later accidental smudging, spray the finished drawing with workable matte fixative. Paper or board with a toothy rather than a smooth surface is best for most types of pencil drawing. Gum, kneaded, and firm-rubber erasers are all useful for cleaning, correction, and modeling purposes.

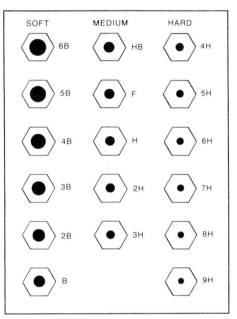

Hardness chart for graphite drawing pencils.

Charcoal.

Charcoal is available in many forms: thin sticks made of natural *vine charcoal,* thick sticks made of *compressed charcoal,* wood-encased *charcoal pencils,* and *charcoal powder.* Sticks and pencils come in various degrees of hardness. Any toothy paper or board is suitable for charcoal drawing, but a paper specially formulated for charcoal is the preferred choice. It is available in many sizes and colors.

Finger tips, facial tissues, a chamois, a kneaded eraser, and stumps (tortillons) are all useful for blending and shading charcoal (stumps are blotter-like paper rolled into pencil form). A kneaded eraser is also used for corrections and cleaning. To avoid smudging, spray the completed drawing with workable matte fixative.

ILLUSTRATION 71

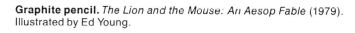

Graphite pencil. *The Lion and the Mouse: An Aesop Fable* (1979). Illustrated by Ed Young.

Graphite pencil and ink. *Fly Like an Eagle and Other Stories* (1978), by Elizabeth Van Steenwyk. Illustrated by Paul Frame.

Graphite pencil. *Femi and Old Grandaddie* (1972), by Adjai Robinson. Illustrated by Jerry Pinkney.

Charcoal. *The Drought on Ziax II* (1978), by John Morressy. Illustrated by Stanley Skardinsky.

Crayons.

Wax crayons, while commonly considered a children's art medium, are frequently used in professional illustration. They are available in sets of from 8 to 64 colors. *Conté crayons* are square, chalky sticks in sanguine (red), bistre (brown), black, and white. Black is available in hard, medium, and soft densities. *Lithographic crayons,* which are black, waxy crayons made for drawing on lithographic stones, are also used for drawing on paper. *Oil crayons* (such as Cray-Pas) are a combination of crayon and pastel in round stick form. They have qualities similar to both pastels and oil paint, and can be worked into with turpentine or paint thinner on a cotton swab or wad.

Mistakes are difficult to correct in waxy mediums. Usually, as much wax as possible is scraped away with a knife or razor blade, and the area is then re-worked with white and/or colors.

Pastels.

Pastel sticks are available in sets of from 12 to over 300 colors, and in soft, medium, and hard densities. The most brilliant colors are produced by the softest sticks, but they are also the most fragile. Pastel colors tend to become muddy when intermixed, and thus the larger the selection of colors, the more successful will be the resulting work. Sets of gray pastel sticks are available for black & white rendering, and sets of colored *pastel pencils* are available for use in conjunction with pastel sticks. Black carbon and charcoal pencils are also used in conjunction with pastel sticks. While any toothy paper or board is suitable for pastel, most artists prefer *pastel paper,* which is available in many sizes and colors.

Fingers, paper stumps (tortillons), facial tissues, and cotton wads and swabs are used for blending and modeling pastel. Cotton wads and swabs tend to remove pastel, and thus are used for lightening plus blending. A stiff-bristled brush will also serve this purpose. A kneaded eraser will remove pastel either entirely or partially, depending upon whether it is rubbed or tamped.

Bond paper masks are frequently used, when applying pastel, to achieve hard edges. They are also used to shield rendered areas when cleaning up with a kneaded eraser. Because pastels are so chalky, they must be sprayed with workable matte fixative to avoid later smudging. This can be done as each shape is rendered, or after the illustration is completed. Two or three light coats are better than one heavy coat.

Acrylics.

These quick-drying colors are extremely versatile, offering the artist a wide range of techniques. They can be used straight from the tube for heavy, opaque, impasto effects similar to that of oil painting, or they can be thinned with water and/or acrylic medium for transparent glazing and watercolor-like effects. A retarder mixed with the paint or applied to the working surface will retard drying. Any porcelain or glass surface can serve as a palette, and colors can be kept moist between working sessions by sealing the palette in plastic kitchen wrap. Almost any painting surface is suitable for acrylics providing it is not oil-primed. This includes illustration board, paper, canvas, and wood panels. Lightweight paper, however, may buckle and should be stretched. Synthetic bristle brushes are necessary for acrylics and are available in brights, flats, and rounds in many sizes. Brushes should be frequently rinsed in water during use. After use, they should be thoroughly washed in soap and water.

Because of the rapid-drying, waterproof-when-dry properties of acrylic paints, successive coats can be quickly applied over one another without intermixing or turning muddy. On the other hand, these properties make it impossible to later blend or rework areas without applying more paint, as would be possible with slow-drying oils, or re-soluble watercolors and gouache. Acrylics are ideal for mixed-media techniques and may be successfully combined with colored pencils, watercolor pencils, watercolor, gouache, ink, dyes, pastel, and pasted-down paper or fabric (collage).

Set of pastel sticks and pencils with facial tissue, cotton wad, kneaded eraser, paper stumps, and workable fixative.

ILLUSTRATION 73

Wax crayon and ink. *Not This Bear* (1968), written and illustrated by Bernice Myers.

Pastel. *The Third Gift* (1974), by Jan Carew. Illustrated by Leo and Diane Dillon. Each shape was masked with frisket paper (see *Air Brush*, page 77) and then rendered and fixed.

Pastel pencils. *Dancing in the Moon* (1955), written and illustrated by Fritz Eichenberg.

Acrylic. *The Seven Days of Creation* (1981), written and illustrated by Leonard Everett Fisher.

Watercolor. *Big Gus and Little Gus* (1982), written and illustrated by Lee Lorenz.

Gouache. *Grimm's Fairy Tales* (1962), edited by Louis and Bryna Unter-meyer. Illustrated by Lucille Corcos. This illustration is for "The Juniper Tree."

Watercolor. *Seven Little Rabbits* (1973), by John Becker. Illustrated by Barbara Cooney.

Gouache.

Gouache, also called *designers color,* is opaque watercolor. It is available in both tubes and pans in dozens of colors. Tube colors are the most popular and must be thinned with water to a creamy consistency before being intermixed or applied. A china or aluminum palette with many small wells is best for thinning and mixing paint. An eyedropper or ear syringe is handy for adding water. Red sable watercolor brushes are most commonly used for application. A good range of sizes for the majority of purposes is #1, #3, and #5 or #6. A slightly toothy illustration board is the best painting surface.

Paper is less suitable because it tends to buckle when large amounts of color are applied to it.

Gouache is an ideal medium for tight rendering as well as for laying flat tones. Being quick-drying and opaque, underlying colors can be easily and quickly covered up, and being water-soluble when dry, the blending and reworking of previously-rendered areas is easily accomplished. To lay a flat tone in one coat with no streaking, first outline the shape with a small brush, and then rapidly flood it in with a large brush well-loaded with paint. If the entire shape is rapidly flooded in, the paint will level itself before drying, thus producing a

dense, streakless coating. This technique works well for small shapes, but large shapes would begin to dry before the flooding-in is completed. They should therefore be masked with frisket paper (see *Air Brush,* page 77) and then painted in with a large brush. Since the mask protects surrounding areas, the paint can be broadly applied and thoroughly brushed out to eliminate streaks.

Watercolors.

Watercolor paints contain very finely ground pigments and gum arabic. Tints are achieved with the addition of water, not white paint, and consequently are

ILLUSTRATION 75

Watercolor and ink line. *The Maestro Plays* (1970), by Bill Martin, Jr. Illustrated by Sal Murdocca and hand-lettered by Ray Barber.

Dyes and ink line. *Jinjero, The Scar-Faced Baboon* (1975), by Cliff Jolly. Illustrated by John Trotta.

very transparent. Because of its transparency, watercolor is a difficult medium to master. In addition to the need for a direct and spontaneous technique, it permits little or no correcting or reworking. Opaque watercolor (gouache) is sometimes used for alterations, but its effect is different from that of watercolors.

Watercolors are available in tube and pan form, the choice being largely one of personal preference. Either aluminum or china palettes are used for mixing and ideally should contain both wells and slant basins. Red sable watercolor brushes in a variety of sizes, plus a large oval, or sky, brush, are most commonly used for watercolor application.

Illustrators usually use heavyweight (double-thick) illustration board for watercolors, whereas fine artists almost always use watercolor paper. Both are available in smooth (hot pressed or HP), medium (cold pressed or CP), and rough (R) surfaces. Watercolor paper, particularly the lighter weights, must be stretched to avoid warping or buckling.

This is done by soaking the paper and then taping it, continuously on all four sides, onto a drawing board. Gummed Kraft package sealing tape is required for this purpose.

Washes may be applied over one another, but more than three may result in dirty color. Unless a loose, wet effect is desired, each wash should dry before another is put down. Work from light washes to dark washes, and from large areas to small areas. Tones may be blended by wetting the surface with a small sponge, blotting to the desired dampness with blotting paper, and then applying color. For details, colors may be used at their fullest strength, with just enough water added to achieve proper brushing consistency.

Dyes.

The technique used with dyes (commonly referred to as *concentrated watercolors*) is similar to that used with watercolors. The difference between watercolor and dye is that watercolor is colored pigment that is laid on the surface of the paper and remains soluble

when dry, whereas dye is a non-pigmented coloring agent that stains the paper and becomes waterproof when dry. Dyes are intensely brilliant and very transparent. Tints can be achieved by adding water. Bottled dyes are available in dozens of colors and are used with watercolor brushes and an aluminum or china palette. Being waterproof when dry, corrections are very difficult, but laundry bleach diluted with water and applied with a cotton swab (never a brush) will remove color fairly well. The bleach must be washed away immediately with a cotton swab dipped in water. Opaque watercolors may be used in conjunction with dyes. Since the dye frequently bleeds through these colors, it may be necessary to first apply a special bleed-proof white. To avoid damaging brushes, rinse them frequently in water during use, and clean them thoroughly with soap and water after use.

Ink and wash. *Miss Suzy* (1964), by Miriam Young. Illustrated by Arnold Lobel.

Ink and wash with flat color tints. *Down the Road* (1978), written and illustrated by Joan Lesikin.

Ink and Wash.

Illustrations combining black ink lines or shapes with gray or colored washes are first drawn in pencil and then inked in with waterproof black ink. Extraneous pencil lines should be erased before washes are added. Water-diluted black ink (either waterproof or non-water-proof), colored inks, dyes, or watercolors are used for washes, and are applied with a watercolor brush.

Color Markers.

Although generally regarded as a layout medium, color markers are also used for finished illustrations. In most brands, at least two nib sizes are available: the broad felt nib and the pointed felt or synthetic fiber nib. A superfine pointed synthetic fiber nib is also available in some brands. Broad-nib and pointed-nib markers are spirit-based dye, while superfine-nib markers may

be either spirit-based or water-based dye. Spirit-based dye is waterproof, whereas water-based dye may be blended, after it is applied, with a water-moistened brush or swab. To blend, soften, or lighten spirit-based dye, it is necessary to use a colorless blender marker.

Because dyes are transparent and stain the paper to which they are applied, marker illustrations cannot

Color markers. *Freedom's Apple Tree* (1970), by Bill Martin, Jr. Illustrated by John Rombola and hand-lettered by Ray Barber.

ILLUSTRATION 77

easily be corrected or modified. For this reason, markers are best suited for styles that are not finicky.

Both marker sketches and finished illustrations are usually executed on layout paper. Work directly on the top sheet of the pad, using an underlying sketch as a guide. Because markers bleed through most layout papers, protect the underlying sketch as well as succeeding sheets in the pad with a piece of acetate cut to the size of the pad. This reusable barrier sheet can be stored at the back of the pad between uses. Layout pads designed especially for marker use are available. The paper is bleedproof and is particularly receptive to markers. Finished illustrations executed on layout paper should be mounted on white board for protection, using either rubber cement, spray adhesive, or the dry mounting process used by photographers.

Finished marker illustrations may also be executed on illustration board. This may be desirable if the markers are combined with other techniques, such as pen and ink, or if frisket paper is used to create hard edges on the marker-rendered shapes. As explained under *Air Brush,* page 77, frisket paper must be cut after it is applied, and this would be very difficult to do on thin layout paper.

Color markers are available individually and in sets of from 12 to 150 colors. Warm and cool grays are also available individually and in sets of 12.

OTHER ILLUSTRATION TECHNIQUES

Air Brush.

An air brush is a small, pencil-shaped spray gun that is operated by compressed air. Ink, dye, watercolor, and gouache can be used in an air brush to create either flat or gradated tones without streaks or textures. A high-quality double-action air brush is necessary for illustration purposes, and its use requires a good amount of experimentation and practice.

Frisket paper is used to mask areas that are not to be sprayed. This is a thin, transparent, waterproof, self-adhesive paper that is available in sheets and

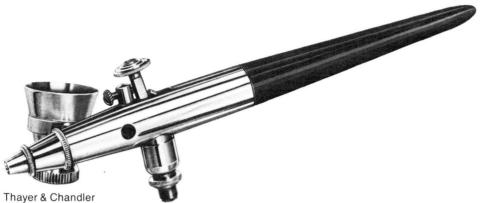

Thayer & Chandler
Model A air brush.

rolls. To apply frisket paper, cut a generous-sized piece from the sheet, using a small frisket or X-Acto knife. Peel off the piece from the backing paper, apply to the artwork, and press down firmly. Then cut out the desired shape with the knife, being careful not to cut into the artwork, and remove the paper in the area to be rendered. If it does not come off easily, squirt some rubber cement thinner under it as it is being peeled off.

While frisket paper is specifically designed for use with an air brush, it can also be used with other mediums and application methods, such as pastel and brush-rendered watercolor, gouache, and acrylics.

Air brush. *Why Mosquitoes Buzz in People's Ears* (1975), by Verna Aardema. Illustrated by Leo and Diane Dillon.

Brush stippling. *Nonna* (1975), by Jennifer Bartoli. Illustrated by Joan E. Drescher.

Collage using real wallpaper. *Splish Splash!* (1973), written and illustrated by Ethel and Leonard Kessler.

Brush Stippling.

Brush stippling is done with a stencil brush, which is a round, stiff-bristled, flat-tipped brush available in five sizes ranging in diameter from ½″ to 1¼″. The brush tip is tamped in ink, dye, pastel, charcoal, or paint, and then tamped on the illustration to create a variety of effects such as dots, striations, and airbrush-like continuous-tone modeling. If the individual dots or striations are sufficiently large and dense they may be reproducible as line copy. Since this is often not the case, however, brush stippling must usually be treated as continuous-tone copy.

Brush stippling is generally combined with other techniques, such as contour-line drawing. Use bond paper or frisket paper (see *Air Brush,* page 77) to mask areas that are not to be stippled. (Also see *Pen Stippling*, page 66.)

Collage.

Pasted-down materials such as paper or cloth may be used alone or in conjunction with other mediums for illustration purposes. Rubber cement is the most popular collage adhesive, but matte acrylic medium is more permanent, and can also serve as a surface coating. Since it contains water, however, it cannot be applied to water-soluble mediums.

Oil Painting.

The slow-drying properties of oil paint make it a somewhat impractical medium for illustration, especially when tight deadlines are involved. However, a new, faster-drying alkyd resin based paint has recently been introduced to help alleviate this problem. Some illustrators prefer oils over acrylics because the longer drying time permits extensive reworking and blending while the colors are still wet.

Oil painting. *The Enchanted Garden* (in progress), written and illustrated by Cecelia M. Laureys.

ILLUSTRATION 79

TREE SOIL

Want to see a clean-up squad?
Take an old sheet.
Put it under a tree.
Put stones at the corners to hold it down.
Come back in a week.
Scoop up a handful of leaves.
You'll see grubs, worms, millipedes
and other tiny creatures
that turn dead brown leaves into soil.

With a magnifying glass you'll see even more.

Collage using colored paper. *The Tremendous Tree Book* (1979) by May Garelick and Barbara Brenner. Illustrated by Fred Brenner.

Eric Carle

Gute Reise, bunter Hahn!

dtv junior

Collage using hand-painted paper. *Gute Reise, bunter Hahn!* is the 1982 German edition of *The Rooster Who Set Out to See the World* (1972), written and illustrated by Eric Carle.

Collage using watercolor-stained paper. *The Golden Swans* (1969), retold by Kermit Krueger and illustrated by Ed Young.

Printmaking.

Printmaking is a general term for any technique involving the use of an inked plate, block, or screen to create printed impressions. Although usually regarded as a fine art, some artists have employed printmaking techniques in the illustration of children's books. A hand-pulled proof is used as the finished art for reproduction.

Relief Printing. Relief, or raised-surface, printing is the oldest, simplest, and least expensive method of making prints. It includes woodcuts, wood engraving, and linoleum cuts (linocuts), all of which can be reproduced as line copy. Woodcuts and linocuts are made in the same way, the only difference being that linoleum is easier to work with because it has no grain. A tracing paper drawing is transferred, in reverse, to the wood or linoleum block, using a sheet of carbon or transfer paper. Wood carving tools are used to cut away the unwanted material, leaving the printing image raised in relief. To print the cut, an inked rubber brayer is rolled over it, which coats the relief areas. A piece of paper is then placed on it and rubbed with the bowl of a tablespoon. A printing press is desirable when many prints are to be made, but for the few prints needed for illustration purposes, a tablespoon is adequate.

Woodcuts are made on the plank, or long grain, of the wood with carving tools, whereas wood engravings are made on the end grain of the wood with engraving tools, or gravers. Wood engravings permit much greater detail and accuracy than woodcuts, but are also much more difficult to make.

Intaglio Printing. Intaglio is a depressed-surface printing method in which the print is taken from ink deposited in the crevices of a metal printing plate. In line engraving, drypoint, and mezzotint, the imagery is achieved by incising or otherwise working the metal with various tools, whereas in etching and aquatint, the imagery is achieved by etching the metal with acid. Printing is done by coating the plate with ink and then wiping it so ink remains only in the crevices. The inked plate is placed on the bed of an etching press, covered

Woodcut (relief printing). *How the Left-behind Beasts Built Ararat* (1978) by Norma Farber. Illustrated by Antonio Frasconi. The illustration in the book is printed in line (two flat colors), but is reproduced here in four-color process.

with a sheet of dampened paper and a felt blanket, and rolled through the press.

Planographic Printing. Lithography is the most common form of planographic printing. In this process, the printing plate or stone is made water-receptive in the non-printing areas, and ink-receptive in the printing or image areas. There is no difference in height between the printing and non-printing areas; both are on the same level or "plane." In the printing operation, the plate or stone is dampened before it is inked so that

the ink will not adhere to the non-printing areas.

Screen Printing. Also known as *silkscreen* or *serigraphy*, screen printing is a stencil method of printing. The stencil is adhered to a fine mesh fabric that has been stretched on a frame, and paint is forced through the open or image areas of the mesh with a rubber blade called a *squeegee*.

There are many books that thoroughly describe printmaking techniques, such as *Printmaking, History & Process* by Donald Saff.

ILLUSTRATION 81

Wood engraving (relief printing). *Stone Soup* (1985), retold by Kenneth Jones and illustrated by Sarah Chamberlain. This hand-bound book was issued in a limited edition of 150 signed and numbered copies.

Metal engraving (intaglio printing). *Perrault's Fairy Tales* (1867), illustrated by Gustave Doré. This is a detail of an illustration for "The Sleeping Beauty."

Lithograph (planographic printing). *Duo* (in progress) by Eudice Charney. Illustrated by Hugh Mesibov.

Silkscreen (screen printing). *Sunflower Garden* (1969) by Janice May Udry. Illustrated by Beatrice Darwin. The illustration in the book is printed in line (four flat colors), but is reproduced here in four-color process.

Photography.

In children's nonfiction books, photographs are often preferable to drawings because they tend to make facts more convincing and believable. Portrait photographs are useful for biographies, and situation photographs are useful to enhance social studies books. You may hire a professional photographer, use stock photos, or take the pictures yourself.

Professional Photographs. A professional photographer can be paid either a flat fee or a share of your royalties. Stock photos can be purchased from companies that specialize in them. They can also be acquired, for little or no fee, from newspapers, news syndications, magazines, libraries, museums, state publicity offices, chambers of commerce, historical societies, tourist bureaus, and various government agencies. Nearly 1,000 picture suppliers who sell, rent, or provide free photographs are listed in a book entitled *Picture Sources,* available for a fee from the Special Libraries Association, 235 Park Avenue South, New York, NY 10003. Picture sources are also listed in *Writer's Market,* which is published by *Writer's Digest.*

It is important to find out whether you may use a photograph freely, or if you need written permission. For example, movie stills that I purchased from a stock picture company and from a museum for use in a book on monsters required additional fees for the written permission of the film company.

Taking Your Own Photographs. The smallest format that should be used for reproduction photography is 35mm. For both black & white and color, slow film is better than fast film because it has a finer grain.

In color photography, printers prefer to reproduce from transparencies, or "chromes," rather than from color prints. The photograph should have moderate contrast, good highlight and shadow detail, and sharp focus. It should also have good color balance, without a bias towards one color (such

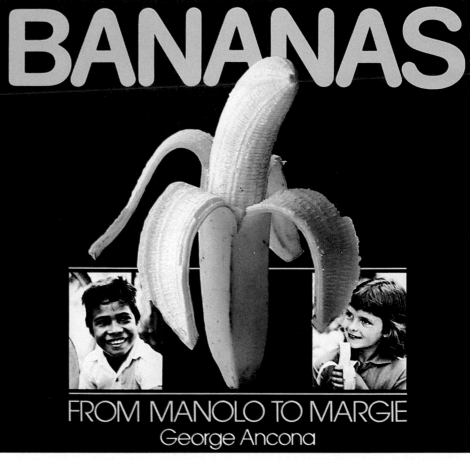

George Ancona visited Honduras to research and photograph material for this book, which is about a boy and his family who live on a banana plantation. Published in 1982.

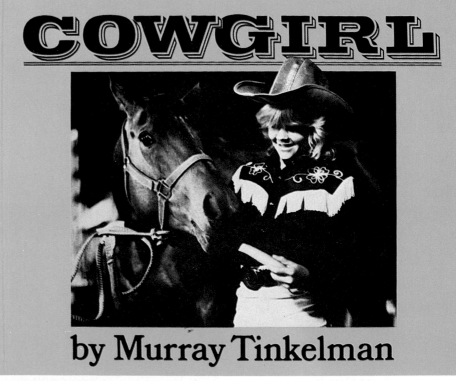

Murray Tinkelman's on-the-scene photographs present a fascinating glimpse of a young cowgirl's debut in a rodeo competition. Published in 1984.

ILLUSTRATION 83

as an overall green tinge). If only a portion of the transparency is to be reproduced, make a black & white photostat enlargement of it to reproduction size, and indicate the cropping on the enlarged print (see *Preparation for Printing*, page 130).

In black & white photography, 8″ x 10″ glossy or matte prints are preferable, although 5″ x 7″ prints are acceptable. The photograph should have sharp focus and a full range of tones from pure white to pure black. Because the screening process used in reproduction tends to reduce contrast, there should be a clear difference between adjacent tones. Also, there should be strong tonal modeling in areas of importance, such as faces. For protection, photographs should be individually mounted on stiff white or gray board that is large enough to provide a 2″ border on all sides. This border is used for crop marks and other specifications for the printer, as described in the chapter, *Preparation for Printing,* page 130.

Veloxes and Line Conversions.
A velox is a halftone reproduction of continuous-tone copy (such as a photo or a wash drawing) that has been printed on photographic paper. Being opaque line copy, the velox can be pasted on the mechanical, which is less expensive than having the printer make the halftone.

Line conversions are similar to veloxes, the difference being that special screens are used to convert the continuous-tone copy (usually photographs) to line copy. These screens are available in a variety of patterns, many of which suggest illustration techniques such as crosshatching, stippling, and scratchboard.

Velox prints courtesy Mask-O-Neg, Inc.
Line conversions courtesy Schaedler/Pinwheel.

Velox—65-line screen.

Line conversion—crosshatch posterization.

Velox—100-line screen.

Line conversion—mezzotint.

Velox—120-line screen.

Line conversion—woodgrain posterization.

COLOR PRINTING

Four-color Process Printing.

Full-color, continuous-tone illustrations and photographs are reproduced by four-color process printing, which involves four printing plates: yellow, magenta (red), cyan (blue), and black. When overprinted in various tonal gradations, these three primary colors plus black will accurately duplicate all colors in the original art.

A color scanner, which is a computerized machine employing light beams and filters, is used to separate the colors of the original art into the four process colors. It produces a film negative for each color, and these are later used to image the printing plates.

While four-color process printing is expensive, it permits the use of unlimited colors and requires no special preparation on the part of the artist. All the printer needs is the original art (or a transparency of it), plus an indication of its cropping, size, and position on the mechanical.

Oil painting reproduced by four-color process. Cover illustration by Seymour Fleishman for *The Boy Drummer of Vincennes* (1972), by Carl Carmer.

Enlarged detail of boy's face.

(Right) These four *progressive proofs,* or *progs,* are used by the printer as a color control guide.

Yellow.

Yellow and magenta.

ILLUSTRATION 85

Magenta (process red) proof.

Yellow proof.

Cyan (process blue) proof.

Black proof.

Yellow, magenta, and cyan.

Yellow, magenta, cyan, and black.

Flat Color Printing.

In flat color (also called match color) printing, the printing plate for each color is made from black & white art that has been color-separated by the artist. In a two-color illustration, for example, the art for one color is executed on illustration board, and the art for the other color is executed, in register, on a hinged acetate or drafting film overlay sheet. This makes it possible for the printer to photograph each piece separately to make his two printing plates.

The printing colors are specified by the artist by pasting color swatches on the mechanical, and the printer mixes his printing inks to match the specified colors. The original art can consist of line copy, continuous-tone copy, and screen tints. Because printing inks are transparent (except black), additional colors can be achieved by overprinting. For example, red printed over blue will produce violet, and blue printed over yellow will produce green. If the original art is continuous-tone, then the printer must photograph it through a halftone screen, and the resulting tonal gradations will be tints of the specified color. If the original art is line copy, flat, ungraded tints can be achieved through the use of dot-pattern shading film applied on the art, or by requesting the printer to apply screen tints on his negatives. Shading film and screen tints are available in 10% increments ranging from 10% (very light) to 90% (very dark).

Flat color printing is usually done in either two or three colors, but sometimes four (or even more) colors are used. When four colors are used, it is generally advantageous that they be the four process colors (yellow, magenta, cyan, and black). Overprinted in various combinations of solids and tints, they produce an unlimited range of colors.

Because the colors are pre-separated by the artist, and because only two or three colors are normally used, flat color printing is much less expensive than four-color process printing. For these reasons, it is the most common method for printing children's picture books. Therefore, while the procedures for preparing color-separated illustrations may seem complicated, it is important for every illustrator to learn them. Further information on this subject is provided in the chapter, *Preparation for Printing,* as well as in such books as *Graphic Design Studio Procedures* by David Gates.

Note: It is important to understand that in printing terminology, black is counted as a color. A one-color job, therefore, means one printing plate and one run on the press, no matter what the color. It does not mean one color in addition to black.

Also, while the three illustrations on this page were originally printed in flat colors, they had to be reproduced here in four-color process.

Four flat colors: yellow, orange, blue, and black.
The Witch Who Wasn't (1964), by Jane Yolen. Illustrated by Arnold Roth.

Three flat colors: wine, yellow ochre, and black.
Tints and overprinting give the appearance of more colors.
This Time, Tempe Wick? (1974), by Patricia Lee Gauch.
Illustrated by Margot Tomes.

Two flat colors: green and black (some pages are orange and black).
The Wonderful Cat of Cobbie Bean (1957), by Barbee Oliver Carleton.
Illustrated by Jacob Landau.

ILLUSTRATION 87

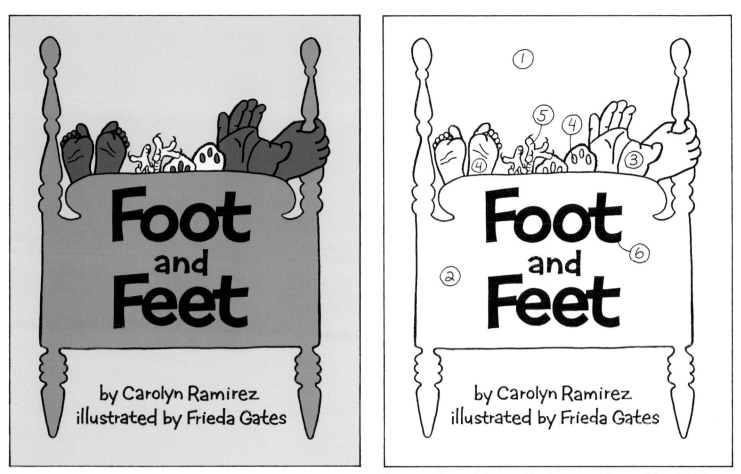

Process colors and tints used for the cover of *Foot and Feet* (1973):

1. 100% Y, 10% C.   4. 100% M.
2. 100% Y, 40% M.   5. 100% Y.
3. 70%M, 50% C.   6. 100% K (code for black).

Using Process Color for Flat Color Printing. As mentioned on page 85, process color may also be used to reproduce black & white line copy in a full range of colors. This technique is commonly used in flat color printing when more than four colors are needed. Rather than using more than four mixed colors, which would require more printing plates and press runs, the four process colors are overprinted in various combinations and tints, thus making an unlimited range of colors possible.

The original art is prepared in the same way as for normal flat color printing, but instead of attaching color swatches for the printer to match, you must provide him with an overlay indicating the process colors and tints required to achieve each color. A color guide that shows all possible overprinting combinations of process colors and tints can be acquired at no charge from some color printing companies. *Color Atlas,* by Harald Kueppers, is an inexpensive process color guide published by Barron's Education Series, Inc.

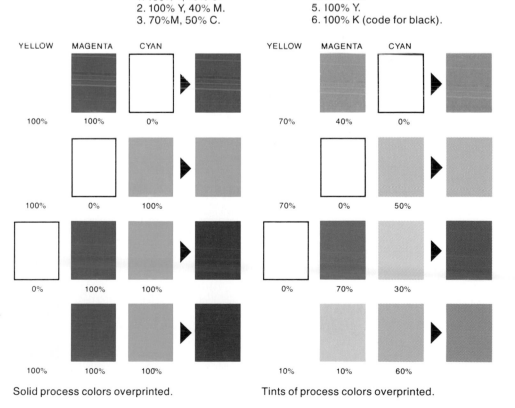

Solid process colors overprinted.   Tints of process colors overprinted.

PORTFOLIO FOR CHILDREN'S BOOK ILLUSTRATORS

An illustrator's portfolio should contain work that demonstrates both competence and versatility. Include only your best work in each style and technique category. It is better to have a thin portfolio containing only excellent work than to have a thick portfolio that is either redundant or interlarded with "near misses." Although a rounded selection is preferable, do not include areas in which you are weak. Editors like to see examples of black & white line art, line art with one and two additional colors, black & white continuous-tone art, and some full-color illustrations. Sketches of children, animals, scenes, buildings, etc., are also desirable. These can be presented as separate sheets or in a sketch book. A well-executed dummy layout of a story you have written, or of a familiar fable or fairy tale, is definitely impressive. At least one of the illustrations in the story should be executed in finished form and presented along with the dummy. If you have the ability to do mechanicals and color separations, it is desirable to include a sample, even if it does not pertain to children's books.

Be sure to have a reproduced example of your work that you can leave with editors so they won't forget you. It can be a business card with a spot illustration, or a larger card or folder showing one or more pieces of your work. There are many companies that specialize in printing full-color, postcard-like reproductions in short runs and at low cost. Be prepared to leave your portfolio with the publisher, as some editors occasionally make such a request.

If you are unable to visit a publisher in person, it is possible to send photostats, slides, and/or color prints of your work by mail. It is advisable, however, to send a query letter first. Always include a self-addressed envelope with proper postage affixed to insure the return of your work.

For further information, the Children's Book Council distributes a pamphlet for illustrators that furnishes information on how to arrange appointments with specific publishers, including what they would like to see, what they would like left with them, their special interests or requirements, and arrangements for illustrators who live outside the publisher's immediate geographic area.

The *Graphic Artists Guild Handbook, Pricing & Ethical Guidelines,* which describes the pricing of artwork, professional practices, business and legal practices for commissioned artwork, ethical standards, etc., is published by Robert Silver Associates, 95 Madison Avenue, New York, NY 10016.

UNTRAINED ARTISTS

Children's book illustrations by untrained artists can be successful if proper supervision is provided. The uninhibited drawings of a young child, for example, can sometimes be more charming and appealing than the sophisticated illustrations of a professional. Even if you ultimately do the illustrations yourself, you might benefit by seeking the help and advice of a child. If nothing else, it could serve to make you less self-conscious.

She Was Nice to Mice (1975), written by Alexandra Elizabeth Sheedy and illustrated by Jessica Ann Levy. Both the writer and illustrator were only 13 years old when they produced this book.

The Dummy

Because pictures play such an important role in children's books, publishers need to see page-by-page layouts in order to make an accurate judgment of a book design. Sometimes these layouts are presented as individual sheets of two-page spreads, but more often they are presented in actual book form. Such a handmade mock-up of a book is called a *dummy*.

Publishers usually employ a designer to lay out the book and prepare the dummy. Working with the editor and illustrator, the designer chooses the typeface and determines the size and location of the type and illustrations on every page plus the cover. However, if you plan to design and illustrate your own book, you must prepare the dummy yourself. Even if you plan to do only the illustrations, or only the writing, a dummy can be very helpful. For illustrators, a dummy aids in determining the number, size, and composition of illustrations. For writers, a dummy, however crudely executed, aids in determining if more or less text is needed, and if the text provides sufficient potential for successful graphic depiction by the illustrator.

BOOK FORMATS

Format refers to the shape, size, and general make-up of a book, and this is determined by the publisher. However, if you are preparing a dummy for a proposed book to be submitted to various publishers for consideration, you must determine the format yourself. Although every publisher has specific format preferences, general publishing guidelines can be acquired by examining a broad variety of children's books at your public library. Since there are many technical considerations that influence page size, it is wise to conform to the size of an already-published book. You will notice that the average picture book, counting each side of the paper as an individual page, contains 32, 40, or 48 pages, the maximum length being 64 pages. Books are bound in signatures of 32, 16, 12, and occasionally 8 pages. A signature is one sheet of paper printed on both sides and folded and trimmed in such a way that it results in a series of consecutive pages.

The first six to eight pages of most books contain "front matter," which includes the half title, title, copyright, dedication, and possibly a table of contents, preface, foreword, introduction, and/or information about the book. Books will vary in the way this information is laid out, but the Library of Congress dictates that the copyright notice appear on the "title verso" page, which is the reverse side of the title page. (In publishing, *recto* means the right-hand page, and *verso* means the reverse, or left-hand page.) The title page generally states the title, author, illustrator, and the name and address of the publishing company. The front-matter section may also include illustrations and/or blank pages.

The last pages of some children's books contain "back matter," which includes biographical information about the author and illustrator, and possibly an index, bibliography, and/or picture credits.

Most hardcover books have endpapers, which are sheets that are glued to the inside of the front and back covers and the binding edge of the first and last pages. They are frequently of heavier stock than the pages and may be either white or colored. Although it is not common to do so, they may be used for illustrations.

CONTENTS

FINGER PUPPETS

Cut the fingers off an old glove.

5

The Library of Congress dictates that the copyright notice appear on the "title verso" page, which is the reverse side of the title page. Here, for economy of space, the table of contents is also placed on the title verso page. *Glove, Mitten, and Sock Puppets* (1978), written and illustrated by Frieda Gates.

THUMBNAIL SKETCHES

The first step in designing a book is to lay out the pages in *thumbnail sketches*, or *thumbnails.* These are rough sketches done in miniature on a pad of layout, or visualizer, paper with a soft pencil. While the thumbnails can be any size that is convenient, it is important that they be in proportion to the actual page size. For example, if your actual page size is 6″ x 9″, then your thumbnail page size should be 2″ x 3″, 3″ x 4½″, 4″ x 6″, etc. An easy way to scale down a page is by the diagonal-line scaling method as described on page 60.

After you have decided on a thumbnail size, a fast and accurate method of drawing page outlines on the layout pad is with a cardboard template cut to the size of a two-page spread. (Thumbnail sketches are always executed as two-page spreads in order to judge the graphic relationship of facing pages.) Use heavy cardboard, such as illustration or mat board, so that a pencil can easily follow its edges, and cut notches in the top and bottom of the template to indicate the centerfold.

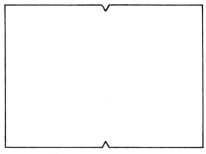

Cardboard template.

Lay out as many two-page outlines as possible on the layout pad, but leave enough room between them for page numbers as well as to avoid visual confusion. Work directly on the pad; it provides a resilient drawing surface and, because layout paper is somewhat transparent, previous sketches and other reference material can easily be slipped under the top sheet for use as a drawing guide. The usual procedure is to first try a number of layout variations on scrap paper. The best one, then, can be slipped under the top sheet and copied. Further layout adjustments can be made by shifting the underlying sketch.

If you or the publisher have decided on the number of pages, then make that many page outlines with the template and number them before proceeding further. If the number of pages has not been decided on, make the page outlines (and number them) as you go along, keeping in mind that the average book length ranges from 32 to 64 pages in multiples of 8.

After you have laid out the page outlines, the next step is to determine how much space the text will occupy. For lengthy stories, the typewritten manuscript has to be character-counted and then converted to typographic measurements. This is called copyfitting, and the procedure is described on page 113. For short stories, the text will occupy such a small space on any one page that an accurate preliminary character count is not necessary. As you lay out the pages you can easily adjust the illustrations to accommodate the type.

To determine how much space is available for illustrations, first indicate the pages that will be used for front and back matter by writing "half title," "title," "blank," etc. in the middle of the appropriate pages on the thumbnail layout. Then count the remaining pages and deduct from them the approximate number of pages that the text would occupy if it were set in full pages. In a 48-page book, for example, there might be 9 pages of front and back matter and 13 full pages of story text, leaving 26 pages for illustrations. Thus, the average page would be two-thirds illustrative and one-third textual. This ratio, of course, can and should vary from page to page, so long as the total book averages out to it.

The final step before starting the page layouts is to read through the manuscript to identify those images and situations that convey the essence of the story and have the best potential for graphic depiction. Small spot, or single-image, illustrations can be interspersed among the larger situational illustrations. Make a numbered list of the potential illustrations using words and/or small sketches, and mark the illustration number at the appropriate place on the manuscript.

At this point you are ready to begin the layout design. As mentioned previously, use a soft graphite pencil, and try out a few layout ideas on scrap paper first. The purpose of thumbnail layouts is to achieve, in a given number of pages, pleasing overall page compositions with well-synchronized words and pictures. Therefore, while the size, shape, position, and subject matter of illustrations are important, the drawing technique and accuracy of details are not. In fact, many illustrators who are fine draftsmen employ a crude, stick-figure technique for thumbnails. The text, too, can be crudely indicated, using a horizontal line to represent each line of type. As with the illustrations, of course, the overall block of type should be reasonably accurate in regard to size, shape, and position. Type larger than 14 points should be block-lettered. Colored pencils or pointed color markers are good mediums for indicating color illustrations.

It is almost always necessary to do a second series of thumbnail sketches. Even if you were lucky enough in the first series to end up on the right page, you will find, upon later overall evaluation, that some spreads are less satisfying than others. A common problem is that two or more consecutive spreads are either so similar in layout as to be boring, or so different as to be discordant. When revising them, try to achieve a pleasing variety of compositions from spread to spread, while at the same time employing certain common factors to provide unity.

Don't rush through the thumbnail sketches, and don't hesitate to revise them one or more times. The most important aspect of a book is its overall graphic structure or "look," which involves the size, shape, and color relationships of elements on individual spreads (the abstract composition), as well as the relationship between the spreads. Beginners tend to believe that beautifully executed illustrations will hide any deficiencies in the layout composition, but just the opposite is true. The better the illustrations are, the more obvious the layout deficiencies become.

Ramirez/Foot and Feet/3

p 7

Foot is a little word with lots of meanings.

A (big dictionary) has two pages of foot words.

Can you think of some?

1-p illus.
book stand
with dictionary

p 8-9

Let's begin at the beginning with just plain foot.

A (foot) is the very best thing to walk on.

A (twelve inch ruler) measures one foot.

A (snail) has a foot that is not used for walking.

It is a long flat sticky foot that can (climb)

and hang on.

2-p illus.
human foot
ruler
snail

p 10

And what about the (foot of the bed?)

and the (foot of a page?)

1-p illus.
bed with cat on it

p 11

(Mountain climbers) wear special footwear to help

them gain a foothold when they scale a (steep cliff.)

1-p illus.
mountain
climber

p 12-13

The (boy) carrying a (football) is walking on the

(footpath) to the (footbridge.)

He is leaving (footprints) in the dust.

Can you hear his footfalls?

They are loud because of his (heavy footgear.)

Across the bridge you can see the (foothills) of

the mountains.

2-p illus.
boy in
football
gear, etc.

A typical method of indicating page distribution and potential illustrations on the manuscript.
Another method is to make a separate list of potential illustrations, using words and/or small sketches.

ROUGH LAYOUTS

When you are satisfied with the thumbnail sketches, you must enlarge them to reproduction size for further refinement before starting the dummy. Working on a layout pad, accurately measure and draw the outlines of two-page spreads, using a ruler, T-square, triangle, and sharp pencil. Then, using a soft layout pencil, roughly lay out the page elements, paying particular attention to their size, shape, and position. Such a conversion from thumbnail to rough layout size is usually done by visual estimation, but if your thumbnails are very tightly executed, you may want to enlarge them by one of the methods described on page 60.

After you have roughly laid out the pages, you can then begin to refine the illustrations in regard to the larger issues of proportions, perspective, and overall composition. Don't be concerned with details and the technique to be used in the finished art; these are issues to be resolved in the finished art itself. As on the thumbnails, the lines of small type are indicated with horizontal pencil lines, while large type (over 14 points) must be block-lettered.

It is usually necessary to do two or three roughs to fully resolve the layout and illustration problems. For color illustrations, therefore, do the earlier sketches in black graphite pencil to resolve the formal composition, reserving color for the later sketches. The best color mediums for roughs are colored pencils, color markers, and pastels. To avoid smudging, spray pastel sketches with workable matte fixative, either as each shape is rendered or when the sketch is finished (see *Pastels*, page 72).

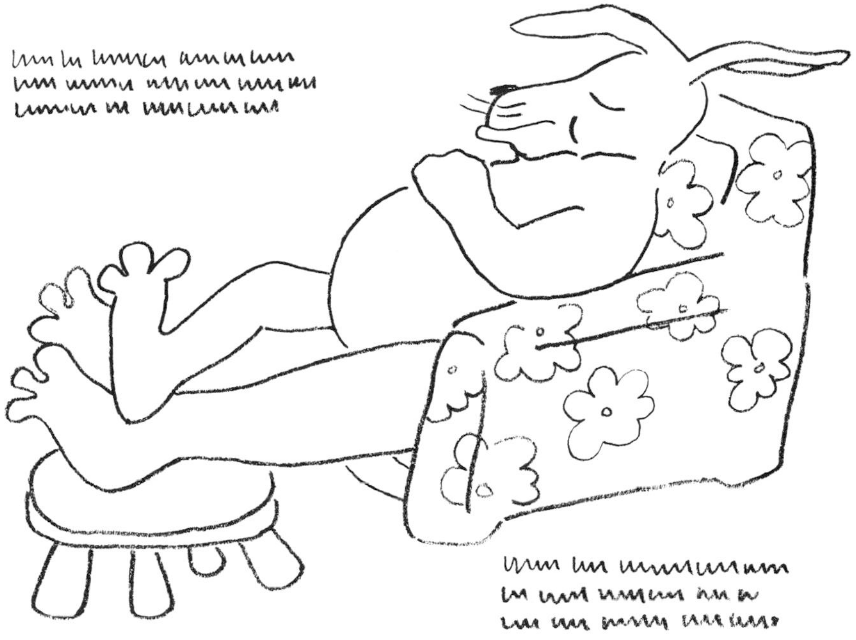

Are there any animals with three feet? Of course not, unless you want to make up one of your own.

How about a plump honnis with ears like a rabbit, and three footweary feet, which he is resting on a footstool.

(Top) A reproduction-size rough layout of pages 26-27 of the thumbnail layout shown at left. (Bottom) A more-refined layout for use in the dummy.

Thumbnail sketches for the first 29 pages of a 48-page book. *Foot and Feet* (1973), written by Carolyn Ramirez and illustrated by Frieda Gates.

(Above left) Portion of dummy illustration for *The Mean Mouse and Other Mean Stories* (1962), written by Janice May Udry and illustrated by Ed Young. (Above right) The same illustration in the printed book.

(Below) Dummy page for *Who Lives Inside?* (1976), written by Lynda Graham Barber and illustrated by Ray Barber.
(Right) The same page in the printed book. Note size and layout change.

What were the Harpers going to do
with such a pile of junk?
Indeed, what *could* be done with it?

Dummy spread for
Milton, the Model A
(1971), written by
Donald J. Sobol
and illustrated by
Joan E. Drescher.

What were the Harpers going to do
with such a pile of junk?
Indeed, what *could* be done with it?

18

19

The above spread
as it appears in
the printed book.

EXECUTING THE DUMMY

Since the dummy is time-consuming to construct and render, you don't want to have to execute it more than once. Therefore, make sure you are fully satisfied with your rough layouts before proceeding further.

There are various methods of constructing a dummy, and each has certain advantages and disadvantages. Read through the following descriptions of some of the most common methods, and select one that best suits your purposes. If your book has already been accepted by a publisher, you will need only an original dummy for presentation. However, if your book will be sent to one or more publishers for consideration, you will need to make a xerographic copy of the dummy, since it would be too risky to send the original.

When planning to make a xerographic dummy, be aware that most office copiers will accept any kind of paper up to 8½" x 14". For pages with color illustrations, do the original art in black, using thin outlines to delineate color areas, and apply the color to the xerographic copy with markers. Of course, you can also make full-color xerographic copies of color pages, but these are substantially more expensive than black & white copies, and are not as easily available. When making a xerographic dummy, keep in mind that you may be able to make copies of your rough layouts, which will eliminate the need to re-execute them for the dummy.

Saddle-stitched Blank Dummy.

This dummy is constructed in the following steps: (1) Carefully measure and draw the outlines of the two-page spreads on white bond paper, adding ¼" to all four sides for later trimming. (2) Mark the hole positions for two staples on the centerfold of each spread, using a strip of paper as a measuring guide to insure that the holes will later align perfectly. (3) Trim the spreads with a sharp blade and a straightedge, puncture the staple holes with a pushpin, and score the centerfolds with the end of a paper clip.

(4) Fold and then unfold the individual spreads, insert the two staples through one spread at a time (from the outside), and bend them over at the center spread. (5) Fold the assembled dummy and trim ¼" off the top, bottom, and unbound side with a sharp blade and a straightedge.

Saddle-stitched blank dummy showing staples clinched at the center spread.

The layouts are not executed directly on this type of dummy. Rather, they are executed separately on thin layout paper (either page by page or spread by spread), rubber cemented onto the dummy, and trimmed to page size (see *Rubber Cementing Procedure,* page 127). The reason for this is that later changes can easily be made by replacing individual pages or spreads. A rubber cemented sheet can be removed with a squirt can of rubber cement thinner. Squirt the thinner between the sheets as they are being pulled apart. Xerographic copies can also be used in this type of dummy. For books over 48 pages, it may be necessary to divide the dummy into two sets of stapled sheets. They can later be bound together with a strip of tape.

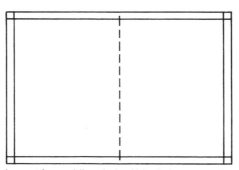
Layout for saddle-stitched blank dummy and cemented-spread dummy. Note the ¼" trim margins on all non-binding sides.

Cemented-spread Dummy.

This type of dummy, which eliminates the need to make a separate blank dummy, is constructed in the following steps: (1) Carefully measure and draw the outlines of a two-page spread on opaque white bond paper, adding ¼" to all four sides for later trimming, and execute the layout on it. Because bond paper is quite opaque, you may need to use a tracing box to see your underlying rough layout (see *Tracing Box Transfer Method,* page 63). (2) Trim the spread with a sharp knife and a straightedge, and score the centerfold with the end of a paper clip. (3) After all the spreads are executed, fold them inwardly, and rubber cement them together, attaching the back of the right-hand page of one spread to the back of the left-hand page of the next spread. (4) Trim ¼" off the top, bottom, and right side of the assembled dummy with a sharp blade and a straightedge.

This is a good method for making a xerographic dummy where the spread size does not exceed 14" x 8½" including trim (6 ¾" x 8" maximum trimmed page size).

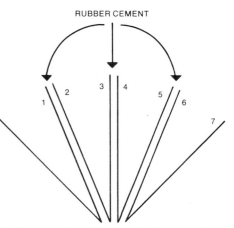
Binding procedure for cemented-spread dummy.

Cemented-page Dummy. This method is used primarily for xerographic dummies where the page size is too large for the cemented-spread method. However, because a ½″ binding tab plus ¼″ trim margins are required, the largest page that can be made from 8½″ x 14″ copier paper is 7¾″ x 13½″ for an upright book (bound on its long dimension) and 13¼″ x 8″ for an oblong book (bound on its short dimension). For page sizes larger than this (up to 8½″ x 14″ in either dimension, you will have to use the saddle-stitched blank dummy described earlier.

Following are the steps required to make a cemented-page dummy: (1) Make a xerographic copy of each page layout, allowing for trim and binding edges as described in the following step. (2) Measure and draw the page outlines on the copies, adding ¼″ at the top, bottom, and right side of right-hand pages, and ¼″ at the top, bottom, and left side of left-hand pages. On the right side of left-hand pages, also add a ½″ binding tab. (3) Trim the pages with a sharp blade and a straightedge, score the binding tabs with the end of a paper clip, and fold them towards you. (4) With rubber cement, attach the back of page 1 (RH) to the back of page 2 (LH); unfold the tab on page 2 and attach the back of page 3 to it; attach the back of page 4 to the back of page 3; and so forth. (5) Trim the assembled dummy at top, bottom, and right side with a sharp blade and a straightedge, and remove any excess cement at the binding edge of pages.

Spiral-wire Dummy. An easy way to make a dummy is with a spiral-wire notebook. The drawback to this method, however, is that the spiral is always visible, and also disrupts two-page illustrations. Use a notebook that has a small spiral and unruled pages. Remove the covers and unneeded pages, trim the notebook to dummy size, and clip off the excess spiral. Execute the layouts on layout paper (or make xerographic copies of the layouts), trim to page size, and rubber-cement them on the notebook pages.

Note: a spiral-wire dummy is illustrated on page 101.

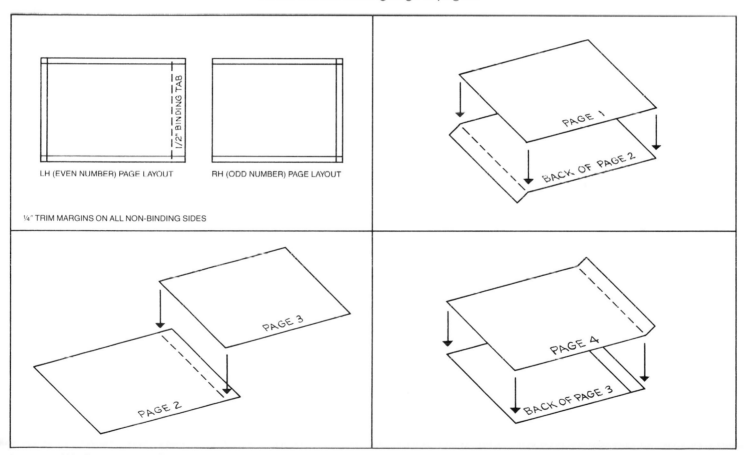

LH (EVEN NUMBER) PAGE LAYOUT   RH (ODD NUMBER) PAGE LAYOUT

½″ BINDING TAB

¼″ TRIM MARGINS ON ALL NON-BINDING SIDES

PAGE 1
BACK OF PAGE 2
PAGE 2
PAGE 3
PAGE 4
BACK OF PAGE 3

Layout and binding procedure for cemented-page dummy.

THE COVER OR JACKET

Some books have a printed cover with no jacket, while others have a plain cover with a printed jacket. The printed cover or jacket is very important because it serves to attract attention to the book. For this reason, even though your book may be limited to one or two colors, most publishers will agree to the use of an extra color or two on the cover or jacket. Keep in mind that it is better to have to eliminate a color after the book has been accepted than to not have the book accepted in the first place because of a drab or otherwise deficient exterior.

The cover of a dummy is of much simpler construction than that of a manufactured book. Usually it is nothing more than a folder made of heavyweight paper that may or may not be attached to the enclosed page dummy. It is possible, however, to simulate a hardcover book by wrapping and gluing the rendered layout around two pieces of cardboard, and reinforcing the interior of the spine with tape. A close examination of a hardcover binding will explain this procedure more thoroughly.

If your book has not yet been commissioned, the only copy required is that for the front cover, which includes the title and the names of the author and illustrator. Spine copy is not required because most dummy covers are single-creased folders that do not have a flat spine. Even on covers with a flat spine (which results when the folder is double-creased to accommodate a thick dummy), spine copy is generally omitted because it is too small to be of significance.

When designing the cover, it is first necessary to construct a trial cover to see that it properly fits the enclosed dummy. As mentioned previously, a simple, single-creased folder is usually adequate, but a thick dummy may require a folder that has been double-creased to form a boxed, or U-shaped, spine. Then open up the folder and accurately draw its outlines and fold(s) on the top sheet of a large pad of layout paper. Note that the front cover is on the right and the back cover is on the left. Make a number of layouts, from rough to tight, before executing the final

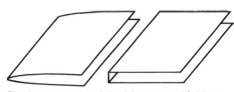

Single-creased and double-creased folders.

dummy cover. For the rough layouts, use a soft graphite pencil to resolve the larger issues of proportions, perspective, and composition. Details and color can be resolved in the tighter layouts, using such mediums as color markers, pastels, and/or colored pencils. Keep in mind that the back cover can be blank or illustrated. Frequently the front-cover illustration extends onto the back cover.

Don't treat type as an afterthought. It is a very important design element that must be included on all the layouts. It can be roughly executed on the rough layouts, but it should be fairly accurate in regard to size, weight, and position. For the tight layouts, find an appropriate type style and size in a type reference book and, using a piece of tracing paper that has been ruled with horizontal guidelines, trace the outlines of the desired letters, shifting the paper to compose them into words. If the type sample is not the right size, it can be enlarged or reduced on an art projector, which is the fastest and most economical method. You can also use a photostat, as well as a xerographic copy made on a copier that enlarges and reduces by 1% increments (see *Enlarging and Reducing Artwork*, page 60).

Transfer the type to the cover design by positioning it under the cover design layout and tracing it. If the layout is not sufficiently transparent to permit this, use one of the transfer methods described on page 62. When executing the type on the cover, use pointed color markers or colored pencils if the background is white or light in value. For white or colored type on a dark background, it is necessary to use gouache (page 74). To obtain maximum brightness, colored type on a dark background must first be painted white. If you fail to follow this procedure, you'll not only be disappointed with the color, but you'll find that any number of additional coats will not improve it.

The final dummy cover can be

executed on layout paper and then cemented onto the cover paper, or it can be executed directly on the cover paper itself. A xerographic copy can also be cemented onto the cover paper, but if the cover is largely in color, only a full-color copy would be worthwhile in regard to rendering time saved. With all methods, don't trim, score, and fold the cover until after the graphics are applied. An excellent cover paper is kid or vellum finish 2-ply bristol board. It is stiff and durable, yet light enough to make crisp, clean folds (score before folding, using the end of a paper clip).

When executing the cover graphics, use the same mediums and techniques recommended earlier for tight layouts. To achieve shapes with sharp, clean edges, mask the surrounding areas with frisket paper before applying the medium. This technique can be used with most mediums, and is described in the section on *Air Brush*, page 77.

The cover can be attached to the enclosed page dummy with strips of tape along the inside binding edges. It can also be attached with endpapers, which are like two-page spreads that are cemented to the insides of the cover and the first and last pages of the dummy.

Note: When your dummy is completed, refer to the evaluation used for review by the Branch Library Media Examination Center, page 37, and see how it scores.

Dummy covers and printed covers. Note layout and copy changes.

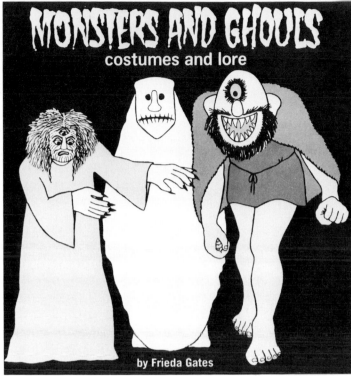

Hand lettering is a slow but accurate method of indicating type on the dummy.
This is the dummy for *"D" is for Rover* (1970), written by Leonore Klein and illustrated by Robert Quackenbush.

PUTTING TYPE ON THE DUMMY

If your book has been commissioned by a publisher, then by the time you do the dummy the editor will have copy edited the manuscript, the type will have been set to your specifications, and you will have received the rough, or galley, proofs. In that case, simply cut up the galley proofs and paste them on the dummy.

If your book has not been commissioned, the easiest way to indicate type on the dummy is to paste in typewritten copy. This is not a very accurate method, but since copy and layout changes are bound to occur after the book is accepted, it is adequate for dummy purposes. Use a typewriter that produces 10 characters per inch (pica size), and set it at single-spacing for normally-spaced paragraphs. This approximates 12 point type, which is a common size used in children's books. To avoid smudging the copy when pasting it on the dummy, spray it lightly with acrylic spray coating, such as Krylon Crystal Clear.

A slower but more accurate method of indicating type is to hand-letter it, using a single-stroke technique. This method is preferable for books that don't contain much copy and thus usually require larger type. Following is the procedure for hand-lettered type indication: (1) Look through children's books or a type reference book to find some type that is the right size and has the right line spacing for your book. Don't be too concerned with the style of the type, since your objective at this time is simply to fit the words into the layouts so that the resulting blocks of type indication look good in regard to overall size, shape, position, texture, and weight. (2) Place tracing paper over the selected type sample and, using a sharp, hard pencil, tick off the "x-heights" of a number of consecutive lines (these are the heights of lower case letters without ascenders or descenders). (3) Place the tracing paper on a drawing board, align a T-square on the tick marks, and rule horizontal guidelines to approximately the page width of your book. Also rule vertical guidelines to indicate the width of your type column. (4) Position the tracing paper layout over each desired letter on the type sample, carefully align the guidelines, and trace the letter, single-stroke, with a pencil whose softness and pointedness approximates the weight and "color," or overall value, of the type. When positioning the tracing paper for each letter, be very careful to use proper spacing within and between words. (5) After you have made a good tracing-paper sketch (which may require two or three tries), measure and draw the type guidelines on the dummy layout before placing the sketch beneath it for transferring. In this way, the underlying sketch can be shifted about for better letter and word composition without damaging the accuracy of linespacing and horizontal alignment.

The soldiers looked in every direction, but the cunning Indians kept themselves concealed behind the trees.

Tracing-paper sketch of an 18-point type layout to be transferred to the dummy.
See page 121 for other methods of indicating type.

CHAPTER I.
A GRUNION RUN

Late on a starlighted spring evening, a bare-
foot teen-ager wearing cut-off blue jeans and carrying an old pillow case ran in and out of the breaking
waves along a southern California beach. An
elderly, white-haired man with a flashlight in one
hand and a gunnysack in the other sauntered not
far behind, waving his light back and forth along
the water's edge. Farther back, a family group hastily gulped hot dogs they had roasted over an open
fire. All up and down the beach, people were wait

If galley proofs are available, they are simply cut up and pasted on the dummy. This is the dummy for *Grunion: Fish Out of Water* (1971), written by Ann Stepp and illustrated by Anne Lewis. Note that this is a spiral-wire dummy.

Tonight is the first time I will race my horse at a rodeo.
We have been practicing all year.

Typewritten copy pasted on the dummy is not a very accurate method of indicating type, but since copy and layout changes are bound to occur after a book is accepted, it is usually adequate for dummy purposes. This is the dummy for *Cowgirl* (1984), written and photo-illustrated by Murray Tinkelman. Xerographic copies of his photographs were used in the dummy.

Submissions

When you are satisfied that your completed manuscript (or manuscript and dummy) represents your best efforts, you are ready to send it off. Refer to the *Members Publishing Programs* from the Children's Book Council (see page 35) to find which publishing houses would be most receptive to your particular book. The Children's Book Council's *Members Listing,* the *Literary Market Place*, and the *Writer's Market* give the names of the current editors at each house. Also refer to *Alternative Ways to Getting Published,* page 108.

SUBMITTING THE MANUSCRIPT

Since your manuscript is unsolicited, publishers are not obliged to read it or even to return it. Therefore, to protect your work, to help get it read, and to insure its return, it is important to conform to the following guidelines:

1. Type your copy on 8½" x 11" opaque white paper, one side only, using double-spacing and generous margins on all four sides. Use a good black ribbon, type neatly, and carefully correct your errors, retyping the page if necessary. Type your last name, one or two words of your book title, and the page number on the top right corner of each page, such as *Gates / Children's /95.* You can submit either the original or a good xerographic copy. If you submit the original, make a copy for yourself.

2. Type a top sheet for the manuscript, putting on it the book title plus your name, address, and telephone number, including area code.

3. Do not staple the manuscript pages together. Rather, put them in a folder or in a clamp binder that permits easy removal (most editors prefer to read loose sheets). For very thick manuscripts, use either a manuscript box or a box that typewriter paper comes in.

4. Include a cover letter, plus a résumé of your work experience if you have one. Also include a stamped, self-addressed return envelope. If you want your manuscript returned by insured mail, you must purchase insurance beforehand and affix the label to the return envelope.

5. Mail the manuscript in a 9" x 12" kraft envelope or, to avoid damage, in a padded book mailer. Address it to the publisher's juvenile department and include the editor's name if you know it. Be sure to put your name and address on the outside of the package.

6. To be certain that your manuscript is received, send it by registered or certified mail and request a return receipt.

7. To be certain that your idea will not be stolen, send a copy of your manuscript to yourself, and *do not open it* when it arrives. If a publisher to whom you submitted your manuscript ever publishes a book like yours, then, you can use the unopened envelope as legal evidence of ownership.

Scriber/Retta's Travels/ 2

Retta was feeling low. She felt so low that she had to look up to see down. "Oh, what a world!" she sighed. "Everything is wrong. Wars, famine, crime, corruption, disasters, and stringy hair. I may as well stay in bed."

And she did. Retta stayed in bed the whole day. She stayed in bed the next day too. Retta stayed in her bed for the rest of the week.

Then one day her friend, Hymie, noticed that he hadn't seen Retta in many days. He asked everyone if they had seen Retta, and of course they had not. So he went to Retta's house. Hymie knocked at the door. He called Retta's name. He banged and he yelled. Finally Retta said that he could come in.

Hymie found Retta still in bed ... with stringy hair. "Why are you in bed? Hymie asked.

"It isn't worth getting up. The world is a lousy place." Retta replied. Then she let out a long loud sigh, and lifted the blankets over head.

Hymie opened the window and told Retta to look out at the world that she was complaining about. The sun was shining. A bird was singing in a blossom-filled tree, and a pretty red flower had just opened its petals. "Now come along!" Hymie said, as he pulled Retta to her feet. "We are going on a trip."

Manuscript page sample.
Note the author/title/page heading, double-spacing, and generous margins.

SUBMITTING THE DUMMY

If you want to illustrate your book, and perhaps also design it, you should submit a dummy along with the manuscript. Don't wait until the manuscript has been accepted before submitting it. Not only may the pictures help to sell the story, but the editor may have decided on another illustrator in the interim. Editors have a stable of illustrators they frequently use, and as they read a manuscript they try to envision whose style would be most suitable. Once they have made this decision it might be difficult to convince them otherwise.

Even if you submit a dummy along with the manuscript, and even if the editor likes your pictures as much as your story, you still may not get to illustrate your book. For promotional as well as economic reasons, publishers sometimes prefer to pair an unknown writer with a known illustrator, or a known writer with an unknown illustrator. Don't let this dishearten you. In addition to having your story published, you may later be commissioned to illustrate someone else's story.

Dummy cover designed and illustrated by Jeanne Brady.

100 Main Street
Suffern, NY 10957
Tel. 914-555-1241

September 11, 1986

Ms. Jeannette Alexander
Lloyd-Simone Publishing Company
32 Hillside Avenue
Monsey, NY 10952

Dear Ms. Alexander:

Enclosed please find my manuscript, dummy, and one finished illustration for Retta's Travels. If you wish, I will send other finished illustrations and my resume.

My background is in art and education, and presently I am coordinator of a YMCA Child Care program. I am also a parent.

Over the years I have read many books to the children in my care (my creations as well as published authors), and this book is a favorite. Although it is written for a beginning reader, it also appeals to younger children.

Thank you for considering my work, I look forward to your response.

Sincerely,

Anne Scriber
Anne Scriber

Enclosures: manuscript, dummy, one piece of finished art, stamped, self-addressed envelope.

Cover letter sample.

It is a good idea to submit, along with the dummy, one or two finished illustrations. You may also include other illustration samples to demonstrate your abilities more fully. Keep in mind that you could be commissioned to illustrate other books. Submit photostats, color prints, and/or transparencies rather than original art, and put your name, address, and telephone number on each piece.

THE COVER LETTER

The purpose of the cover letter is to describe the objectives of your project and provide any important background information relating to it. You may, for example, describe what inspired you to write the story, or you may touch on your experiences with children as a teacher, a librarian, a parent, etc. If your book has potential as a series, briefly describe what the other books in the series might be. Publishers may be more receptive if your book is not merely a one-shot deal. The cover letter is a sales pitch for yourself and your project, so spend time honing it to perfection.

```
                Anne Scriber
                100 Main Street
                Suffern, New York 10957
                Tel. 914-555-1241

                RESUME

                EDUCATION
                       Central State College BA
                       City Acting School
                       Continuing Education Art Courses

                FIELD OF INTEREST
                       Working with children.  Creating educational and
                       entertainment projects, with and for children.

                MAJOR WORK EXPERIENCE
                       Teaching and Counseling
                       Summer camp counselor.  Nursery School teacher.
                       Girl Scout Brownie assistant leader.  YMCA Child
                       Care-program coordinator.

                       Writing and Art
                       College publications.  Posters, direct mailers, etc.
                       for PTA and various community groups.

                INTERESTS AND ACTIVITIES
                       Children's theater (director), local adult theater
                       group, folk music, aerobics, cooking, arts and
                       crafts, travel.
```

Résumé sample.

THE RÉSUMÉ

As with the cover letter, the résumé is a sales pitch about you. It is not written in letter form, however, but is a brief listing of facts. It need not be of the type used when applying for a job, although it should include your educational and work experiences. Describe your contacts with children, where you have lived or traveled, and your hobbies or special interests, particularly if they relate to your writing and/or illustration activities. If you have been published, list the publications, their dates, and the work of yours they contain. Copies of reviews or other personal publicity may be attached to the résumé.

THE QUERY LETTER

The query letter is a brief description of a proposed book, its purpose being to receive permission to submit the manuscript (or manuscript and dummy) for consideration. Since query letters are often ignored by editors, many writers don't bother securing permission before submitting manuscripts. However, if an editor sends a positive reply, then the manuscript is assured of consideration. Moreover, although manuscripts, dummies, and artwork are seldom lost, publishers are responsible only for solicited work.

In addition to a brief description of the proposed book, the query letter might also include an outline, if appropriate, and a sample piece of writing. Enclose a stamped, self-addressed envelope to encourage the editor to reply.

```
                                    100 Main Street
                                    Suffern, NY 10957
                                    Tel. 914-555-1241

                                    September 11, 1986


Ms. Jeannette Alexander
Lloyd-Simone Publishing Company
32 Hillside Avenue
Monsey, NY 10952


Dear Ms. Alexander:

     I would like to submit my manuscript and dummy
for Retta's Travels.  If you wish, I will also send
samples of finished illustrations and my resume.

     Retta's Travels is a story about a depressed ant
who refuses to get out of bed.  Her friend, Hymie,
persuades her to take a trip and observe all the nice
things in life.  The message, however, is that happiness
comes from within.  The illustrations are black and
white line drawings.  Humor is a strong point in both
text and art.

     As coordinator of a YMCA Child Care program, I
have read many stories to children (my creations as
well as published authors), and this book is a favorite.
Although it is written for a beginning reader, it also
appeals to younger children.

     Thank you for your attention.

                              Sincerely,

                              Anne Scriber
                              Anne Scriber
```

Query letter sample.

AGENTS

A list of agents is available from the Society of Author's Representatives, 101 Park Avenue, New York, N.Y. 10017. Enclose a stamped, self-addressed envelope with your request.

It is not necessary to have an agent. In fact, it is often difficult for an unpublished author to obtain one. There *are* agents who solicit new authors, but they charge a reading fee to review manuscripts. The fee is usually deducted from their commission if they sell the manuscript. Most literary agencies offering this service employ a reading staff made up of writers, journalists, and/or teachers, who may or may not know much about children's books.

A knowledgeable and experienced agent can be of great benefit. Having many acquaintances among editors and publishers, the agent is better than the author at selling manuscripts, and also has the expertise to secure optimum contractual terms. The agent's fee is a percentage of the author's earnings.

MULTIPLE SUBMISSIONS

The ready availability of office copiers makes it easy to submit materials to more than one publisher at a time. The advantage to this is that it eliminates the need to wait weeks or months for a reply and the return of materials before they can be sent out again. Also, if more than one publisher expresses interest, you are in a good negotiating position. There is even an advantage when all your replies are negative, for you have not lost much time in coming to realize that your project probably needs to be re-evaluated. Multiple submissions used to be frowned upon, but they are more acceptable now, especially for scripts dealing with topical subjects.

REPLIES TO SUBMISSIONS

Soon after receiving submissions, some publishers send a form acknowledging receipt of the material and sometimes disclaiming responsibility for its safety. The manuscript is put into the "slush pile" (meaning unsolicited) to await reading. A reader can be an editor, an assistant editor, an inhouse manuscript reader, or an outside manuscript reader. The amount of time a publisher keeps a manuscript depends upon the number of readers it employs and the number of readers a script may require. If there is interest, the editors have to consider how it fits into their list of titles, how much editing it requires, how marketable it is, and what its production costs will be. It takes anywhere from three weeks to three months—sometimes longer—before a decision is reached. If two months elapse without word, you might send a brief note of inquiry to the editor. Perhaps it is still being considered, or perhaps it is buried in the slush pile.

Lloyd-Simone
Publishing Company

32 Hillside Avenue
Monsey, New York 10952
(914) 356-7273

L-S

November 20, 1986

Anne Scriber
100 Main St.
Suffern, NY 10957

Dear Ms. Scriber:

I presented your manuscript and dummy to our editorial board last Thursday and I'm happy to tell you that they responded favorably. I would therefore appreciate meeting with you at your earliest convenience to discuss contractual terms and publication schedule.

Looking forward to hearing from you.

Sincerely,

Jeannette Alexander

Jeannette Alexander
Editorial Director

Lloyd-Simone
Publishing Company

32 Hillside Avenue
Monsey, New York 10952
(914) 356-7273

L-S

Thank you for the opportunity to examine the enclosed material and consider it for publication. We have looked at it carefully with regard to our current needs. We regret that we cannot use it at this time.

Our returning your material need not imply that we think it lacking in merit. In many cases the reason is merely an overlapping of subject area. Due to the volume of materials sent to us, we regret that a personal evaluation or explanation is not possible.

With every good wish,

The Editors

Samples of replies
to submissions.

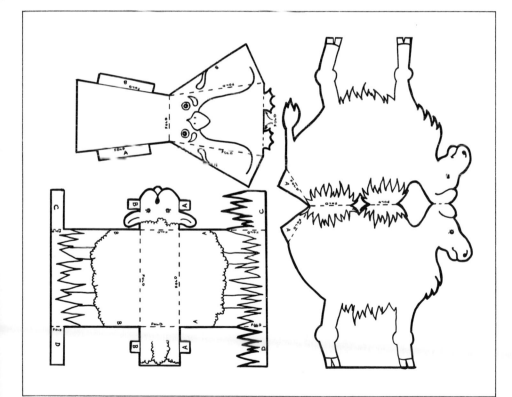

Illustrations from *Young Life* magazine for craft projects by Susan Gelb.
(Top) Cutout puppets for "The Bare Bear," adapted by Barbara Heckman from the story by Kathryn Jackson. (Bottom) Display cutouts for making Noah's Ark.

MAGAZINE SUBMISSIONS

Although magazines do not pay well, they provide a good way for getting your work into print. Approximately forty juvenile magazines are published in the United States, and they are listed in the *Literary Market Place*, available at the public library. Most juvenile magazines are interested in fiction (including easy-to-read), non-fiction, articles, poems, plays, crafts, puzzles, games, drawings, cartoons, and photographs. Holiday and seasonal material is welcome at most magazines, but should be submitted at least six months in advance of the holiday or season. Some magazines have specific vocabulary, content, and/or style requirements, and it is therefore wise to familiarize yourself with a magazine before submitting anything to it. If copies are not available at the library, write to the magazine for a sample copy and guidelines for submission. Include a stamped, self-addressed envelope with your request.

REJECTION

Everyone is disheartened by a rejection notice, and a third or fourth rejection is no less—and often more—disheartening than the first. It may be consoling to know, however, that many successful books—even some award-winners—were rejected by several publishers before finally being accepted. Also, it is not only new authors who receive rejection notices; many seasoned authors receive them as well.

The form letters or cards returned with rejected manuscripts are not meant to be rude or insulting. Editors simply do not have the time to write a critique or explanation for every manuscript they cannot accept. If a manuscript is held for a fairly long time, or if the editor sends a personalized rejection letter, it is usually a fair indication that there was at least *some* interest in it. An editor sometimes asks to see a manuscript again after certain changes are made. This doesn't guarantee acceptance, but it is encouraging.

After a few rejections, carefully re-examine your material. Not having worked on it for a while, you can be more objective and you may see ways for improving it.

ALTERNATIVE WAYS TO GETTING PUBLISHED

Publishers cannot possibly publish all the properties submitted to them, and many good manuscripts therefore go unpublished. Major publishing houses are usually the first choice of authors because of their promotion, sales, and distribution capabilities. If none of them shows interest in your project, there are a number of publishing alternatives— small press, or independent, publishers, vanity presses, and self-publishing.

Small Press Publishers. An increasing number of small presses in the United States are producing many fine and unusual books. Although the promotion, sales, and distribution capabilities of these publishers are often limited, they have a reputation for being more adventurous than the major houses.

The Cooperative Children's Book Center (CCBC), a children's book examination center and children's literature research library at the University of Wisconsin, publishes a directory of small presses entitled *Alternative Press Publishers of Children's Books.* This directory lists over 170 small press publishers and includes addresses, telephone numbers, and the names of persons to contact. It also provides information on the type of books each publishes including genre, age group, and special emphasis. If you are not able to obtain this directory from the library, it can be ordered for a small fee from The Friends of the CCBC, Inc., (ATTN: Directory), P.O. Box 5288, Madison, WI 53705.

Vanity Presses. There are different types of vanity presses. Some handle only designing, printing, and binding— at your expense—and send you all the copies for you to promote and sell yourself. Others, sometimes referred to as *subsidy* publishers, handle promotion, advertising, distribution, and bookkeeping in addition to designing, printing, and binding. You pay for the book's manufacture, and you receive a royalty on books sold. The advantages and disadvantages of dealing with vanity and subsidy presses are described in *The Writer Publisher*, by Charles Aronson, and *The Writer's Legal Guide,* by Tad Crawford.

The Gallopade Publishing Group, a small press publisher, was founded in 1979 by Carole Marsh. A writer and photographer, Ms. Marsh has published many books of her own as well as those of other authors. Her children and their neighborhood friends help with research and inventory, and are often identifiable as characters in her books. *The Mystery of the Biltmore House* was published in 1982.

Self-publishing. Self-publishing means that you arrange and pay for all services relating to the editing, design, and manufacture of a book, as well as for all services relating to its promotion and distribution. If you have the time, interest, and expertise, you can do everything yourself (a few self-publishers even do their own typesetting, printing, and binding). Otherwise, you can farm out whatever operations you cannot or choose not to do. Many self-publishers, for example, arrange to have a larger publisher or book distributor handle promotion, distribution, and book-keeping.

The most important factor in self-publishing is the money needed for production costs, which must be paid *before* you begin to receive proceeds from the book sales. Expertise is not so important. You can either pay someone to do certain jobs for you, or you can learn how to do them yourself through discussions with people in publishing and printing, most of whom are eager to be of help to a novice. Also, there are dozens of books available on every aspect of production and publishing, as well as a number of books on self-publishing, such as *The Publish-it-Yourself Handbook* by Bill Henderson, *The Writer Publisher* by Charles Aronson, *How to Publish Your Own Book* by L. W. Mueller, and *The Self-Publishing Manual* by Dan Poynter. A catalog of books on writing, editing, graphic arts, and publishing is available from the Ross Book Service, Box 12093, Seminary Post Office, Alexandria, VA 22304.

Daniel clutched his stomach. All of a sudden he felt like he had a bad tummy ache. "Oh, Mommy, that hurts," he groaned.

A page from *Daniel's Question: A Caesarean Birth Story* (1981), written by Elaine Sussman Allinson and illustrated by Judith DeBiase. This book was published by Willow Tree Press, a small press publishing company founded by Mrs. Allinson in 1981.

No sooner had they tasted the candy canes than the strangest things started happening. The elves were giggling and laughing and dancing around the room. Even Old Bob was rolling all over the floor from laughter.

"They're the happiest souls I've ever seen!" exclaimed Mrs. Claus.

'Ho-Ho-Ho", laughed Santa. "Those candy canes have enough joy, happiness and love flavoring in them to last a child all year. But there's also a bonus." He walked over to Tom.

A page from *Candy Canes and Dandy Planes* (1981), written by Rosemary Capozza and illustrated by Susan J. Ghezzi. This is a self-published book. Ms. Capozza paid Ms. Ghezzi to illustrate and design it, and paid a printer to manufacture it. She distributes it herself.

Upon Acceptance

THE CONTRACT

When a manuscript is accepted, the publisher generally offers a standard contract into which is written the amount of the advance payment, the payment dates, the royalty rate (usually 10%), the approximate length of the manuscript, the requirements for the illustrations and/or photographs if they are the author's responsibility, and the delivery dates for the finished manuscript and artwork. It is unwise to be so overjoyed with being published that you will sign *anything*. Read your contract carefully to make sure you understand what to expect and what is expected of you. If possible, discuss the terms with acquaintances who have publishing experience. Pamphlets containing advice for authors are available from the Authors Guild, 234 West 44th Street, New York, NY 10036, and from the Society of Children's Book Writers, P.O. Box 296, Mar Vista Station, Los Angeles, CA 90066. Additional advice can be found in the books, *The Writer's Legal Guide* and *Legal Guide for the Visual Artist*, both by Tad Crawford.

If a clause or subclause is unacceptable to you, cross it out and write your initials next to it. It is wise, however, to first discuss any changes with your editor. Upon agreement, the publisher will also initial the changes, indicating approval. As many authors do, you should eliminate the clause that gives the publisher the option to publish your next book. If you are satisfied with a publisher you would most likely give them this option anyway. Conversely, if you become dissatisfied you should be free to submit your future work elsewhere.

ADVANCE AND ROYALTIES

The advance is the money that a publisher pays an author prior to a book's publication. It is recouped by the publisher from the first royalties earned on the book. The amount of the advance is based on estimated book sales for the first year, and therefore a new author usually receives less than a published author, whose sales can be more accurately projected because of previous books. The total advance may be paid when the contract is signed, but more often it is paid in two installments; upon the signing of the contract and upon the delivery of the manuscript. If a third installment is involved, it is paid upon the publication of the book. However, such a late payment is considered unreasonable by many legal experts, since the author's commitments are fulfilled with the delivery of the manuscript.

The royalty rate is a percentage of the book's list, or retail, price. Ten percent is standard for hardcover books. New authors sometimes receive a lower rate, but it should be no less than 7 percent. If the royalties are to be shared by a writer and illustrator, the minimum rate should be 10 percent, usually divided equally between them. Some publishers' royalty rates increase with the number of books sold. A typical rate would be 10 percent for the first 5,000 copies sold, 12½ percent for the second 5,000 copies sold, and 15 percent for all copies sold in excess of 10,000. Most publishers issue royalty payments twice a year. Each payment should be accompanied by a detailed sales report.

About the . . .

SOCIETY OF CHILDREN'S BOOK WRITERS

A professional organization for writers and illustrators of children's literature

WRitkin@G BoɯoKs for ᚷChilDr en and YO?ung adulᚷts

THE CHILDREN'S BOOK COUNCIL
67 Irving Place
New York, New York 10003

The Society of Children's Book Writers and The Children's Book Council are two of the many sources of publishing information for authors.

COPYRIGHT

The purpose of the copyright is to protect the writer, illustrator, and publisher from unauthorized editions or reprints, as well as from plagiarism of any part of the book. While it is the responsibility of the publisher to obtain the copyright, it should be in the writer's name. This is to protect the writer from such eventualities as the publisher's unauthorized sale of rights, unauthorized use of part of the book in another work, bankruptcy, etc.

To obtain the most-current copyright information, write to the Copyright Office, Library of Congress, Washington, DC 20559, and ask for a free *Copyright Information Kit.*

SUBSIDIARY RIGHTS

Subsidiary rights refer to the licensing terms for the use of an author's work in abridgments, anthologies, digests, serializations, paperback editions, book club and other special editions, foreign editions, cartoon strips, radio, television, video cassettes, cable television, film strips, and movies. Since these rights define the publisher's powers as well as the division of licensing proceeds, it is important that you carefully study all the terms of the contract before signing it.

PROCEDURE AFTER SIGNING THE CONTRACT

A juvenile book department is made up of editors, an art and production staff, and sales promotion people. Large publishing houses employ many people to fill these positions, but in smaller houses with fewer employees, one person may do more than one job. Writers generally deal only with the editorial staff, but writer-artists will also have contact with the art director and designer, and sometimes the production manager.

Initially you will work with an editor to discuss the title, structural changes, copy revisions, format, and the book's layout and illustrations. If someone else is to do the illustrations, the editor and the art director will determine candidates. When an illustrator is chosen (usually after submitting sketches and/or representative samples of finished illustrations), he or she works with the designer on the page layouts. If you plan to do your own artwork, then you will work with the art director, designer, and production manager. You may do the illustrations; the illustrations and the design; or the illustrations, the design, and the preparation of mechanicals. These arrangements should be agreed upon beforehand and set forth in the contract.

The production manager will determine the kind of paper and binding to be used, as well as the number of colors and other factors that influence production costs. Both the production manager and the designer will guide you in preparing the mechanicals. It is important to check with them every step of the way, for an error or misjudgment can result in costly and/or time-consuming corrections.

SALES PROMOTION

The promotion of a book begins before it is published. So that sales representatives have something to show to their customers, the book jacket is printed in advance of the book. The blurb on the front flap describes the book's content, and the blurb on the back flap usually has information about the author and illustrator. The editor generally writes the blurb copy, but the author and illustrator must provide pertinent personal facts that may help to sell the book. Also before publication, sales promotion pieces such as posters or bookmarks may be distributed to schools and libraries to familiarize them with a forthcoming book.

After publication, the author may be asked to make personal appearances at book stores, schools, public libraries, club meetings, etc. If such appearances are not planned by the publisher, they may be initiated by the author. Libraries and schools are usually eager to have an author speak at gatherings, and local organizations as well as television and radio stations are always interested in hometown celebrities. Publicity sells books, so it pays to actively and imaginatively pursue it.

REVIEWS

Adult books that are largely verbal can be reviewed from galley proofs, and sales often begin before a book is actually published. Most children's books, however, cannot be accurately reviewed before they are printed because of the importance of illustrations. Since the reviews for a children's book do not appear until weeks or even months after the book is published, its sales usually start slowly and begin to rise by the end of the first year.

New authors tend to overreact to negative criticism, permitting one bad review to outweigh ten good reviews. Reviewers are only human, and even the best of them can be affected by personal bias. One reviewer may say that a book is too simple, while another may say it is too complex. Similarly, one reviewer may regard the illustrations as crude, while another may find them charmingly quaint. As with a rejection notice, the author has to learn to not take a bad review too seriously, for it is the opinion of only one person.

The *Kirkus Reviews* are published semimonthly, and are aimed at librarians to help them select books for their collections. Most of the books that they review are in galley form. Kirkus has a reputation of being somewhat negative and glib, and since they are often the first to publish a review of an author's book, this can be disheartening. Whereas Kirkus has a paid staff of reviewers, the *School Library Journal* employs librarians whose only payment is possession of the book they review. These unpaid reviewers are slow to submit their evaluations and are not always objective. Too often, their reviews reflect personal tastes. *Horn Book* and *Booklist* publish fewer reviews, and mostly of books that their staffs consider worthy of comment. Their reviews are often negative. A review in *Publishers Weekly*—good or bad—is beneficial because it serves to bring the book to the attention of bookstore buyers.

All books are usually reviewed within the first two years of publication. If your book receives poor reviews in the beginning, take heart. It is not uncommon for a book to catch on slowly, and ultimately to even win awards.

AWARDS

As a new author, your only aspiration may be to get published. However, if your book was good enough to be published, it may also be worthy of an award. There are many awards and prizes in the children's book field that are given by organizations, schools, publishers, and newspapers in the United States and other countries. A complete listing of honors and awards is available for a fee from the Children's Book Council.

The most coveted U.S. awards given annually are the Newbery Medal for writing, the Caldecott Medal for illustration, and the $1,000 National Book Award for the most distinguished contribution to literature for children. The Laura Ingalls Wilder award is given every five years to a children's author or illustrator whose books have made a substantial and lasting contribution.

These books must have been first published in the United States, and the recipients must be U. S. citizens. Other awards are given by the *Horn Book*, *School Library Journal,* the American Institute of Graphic Arts, *The New York Times, The Boston Globe,* and Bank Street College.

The Hans Christian Andersen Medal, given biennially, is the best known international award. An award especially for new authors is given annually by The International Reading Association. England's major awards are the Carnegie Medal, given to an author, and the Kate Greenaway Medal, given to an illustrator, by the British Library Association. The Canadian Library Association awards two medals annually, one for a children's book published in English, and the other for a children's book published in French.

RESERVE COPIES

When a book is published, the publisher sends a few complimentary copies to the author, and the author may purchase additional copies at a 40% discount. In the past, children's books were printed in large quantities and were available for many years. Today, printing runs are smaller, and the average life span of a children's book is five years. After this period, the publisher may decide not to reprint the book if its current sales are too low. Since the publisher doesn't usually notify the author of this decision before the last printing is sold out, it is important for the author to always keep a supply of reserve copies on hand. In addition to their use for personal and portfolio purposes, they may be needed for selling reprint rights to another publisher. Most contracts give the author the right to sell a book to another publisher if the original publisher chooses not to reprint it. Also, the printing plates or negatives can usually be purchased at one-half to one-third of their original cost.

Finding a publisher to reprint a book is not easy, particularly if recent royalty statements indicate low sales. If major publishers are not interested, look into small presses, vanity presses, and self-publishing, as described on page 108.

The Newbery Medal is awarded annually by The Association for Library Service to Children, The American Library Association. Named after John Newbery, the famous 18th century publisher of children's books, it was first offered in 1921 by Frederic G. Melcher (1879-1963) as an incentive for better quality in children's books. The award is now donated annually by Daniel Melcher, son of the original donor, to the author of the most distinguished contribution to American literature published during the preceding year.

The Caldecott Medal is awarded annually by the Association for Library Service to Children, The American Library Association. In 1938, the first Caldecott Medal donated by Frederic G. Melcher was awarded to the artist of the most distinguished American picture book for children published in the United States during the preceding year. The name of Randolph Caldecott, the famous English illustrator of books for children, was chosen for the medal because his work best represented "joyousness of picture books as well as their beauty." The horseman on the medal is taken from one of his illustrations for "John Gilpin."

Copyediting, Copyfitting, and Typesetting

COPYEDITING

After your manuscript meets the editor's approval in regard to overall structure and content, it is ready to be copyedited. The copyeditor is a specialist who checks manuscripts for consistency as well as correct grammar, spelling, and punctuation. A book dealing with a particular subject may also require an expert in that field to check the accuracy of information.

When the copyedited manuscript is returned to you for approval, carefully examine all revisions. If you disagree with any of them, don't put your comments or corrections on the manuscript itself. Rather, make a list of the questioned revisions, identifying them by page and line number, and explain your reasons for disagreement. If neither your original text nor the copyeditor's revision are satisfactory, perhaps you can suggest another alternative. Return this list with the manuscript, and if your revisions are approved, they will be incorporated into the manuscript by the editor. If there is still a disagreement, the editor will discuss it with you, and perhaps even secure the opinions of other people. Ultimately, of course, the editor always has the final say.

Because the typewritten manuscript is double-spaced, the copyeditor is able to make most copy changes by writing in the new copy directly above the typed copy. In some cases, however, the copyeditor will use symbols to indicate changes. These symbols are called *proofreaders' marks* and are listed on page 124. Refer to this list as you are reading the copyedited manuscript, and make a habit of using these marks yourself whenever you are editing copy. Not only do they insure against misunderstandings and confusion, but their use is essential when proofreading and correcting copy that has been typeset, where the space between lines is too small for anything more than symbols.

A page (reduced in size) from *Type*, by David Gates. This type specimen book contains complete fonts, in all point sizes, of the major typefaces. It also contains character count charts as well as hundreds of other typefaces in one or more display sizes.

COPYFITTING

The process of converting typewritten manuscript copy into typographic form to fit the page layouts is called copyfitting, and is done by the designer of the book. In order to do copyfitting, you need a type specimen book that contains complete fonts, in all sizes, of at least the major typefaces. A complete font includes capitals, lower case letters, numbers, and punctuation marks. The book should also contain charts showing the number of characters per pica for text, or body, sizes. Most typographers have such books or catalogs that they give to customers. You may also buy one at an art supply store, or borrow one at a library. Recommended books are *Type* by David Gates, and *Type and Typography* by Ben Rosen. Another necessity is a type gauge, which is used for pica measurements as well as for line spacing and column depths. Some typographers have cardboard type gauges that they give to customers, or you can purchase a plastic *Haberule Type Gauge* at an art supply store.

OLD STYLE
GARAMOND

ABCDEFGHIJKLMNOPQRSTU VWXYZ&abcdefghijklmnopqrstuvw xyz1234567890$.,"-;;!?

48 POINT GARAMOND ITALIC

ABCDEFGHIJKLMNOPQRSTUVWXY Z&abcdefghijklmnopqrstuvwxyz1234567890 $.,"-;;!?

36 POINT GARAMOND

ABCDEFGHIJKLMNOPQRSTUVWXYZ& abcdefghijklmnopqrstuvwxyz1234567890$.,"-;;!?

36 POINT GARAMOND ITALIC

ABCDEFGHIJKLMNOPQRSTUVWXYZ&abcd efghijklmnopqrstuvwxyzfifl1234567890$.,"-;;!?""

30 POINT GARAMOND

ABCDEFGHIJKLMNOPQRSTUVWXYZ&abcdefgh ijklmnopqrstuvwxyzfifl1234567890$.,'-;;!?""

30 POINT GARAMOND ITALIC

ABCDEFGHIJKLMNOPQRSTUVWXYZ&abcdefghijklmno pqrstuvwxyzfifl1234567890$.,"-;;!?""

24 POINT GARAMOND

64

Another requirement for copyfitting is a reasonably good knowledge of typographic criteria, terms, and measurements, which are described on the following pages. Be sure to familiarize yourself with this information before attempting the copyfitting procedure described on page 120.

Type Measurements.
The basic units of measurement in typography are points and picas. There are 12 points to a pica, and approximately 6 picas to an inch (which means that 1 point is approximately 1/72″). Points are used to designate typeface sizes, as well as the amount of added space, or leading (pronounced *ledding*), between lines. Picas are used to designate the width of the line or column of type, as well as the length of rules and borders. To measure picas on a type gauge, use the 12 point scale.

The point size of a typeface is measured from slightly above the top of a lower case ascender (or a capital) to slightly below the bottom of a lower case descender. Thus, because the lengths of ascenders and descenders differ with each typeface, typefaces of the same point size differ in actual letter height. For example, Caslon 540 letters, having very short ascenders and descenders, are much larger than Garamond letters of the same point size. Since it would be very difficult to accurately measure a typeface by the

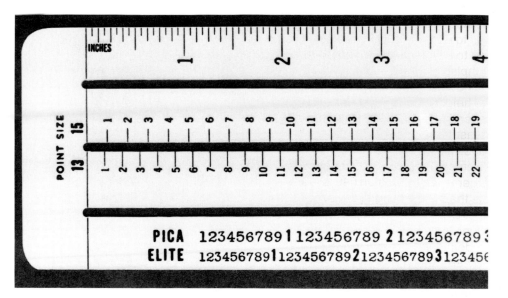

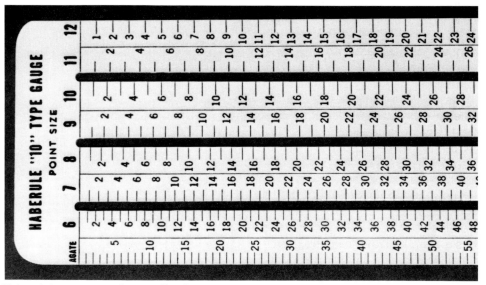

Haberule type gauge—front and back.

1 INCH
12 points equal 1 pica.
6 picas equal .996 inch.

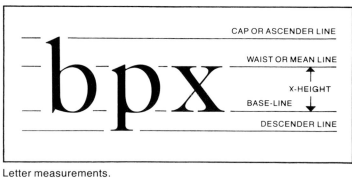

Letter measurements.

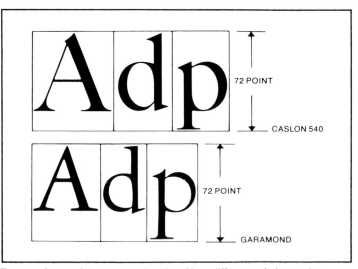

Two typefaces of the same point size. Note difference in letter sizes.

method described above, the only sure way to determine point size is by referring to a type specimen book that has samples of all sizes.

The *x-height* of a typeface refers to the height of lower case letters without ascenders and descenders. This measurement is very important because it establishes the legibility of a typeface. For example, because of its larger x-height, Caslon 540 is more legible than Garamond of the same point size. Of course, the capitals, too, are larger, but since lower case letters are predominant in text applications, it is *their* size that most influences legibility.

Another unit of measurement in type is the *em,* or *em quad.* It is used to designate the amount of indentation, the width of dashes, and the space between words. It is the same width as the point size of the type being used. For example, an em in 14 point type is 14 points wide, an em in 12 point type is 12 points wide, etc. One-half of an em is called an *en,* or *en quad,* and 1/3, 1/4, and 1/5 of an em are called *3-em, 4-em,* and *5-em spaces* (not quads). Ems and ens are used in both metal and photographic typesetting, but phototypesetting uses *units* for measuring small divisions of the em. Most phototypesetting systems employ 18 units to the em, and thus a 3-em (1/3 of an em) space in metal type would be 6 units in most phototype.

Em quad is the square of the point size of the type.

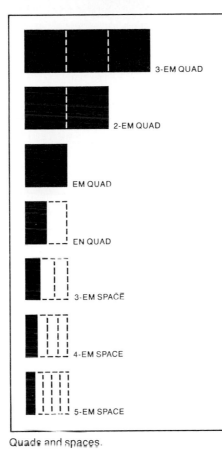

Quads and spaces.

Letterspacing.
In metal typesetting such as Linotype, the space between letters is automatically determined by the "set," or width, of the metal type body of each letter. It can be increased by inserting metal spaces between letters, but it can't be decreased. In phototypesetting, however, since there is no metal type body to contend with, the space between letters can be decreased (tight or minus letterspacing) as well as increased (open, loose, or plus letterspacing). While tight letterspacing is commonly used today, it does not provide maximum legibility. For children's books, therefore, where maximum legibility is of utmost importance, it is best to specify "normal setting" when ordering phototype. In fact, since the traditional Linotype setting is slightly more open, or looser, than the normal setting in some phototype systems, many book designers using those systems specify "Linotype setting" because they believe that the slightly looser setting provides superior legibility.

Two typefaces with normal, tight, and very tight letterspacing.

14 pt. n   The main purpose of letters is the practical one of making thoughts visible.
ABCDEFGHIJKLMNOPQRSTUVWXYZ $1234567890

minus ¼   The main purpose of letters is the practical one of making thoughts visible.
ABCDEFGHIJKLMNOPQRSTUVWXYZ $1234567890

minus ½   The main purpose of letters is the practical one of making thoughts visible.
ABCDEFGHIJKLMNOPQRSTUVWXYZ $1234567890

CASLON 540

14 pt. n   The main purpose of letters is the practical one of making thoughts visible.
ABCDEFGHIJKLMNOPQRSTUVWXYZ $1234567890

minus ¼   The main purpose of letters is the practical one of making thoughts visible.
ABCDEFGHIJKLMNOPQRSTUVWXYZ $1234567890

minus ½   The main purpose of letters is the practical one of making thoughts visible.
ABCDEFGHIJKLMNOPQRSTUVWXYZ $1234567890

HELVETICA

Linespacing (Leading).

Linespacing is the vertical distance between lines of type. A certain amount of linespacing is automatically provided when type is "set solid," but this is not usually adequate for optimum legibility. Depending on the size, style, and line length of the type, linespacing must usually be increased one or more points in a process called *leading* (pronounced *ledding*).

The rule of thumb for leading is that it should be increased as the length of line increases. Generally, a column 12 picas wide is leaded 1 or 2 points, a column 20 picas wide is leaded 2 or 3 points, and a column 30 picas wide is leaded 3 or 4 points. A typeface with a large x-height (see *Type Measurements*) requires more leading than one with a small x-height. While this guideline is adequate for most purposes, the surest method of determining linespacing is to compare sample columns of type having differing amounts of leading. Some type specimen books contains such comparison charts.

If you want to find the amount of leading used in someone else's book, you must first identify the typeface style and size by referring to a type specimen book. Then find which point size on the type gauge matches the line spacing, measuring from baseline to baseline. If the distance between baselines is 12 points, and if the type size is 10 points, this means that there are 2 points of leading.

When ordering type, the amount of leading is specified by first stating the point size of the type, then stating the distance between baselines. For example, if 10 point type is leaded 2 points, there will be 12 points between baselines, and the specification would be stated as "10/12" (orally stated as "10 on 12"). If there is no leading (set solid) the specification would be stated as "10/10."

12/12

There was a time when typesetting was only the process of assembling individual pieces of type by hand. Gutenberg printed his Bible from movable type in the middle of the Fifteenth Century in this way. The first

12/13

There was a time when typesetting was only the process of assembling individual pieces of type by hand. Gutenberg printed his Bible from movable type in the middle of the Fifteenth Century in this way. The first

12/14

There was a time when typesetting was only the process of assembling individual pieces of type by hand. Gutenberg printed his Bible from movable type in the middle of the Fifteenth Century in this way. The first

GARAMOND NO. 3

12/12

There was a time when typesetting was only the process of assembling individual pieces of type by hand. Gutenberg printed his Bible from movable type in the middle of the Fifteenth Century

12/13

There was a time when typesetting was only the process of assembling individual pieces of type by hand. Gutenberg printed his Bible from movable type in the middle of the Fifteenth Century

12/14

There was a time when typesetting was only the process of assembling individual pieces of type by hand. Gutenberg printed his Bible from movable type in the middle of the Fifteenth Century

CASLON 540

12/12

There was a time when typesetting was only the process of assembling individual pieces of type by hand. Gutenberg printed his Bible from movable type in the middle of the Fifteenth Century

12/13

There was a time when typesetting was only the process of assembling individual pieces of type by hand. Gutenberg printed his Bible from movable type in the middle of the Fifteenth Century

12/14

There was a time when typesetting was only the process of assembling individual pieces of type by hand. Gutenberg printed his Bible from movable type in the middle of the Fifteenth Century

HELVETICA REGULAR

Garamond No. 3 has a small x-height, Caslon 540 has a medium x-height, and Helvetica Regular has a large x-height. This influences the amount of leading necessary for good legibility.

Column Width (Line Length).

For good legibility, the column width (called the *measure*) should be proportionate to the size of the type. As a general rule, there should be 30 to 60 characters per line, with 40 to 50 providing maximum legibility. If there is not much copy per page, as would be the case with some children's books, it is not usually necessary to follow this rule.

The specification for column width is an "X" followed by the pica measurement. For example, "X20" means a column 20 picas wide.

Too narrow a column (9/10 X6).

Too narrow a column makes rapid scanning impossible, and an excessive number of words must be divided at the ends of lines. Also, if the column is justified (set flush left and right), wordspacing will be very uneven from line to line.

For good legibility, the width of the column should be proportionate to the size of the type. As a general rule, there should be 30 to 60 characters per line, with 40 to 50 providing optimum legibility. This is not a hard and fast rule, and may be modified to a certain extent. Too wide a column makes it difficult for the eyes to follow a line, and also to locate the succeeding line. If a column must be widened beyond normal limits, additional leading may help to maintain good legibility.

Too wide a column (9/10 X38).

Column Arrangements.

Justified (Flush Left and Right). This is the most common column arrangement. All lines are made equal in length (justified) by adjusting wordspacing. If done well, the varying amounts of wordspacing from line to line are not noticeable. In phototypesetting, if the line length cannot be successfully adjusted with wordspacing, letterspacing may also be adjusted.

Flush Left/Ragged Right. In this column arrangement, which is also commonly used, the lines are unjustified, which means that each line is a different length. Many designers prefer this arrangement to justification because wordspacing remains consistent, and fewer words need to be hyphenated at the ends of lines. The specification for this arrangement is usually stated simply as *ragged right*.

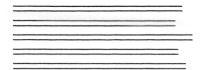

Flush Right/Ragged Left. This arrangement is not used for large amounts of copy because it is difficult to read. It is frequently used for picture captions, however, because it often makes a better page composition.

Centered. This arrangement is used primarily for titles and other headings. In order to achieve a pleasing combination of line lengths, it is necessary to make a word-by-word character count, and to indicate the line breaks on the manuscript.

Asymmetrical. In this arrangement, lines of varying length are staggered over one another. In addition to indicating the line breaks on the manuscript, the typographer must be provided with a layout indicating line positions.

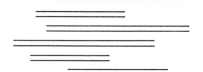

Runaround. In this arrangement, the column is shaped to fit around an illustration, photograph, or decorative initial. The line breaks must be indicated on the manuscript, and the typographer must be provided with a layout. In some phototypesetting systems, it is not necessary to indicate line breaks.

Contour. In this arrangement, the type is fitted into a circle, triangle, diamond, or other shape provided by the designer. As with a runaround, you may not need to indicate line breaks on the manuscript, but a careful character count is necessary to insure that you have exactly the right amount of copy to fill the shape.

Character Counting the Manuscript.
Copy that is to be set in 18 point or larger type does not need to be character counted because it is rendered letter by letter on the layouts, using a type specimen book as a guide. Type smaller than 18 points, however, is indicated on the layouts with ruled lines that represent the type height, line length, and number of lines. To determine the line length and number of lines for a specific size of type, it is first necessary to character count the manuscript.

The total number of characters in a body of manuscript copy is found by multiplying the number of characters per line by the number of lines. Since it would be too time-consuming to count the characters in every line, the follow-

ing method of averaging is used:

To determine the average number of characters per line, vertically position a transparent ruler or triangle on the right side of the typewritten manuscript, adjust it so that there are approximately as many characters to the right of the ruler's edge as there are blank spaces to the left, and lightly draw a vertical pencil line through the copy. Then, in any one line, count the number of characters that fall to the left of the vertical guideline, including periods, commas, spaces, etc. This gives you the average number of characters per line, which you multiply by the number of lines to find the total number of characters in the copy. Record this total at the bottom of the page.

To count the number of characters in a line, use the typewriter scale on the type gauge. The *pica* scale is for typewriters that produce 10 characters per inch, and the *elite* scale is for typewriters that produce 12 characters per inch.

Choosing a Typeface.
For most applications, the "look" or aesthetic quality of type is at least as important as legibility. For children's books, however, legibility must be the primary consideration. The typefaces that are easiest to read have generous serifs, sturdy strokes, and simple, clearly-articulated structures. There are dozens of typefaces with these characteristics, some of the most popular for children's books being Caslon, Century Oldstyle, Garamond, Goudy Oldstyle, Times Roman, Baskerville, Century Schoolbook, Bookman, and Clarendon. While you should avoid sans serif typefaces for lengthy texts, they are quite legible when used in large sizes for short texts. Choose a sans serif face that has simple structures, generous counters (the white shapes inside the letters), and strokes that are neither too thin nor too thick, such as Futura Book, Folio Book, Helvetica Regular, News Gothic, and Univers 55.

The size of the type is usually determined by the amount of copy, which in turn is determined by the age of the reader. For example, a book for a very young child would have few words and large type, whereas a book for an older child would have more words and smaller type. Generally, 11 point type is the smallest size used in children's picture books, with 12, 14, and 18 point being more typical.

When choosing a typeface style and size, also decide on the amount of leading to be used, as this greatly affects legibility. Too little leading makes it difficult for the eyes to follow a line and to locate the succeeding line. In some typefaces, in fact, it is easier to read 10 point type with 2 points of leading than 12 point type with no leading. As mentioned on page 116, the amount of leading should be increased as the length of the line increases.

```
                                        Copyfitting  p. 1

Copyfitting
                                                            50

Copyfitting, also known as copy casting, is the

process of converting written words, or copy, into

typographic form.  The copy, which is usually pre-

pared and/or written by a professional copywriter,

is furnished to the designer, along with other

specifications, at the time that he receives the

design commission.  It is always typewritten, and

is variously referred to as the copy, the typescript,

or the manuscript.  It contains every word that is

to be printed, such as the headline, the sub-head

(line), and the body copy or text.

    Copyfitting is done during the layout stage of

designing.  Using the manuscript as a guide, the

designer experiments with various styles, sizes, and

arrangements of the typographic elements, taking

into account their relationship to the entire design.

When he has arrived at a good solution, he writes

his specifications on the manuscript and sends it -

plus the layout - to the typographer for typesetting.  19


                                                            950
```

This copy averages 50 characters per line. Multiplied by 19 lines, the total character count for the page is 950.

Caslon 540 ABCDEFGHIJKLM 125&	Bookman ABCDEFGHJKLMN 125&
Century Oldstyle ABCDEFGHJK 125&	**Clarendon Reg ABCDEFGHI 125&**
Garamond ABCDEFGHJKLMNOPQRS 125&	Futura Book ABCDEFGHIJKLMNOPQRS 125&
Goudy Oldstyle ABCDEFGHJKL 125&	Folio Book ABCDEFGHIJKLMNOPQR 125&
Times Roman ABCDEFGHJKLMN 125&	Helvetica ABCDEFGHJKLMNOP 125&
Baskerville ABCDEFGHIJKLMN 125&	News Gothic ABCDEFGHIJKLMN 125&
Century Schlbk ABCDEFGHJL 125&	Univers 55 ABCDEFGHIJKLMNOP 125&

Some of the most popular typefaces for children's books.

11 PT.
The main purpose of letters is the practical one of making thoughts visible.
ABCDEFGHIJKLMNOPQRSTUVWXYZ $1234567890

12 PT.
The main purpose of letters is the practical one of making thoughts visible.
ABCDEFGHIJKLMNOPQRSTUVWXYZ $1234567890

14 PT.
The main purpose of letters is the practical one of making thoughts visible.
ABCDEFGHIJKLMNOPQRSTUVWXYZ $1234567890

18 PT.
The main purpose of letters is the practical one of making
ABCDEFGHIJKLMNOPQRSTUVWXYZ $1234567890

CENTURY SCHOOLBOOK

11 PT.
The main purpose of letters is the practical one of making thoughts visible.
ABCDEFGHIJKLMNOPQRSTUVWXYZ $1234567890

12 PT.
The main purpose of letters is the practical one of making thoughts visible.
ABCDEFGHIJKLMNOPQRSTUVWXYZ $1234567890

14 PT.
The main purpose of letters is the practical one of making thoughts visible.
ABCDEFGHIJKLMNOPQRSTUVWXYZ $1234567890

18 PT.
The main purpose of letters is the practical one of making
ABCDEFGHIJKLMNOPQRSTUVWXYZ $1234567890

UNIVERS 55

Typical point sizes used in children's picture books.

Copyfitting Procedure.

After you have character counted the manuscript and chosen a type style and size, you must determine how much space these characters will occupy on the layout when converted to type. To do this, you need to refer to a character count chart for the type style and size that you plan to use, which indicates the average number of typeface characters per pica. Most type specimen books contain such charts, and you can also secure them from your typographer.

When you have found the number of characters per pica (CPP) for your typeface, multiply it by the pica width of your column to find the number of characters per line (CPL). For example, if there are 2.5 CPP, and your column width is 20 picas, there will be 50 CPL. (Some character count charts indicate the CPL for all column widths, which makes the foregoing multiplication procedure unnecessary.)

After determining the number of characters per line, divide this number into the total number of characters in the manuscript copy to find the number of lines in the column. For example, if there are 50 CPL, and if the manuscript totals 1150 characters, there will be 23 lines in the column.

Now you are ready to draw the column shape on your layout. Use the 12-point (pica) scale on the type gauge to measure the column width, and use whatever point scale is appropriate to measure the column depth. For example, if your type size is 11 points with no leading, you would use the 11-point scale because there are 11 points from baseline to baseline. If your type size is 11 points with 2 points of leading, you would use the 13-point scale because there are 13 points from baseline to baseline. If the resulting column depth does not properly fit your layout, either try other column widths or rearrange other layout elements. You could, of course, also change the type size and/or leading, but this is not always possible in a book, where the type size and leading are usually the same on all pages.

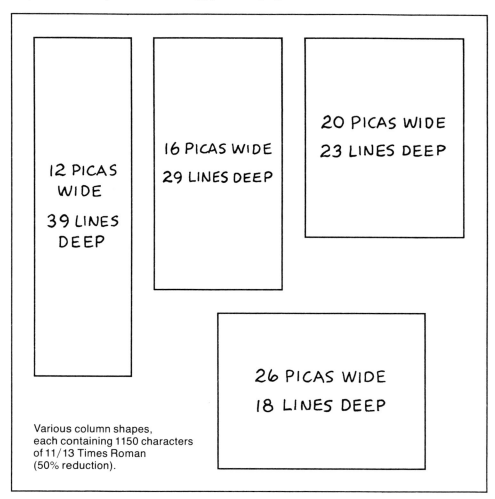

Various column shapes, each containing 1150 characters of 11/13 Times Roman (50% reduction).

Times Roman
Times Roman Bold
Times Roman Italic

Size	6	7	8	9	10	11	12	14
Picas								
10		36	33	31	29	27	25	23	22
12		43	40	37	34	32	30	28	26
14		50	46	43	40	37	35	32	30
16		58	53	49	46	42	40	37	34
18		65	59	55	51	48	45	41	39
20		72	66	61	57	53	50	46	43
22		79	73	67	63	58	55	51	47
24		86	79	73	68	64	60	55	52
26		94	86	79	74	69	65	60	56
28		101	92	85	80	74	70	64	60
30		108	99	92	86	80	75	69	65

A character count chart showing characters per line for all column widths. If you want to know the characters per pica, put a decimal point between the numbers on the 10-pica scale. For example, 11 point Times Roman has 25 characters per 10-pica line or 2.5 characters per pica.

Type Indication.

After you have drawn the outlines of the type column on your layout, you may also want to indicate the lines of type. To do this, use the same point scale on the type gauge to tick off the baselines for every line along the left side of the column with a hard, sharp pencil. Then mark the waistline measurement of the typeface above the first baseline, align the same point scale on it, and tick off the waistlines for every line. Finally, align a T-square on the tick marks and use a pointed, medium-soft pencil to draw the type indication lines. The pencil should be blunt enough so that the two lines (waistline and baseline), plus the space between, accurately represent the "color," or value, of the type. Also, the outsides of the two lines should coincide with the tick marks to accurately represent the x-height of the type. On a highly-finished layout, a ruling pen adjusted to the right line-width can be used to indicate the type in ink.

Rather than using two thin lines to represent the x-height and "color" of the type, you can use one thick line. To do this, use a sandpaper pad to form a chisel point on a medium-soft pencil (2B or HB), making the chisel width exactly the same as the x-height. In this method (which can only be used for pencil layouts), there is no need to tick off the waistline measurements.

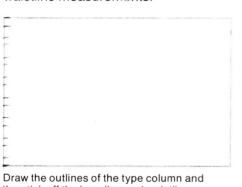

Draw the outlines of the type column and then tick off the baseline and waistline measurements along the left side.

Ruled lines in pencil. The pencil should be blunt enough so that the two lines (waistline and baseline), plus the space in between, have the same "color" as the type.

Ruled lines in chisel-point pencil. Make the chisel width exactly the same as the x-height of the type. Only baseline measurements need to to be ticked off.

Ruled lines in ink. Adjust the ruling pen so that the two lines, plus the space in between, have the same "color" as the type.

Once upon a time there was a giant ogre who had

For small amounts of copy, you may want to hand-letter the type rather than just indicating it with lines. If you plan to do it in ink, make a pencil layout first.

Type Specifications.
After the copy has been fitted to the layouts, you must write the type specifications on the manuscript. They should be clearly written or lettered, preferably in the left margin, with lines pointing to or bracketing the copy being specified. If possible, use a colored pencil or pen for specifications so that they are clearly differentiated from copy corrections, which ideally should be in black. Specifications should be concise and precise, using standard terminology, abbreviations, and symbols. Following is a checklist of the specifications that must be provided to the typographer.

Typeface Name. The full typeface name should be written just as it appears in the type specimen book. Include any number that appears, for this usually denotes a specific version or weight of the typeface.

Capitalization. If the copy is to be set in all capitals, write "caps" after the typeface name. If it is to be set in upper and lower case, write "U&lc" after the name.

Typeface and Line Leading Size. If, for example, 11 point type is to be leaded 2 points, write "11/13" before the typeface name. If 11 point type is to be set solid (no leading), write "11/11" before the typeface name. The first number indicates the typeface size, and the second number indicates the typeface size plus the leading (the baseline to baseline measurement).

Column Width and Arrangement. For most column arrangements, the column width follows the typeface/leading size specifications, and is designated by an "X". For example, in the specification "11/13 X20", the "X20" means a column 20 picas wide. The column arrangement, such as "justified" or "flush left/ragged right", is the last specification written. When a layout is furnished for an unusual column arrangement, indicate this in the specifications, such as "runaround—see layout."

Extra Leading. If, for example, your normal line leading is 2 points, and you want a total of 6 points between certain lines, write "+4" in the margin at the point of insertion. Since the typesetting machine is pre-set to automatically lead 2 points, the typesetter needs to know the amount of *additional* leading, not the total amount. Be sure to include the plus sign, for otherwise the typesetter won't know if you mean "additional" or "total."

Manuscript copy with type specifications and copy corrections.

COPYFITTING

Copyfitting, also known as copycasting, is the process of converting written words, or copy, in to typographic form. The copy, which is usually prepared and/or written by a professional copywriter, is furnished to the designer, along with specifications, at the same time that he receives the design commission. It is typewritten always, and is variously referred to as the copy, the typescript, or the manuscript. It contains every word word that is to be printed, such as the headline, the subhead(line) and the body copy or text. Copyfitting is done during the layout stage of design. Using the manuscript as a guide, the designer experiments with various styles, sizes and arrangements of typographic elements, taking in to account their relationship to the entire design.

When he has arrived at a good solution he writes his specifications on the manuscript and sends it —plus the layout— to the typographer for type-setting.

mark	
lc	(AA)
fl # / #	(AA)
⌢ / ⌣	(PE)
rom	(AA)
other	(AA)
&	(PE)
tr	(AA)
&/ital	(PE)
ital/&	(PE)
⌃ / =/	(PE)
# / t	(AA)(PE)
ing	(PE)
x	(PE)
↑	(PE)
c/tr	(PE)
no #	(AA)
⌃	(PE)
⅟M	(AA)

Galley, or rough, proof with errors indicated. Errors shown are for demonstration purposes only, and would not be so excessive in normal typesetting.

Copyfitting

Copyfitting, also known as copy casting, is the process of converting written words, or copy, into typographic form. The copy, which is usually prepared and/or written by a professional copywriter, is furnished to the designer, along with other specifications, at the time that he receives the design commission. It is always typewritten, and is variously referred to as the *copy,* the *typescript,* or the *manuscript.* It contains every word that is to be printed, such as the headline, the sub-head(line), and the body copy or text.

Copyfitting is done during the layout stage of designing. Using the manuscript as a guide, the designer experiments with various styles, sizes, and arrangements of the typographic elements, taking into account their relationship to the entire design. When he has arrived at a good solution, he writes his specifications on the manuscript and sends it—plus the layout—to the typographer for typesetting.

TYPESETTING AND PROOFREADING

After the type has been set, the typographer makes as many sets of *galley,* or *rough,* proofs as the publisher requests. Usually four sets are needed: one for the proofreader (the master copy); one for the author; one for the subsidiary rights director; and one for the designer to paste onto the dummy. When you receive your set of author's galleys, read through them carefully, marking any errors or changes in colored ink (red is best). Use standard proofreaders' marks, and write the corrections in the margin, with a mark in the text at the point of correction. Corrections are usually made in the right margin, but the left margin, or both margins, may be used if necessary. Next to the marginal correction, an encircled PE is used to indicate a printer's error, and an encircled AA is used to indicate an author's (or editor's) alteration. The cost of making AA's is added to the type-setting bill.

The editor reads both the author's and the proofreader's corrected galleys, adding any approved author's changes to the proofreader's master copy. This master copy is returned to the typographer, who makes corrections and pulls one or more sets of reproduction proofs, or "repros." After the editor checks the repros to see that the corrections have been properly made, they are given to the designer or paste-up artist for use on the mechanicals.

Reproduction (or repro) proof with errors corrected.

PROOFREADERS' MARKS

Correction desired	Marginal mark	Mark in text at point of correction
Comma	⌄⸍	∧
Semicolon	;/	∧
Colon	⊙	∧
Period	⊙	∧
Apostrophe	⌄	∧
Open quotes, close quotes	⸌⸍ ⸌⸍	∧
Hyphen	=/	∧
Dash—show length	$\frac{1}{N}$ $\frac{1}{M}$ $\frac{2}{M}$	∧
Brackets, parentheses	[ ] ( )	∧
Delete	℘	/ or ℓ or ——— through characters
Substitute or insert character(s)	new character(s)	/ through or between characters
Insert omitted copy	out-see copy	∧
Disregard correction—let stand as printed	stet	dot under each character to be retained
Paragraph	¶	∧
Flush paragraph	fl ¶	∧
Indent (show no. of ems)	□ ⊓ ⊔⊔⊔	⅂
No paragraph, or run in	no ¶ or run in	(run-in mark)
Move right or left	⅃ or ⊏	⅃ or ⊏
Raise or lower	⊓ or ⊔	⊓ or ⊔
Center	ctr	⌐ ¬
Flush left or flush right	fl L or fl R	[or]
Align horizontally	═══	lines above and below defect
Align vertically	‖	lines to the left and right of defect
Transpose	tr	had first miss or hit
Insert space	#	∧
Equalize space	eq sp	∧ ∧ ∧
Close up	⌒	⌒
Wrong font	wf	encircle
Lower case	lc	/ through characters, or encircle
Capitals	cap	triple underline
Small capitals	sc	double underline
Roman	rom	encircle
Italic	ital	single underline
Bold face	bf	jagged underline
Superior or inferior character	⌄² or ₂⌃	∧
Broken type	✕	encircle
Invert type	↺	encircle
Push down type	⊥	encircle
Spell out	spell out or sp	encircle
Query to author	who?	∧ or encircle
Line break	break	∫ between characters

Preparation for Printing

THE PRODUCTION PROCESS

The mechanical, or paste-up, is the final stage in preparing art for offset lithography, which is the method of printing used for almost all children's books. The mechanical is a two-page layout, precisely executed on white board, that contains all line copy, such as type and pen and ink drawings, pasted into printing position. Continuous-tone copy, such as photographs and wash drawings, is not pasted on the mechanical because the printer must photograph it separately as halftone copy. However, its size and position must be accurately indicated so that the halftone negatives can later be stripped into the line negative of the mechanical. If more than one color is involved, the copy for the additional colors is placed on acetate overlays that are hinged, in register, over the base, or key, mechanical board (see *Flat Color Printing, page 139*).

Graphic arts copy camera (Consolidated).

Using a large copy camera, the printer makes line negatives of the mechanicals and overlays, and halftone negatives of the continuous-tone copy. In a light-table procedure called *stripping*, he tapes the line negatives in position on large sheets of lightproof, yellow-orange paper called *goldenrod*, and cuts windows in the paper where light must pass through the negatives. Since the mechanicals are laid out as two-page spreads, the negatives must be cut in half and arranged in such a way that when the sheet of printed pages (the signature) is folded and trimmed, the pages will be in correct sequence. This is called *imposition* or *press layout*. Finally, after the page negatives for one side of a signature have been impositioned on a sheet of goldenrod, the halftone negatives and screen tints, if any, are stripped in.

The completed assemblage of negatives on goldenrod is called the *flat*, and is used to make the printing plate. In offset lithography, this is done by positioning the flat over a printing plate that has a light-sensitive coating, and exposing it to light in a platemaking device called a *vacuum frame*. With further chemical processing, the exposed, or image, areas become ink-receptive, and the unexposed areas become water-receptive. In the printing operation, the plate is dampened and then inked with each revolution of the

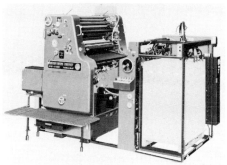

One-color offset press.

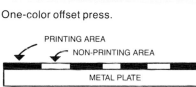

Offset lithography printing plate. There is no difference in height between the printing and non-printing areas. The plate is chemically treated so that the non-printing areas absorb water during the printing process, and thus will not accept ink.

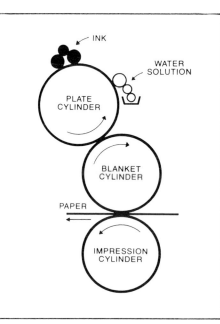

Offset lithography printing process.

plate cylinder. The inked images are transferred, or offset, onto a rubber blanket cylinder, and from there onto the paper.

After the sheets are printed, they are folded into signatures, and the signatures are gathered, or collated, in correct sequence for binding. For hardcover books, the signatures are usually sewn together with thread, either through the backbone of each signature (Smyth-sewn), or through the entire book, ⅛″ in from the binding edge (side-sewn). For paperback books, the signatures are usually bound together with adhesive (perfect binding). In perfect binding, the paper cover is glued on before the book is trimmed, whereas in sewn binding, the bound signatures are trimmed before the separately-manufactured cover is attached.

There are many variations to these binding methods. For example, perfect binding is sometimes used for hardcover books, and sewn signatures are sometimes used for paperback books. Also, staples are sometimes used instead of thread for side-stitching.

1	16	6	8
4	13	12	5
3	14	11	9
2	15	10	7

Press layout of pages on a printing plate. The same plate is used to print both sides of the sheet, which results in two 16-page signatures. The sheet is cut on the dash line before folding as shown below.

LAYING OUT THE MECHANICAL

Sometimes a publisher will furnish you with mechanical boards that are printed with light blue guidelines indicating page size, folds, etc. If such "bluelines" are not available, you must make your own mechanical boards, following the publisher's size specifications. Use smooth illustration board or 2-ply kid-finish bristol board that is 2″ larger on all sides than the trim size of a two-page spread. Attach it to your drawing board with pushpins or tape after aligning it with a T-square. Then, from the top center of the spread, accurately measure the page widths and depth, and draw their outlines, using a sharp 5H pencil, T-square, and triangle. Finally, draw fine, black trim marks with either a ruling pen or technical fountain pen. For book mechanicals, most printers recommend that the trim marks be crossed lines, ½″ to ¾″ long, placed at the outside corners and top and bottom centers of the two-page spread. (If you are using blueline mechanicals furnished by the publisher, you must add these trim marks to them.)

Since the black pencil lines delineating page outlines must be erased after the mechanical is finished, some designers draw them in light blue, which does not reproduce on lithographer's film. Non-reproducing (non-repro) blue pencils and ball point pens are available in art supply stores. In addition to their use for page outlines, they are handy for other guidelines as well as for writing specifications within the reproduction area of the mechanical.

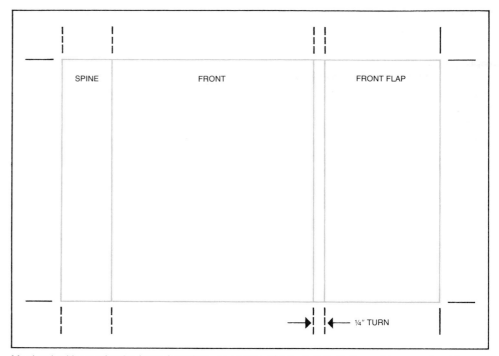

Mechanical layout for the front, front flap, and spine of a book jacket. To avoid an overly-wide mechanical, the back and back flap are placed on another board. This method of indicating trim size and folds is used for all graphic design work except book and booklet pages. Trim marks are fine black lines, about ½″ long, placed about ⅛″ outside the trim dimensions. Fold marks are dash lines of the same weight and length as trim marks. The trim dimensions and folds, shown here in gray, are drawn in pencil or non-repro blue ink. Pencil lines must later be erased.

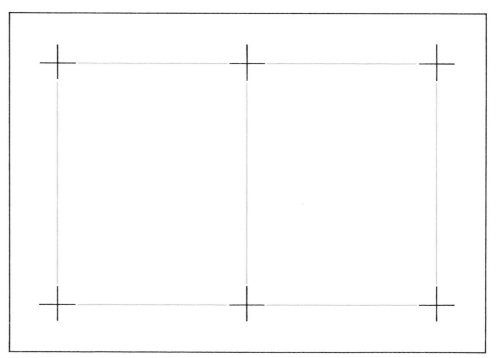

Mechanical layout for book and booklet pages. As explained on page 125, the negatives of page mechanicals must be cut in half and trimmed to page size in order to achieve correct press layout, which means that trim marks will be cut off if they are placed outside the trim dimensions. To avoid this problem, use fine, crossed black lines, ½″ to ¾″ long, at the outside corners and top and bottom centers of the two-page spreads (printers usually refer to these marks as corner and center marks, not trim marks). Page outlines, shown here in gray, are drawn in pencil or non-repro blue ink. Pencil lines must later be erased.

RUBBER CEMENTING PROCEDURE

Rubber cement is the most commonly used adhesive for paste-ups. It dries rapidly and will not penetrate, stain, wrinkle, or shrink paper. Dried cement may be removed with a rubber cement pick-up, which may be purchased or may be made by rolling bits of dried cement into a ball. Also, previously-cemented material may be removed by squirting rubber cement thinner beneath it as it is being pulled off. To do this, you need an oil can or other squirt-type container with a small opening. Since the thinner evaporates rapidly, seal the top between uses with a piece of rubber eraser. Sealable-spout thinner dispensers are sold in art supply stores.

Rubber cement may be purchased in a small can with a brush in the cap, or it may be purchased in a larger can and poured into a glass or plastic dispenser with a brush that adjusts to the level of cement in the jar. Since the vehicle used in rubber cement evaporates rapidly, the cement must occasionally be thinned to return it to proper brushing consistency. When buying rubber cement, therefore, also buy a can of thinner. (As mentioned before, thinner is also necessary for removing previously-cemented material.)

For proper adhesion, rubber cement must be applied to both surfaces. For paste-ups, the best procedure is to coat the back of the piece to be mounted and let it dry. Then coat the mounting surface (the mechanical) and immediately place the piece to be mounted on the wet cement, using a T-square to align it. The cement will begin to take hold within a minute or two, but wait 20 to 30 minutes before removing the excess cement around the mounted piece to avoid disturbing it.

When cementing very large pieces, the cement on the mounting surface will begin to dry before the piece to be mounted can be placed on it, thus making accurate alignment impossible. In that case, let both surfaces dry thoroughly and place a sheet of tracing paper on the mounting surface so that it covers all but a narrow band of cement along the top edge. Then position the piece to be mounted, adhere it to the

Rubber cementing equipment. A *Valvespout* thinner dispenser and a purchased rubber cement pick-up are shown in the foreground.

band of exposed cement, and slowly pull out the tracing paper, pressing the cemented surfaces together with your hand or the edge of a triangle as you proceed. This "slipsheet" method is also used when mounting very thin or easily-wrinkled materials. If a wrinkle still occurs, detach the material either partially or fully by squirting thinner beneath it, let the cement dry again, and repeat the slipsheet procedure.

In addition to regular, or two-coat, rubber cement, there is a one-coat rubber cement that is applied only to the material being mounted. Because it contains wax it remains tacky indefinitely, and mounted work can easily be removed or repositioned without thinner. It is useful for making dummies, but is not desirable for mechanicals because it has a weak bond and because excess cement is difficult to remove.

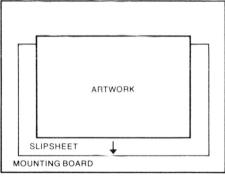

Single slip sheet.

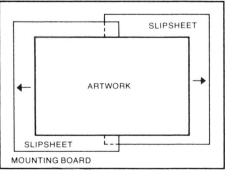

Two slip sheets are necessary for very large work.

PASTING UP LINE COPY

Line copy includes type as well as any art composed of solid blacks and whites with no intermediate gray tones, such as pen and ink illustrations (see *Techniques*, page 64). Since the type is always set at reproduction size, the proofs are simply cut up and pasted on the mechanicals. Illustrations, however, are usually executed larger than reproduction size (see *Working Size*, page 59), which means that photostat prints of them must be used on the mechanical. For information on ordering photostats, see page 134. If original art is used on the mechanical, it must be on board no thicker than 3-ply bristol. Work on illustration board must either be photostatted or stripped off the backing board. To strip the face paper off the backing board, peel up a corner of the paper and diagonally position a large-diameter mailing tube over it. Then grasp the tube with your palms, press the peeled-up paper against it with your thumbs, and roll off the rest of the sheet. Sand the back of the paper to remove backing-board residue before trimming and pasting it up. If this procedure sounds risky, try it first on a scrap of board. You will find that it is both safe and easy.

A good T-square is necessary for doing mechanicals. Since it is used for cutting as well as for drawing lines and aligning paste-up elements, a steel T-square is best because it can't be nicked. For cutting with the T-square,

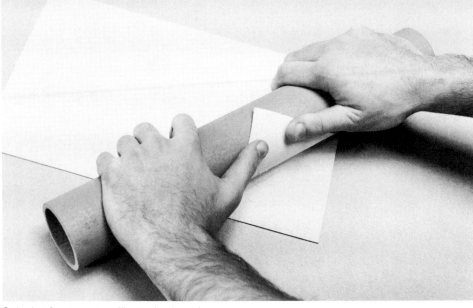

Stripping face paper on illustration board.

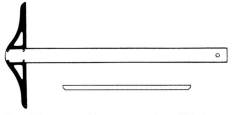

Steel T-square with cross-section of blade. Note that the blade is beveled, which prevents ink run-under.

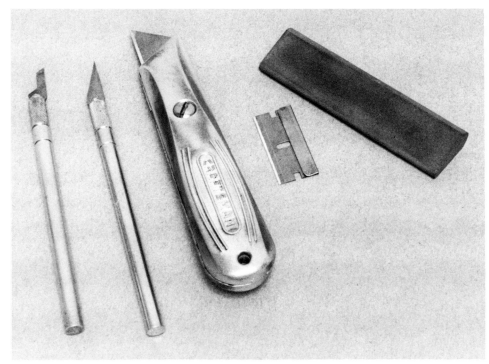

(Left to right) The #1 X-Acto knife with #16 blade is used for freehand-curve cutting; the #1 X-Acto knife with #11 blade is used for straight-line precision cutting; the mat knife is used for cutting mat and illustration board; the industrial razor blade is used for general straight-line cutting; the slip stone is used for sharpening blades.

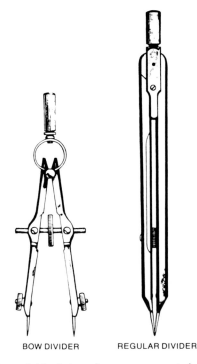

BOW DIVIDER   REGULAR DIVIDER

Use a divider to transfer measurements from the layout to the mechanical. The regular divider is faster to use because of its friction-joint adjustment mechanism.

use a single-edge industrial razor blade or a #1 X-acto knife with a #11 blade. Free-form shapes should be cut with scissors before pasting up. Because small bits of paper are difficult to pick up and position, some designers use tweezers. Another method is to jab the cutting blade into a blank corner of the paper. A divider is very handy for transferring measurements from the dummy to the mechanical, centering type, etc. In lieu of a divider, tick off the measurements along the edge of a sheet of paper. Don't use a ruler, for your measurements will very seldom coincide with the ruler markings.

Because the mechanical is attached to the drawing board, you need a cutting board for trimming paste-up elements, such as a piece of illustration board or the back of a used-up paper pad. You also need a similar board for applying rubber cement to the back of pieces to be mounted. Don't use the same board for both purposes: you often have to trim elements after they have been backed with cement, and they would stick to a board that has cement on it.

Type proofs generally contain a number of type elements that must be cut apart for use on the mechanical. The best way to do this is to rubber cement the entire proof before cutting it up. After it has dried, place it on the cutting board, carefully align it with a T-square, and make all the horizontal cuts. Extend the cuts beyond the type, but not the full width of the proof. By leaving the ends of the strips attached, the type will remain in alignment for the vertical cuts, which are made by turning the board sideways. The vertical cuts can be

made all at the same time or just before each piece is to be pasted up. Cutting them out as needed is best when many small elements are involved, because it insures against loss or mix-up. Be careful to accurately align the cuts with the type, for crooked cut marks on the mechanical make it seem as if the type is crooked.

For both type and illustrations, don't cut closer than ⅛″ to the images unless it can't be avoided. Cut marks sometimes reproduce on the printer's negative, and if they are very close to the images they cannot easily be opaqued.

After the paste-up is completed and the rubber cement is thoroughly dry, remove the excess cement with a pickup, being especially careful to remove the bits that cling to cut edges. Then closely examine the type and other line copy for flaws, and retouch them with lampblack watercolor and/or zinc white gouache or retouch color applied with a small brush. A magnifying glass is useful for small corrections such as broken letters. If a type flaw cannot be successfully retouched, the typographer will provide you with another proof, usually at no charge.

Free-form shapes can be trimmed with scissors. Try to make at least one accurate vertical or horizontal cut so that the shape can be easily aligned on the mechanical.

Crooked cut marks make it seem as if the type is not aligned properly.

Non-repro blue guidelines drawn on the mechanical and at the edge of the type proof make it easy to position the type.

When cutting type proofs, use a steel T-square for horizontal cuts, and a steel T-square and metal-edged triangle for vertical cuts (as shown). If you don't have a metal-edged triangle, turn the proof sideways and use the steel T-square.

INDICATING CONTINUOUS-TONE COPY

To reproduce continuous-tone copy, the printer must photograph it through a halftone screen. This converts the tones to minute dots of varying sizes which, when printed, optically mix with the white of the paper to simulate the tones of the original art. Since the continuous-tone copy must be photographed separately from the line copy, it cannot be put on the mechanical even if it is the right size (which it seldom is). Therefore, it is submitted separately to the printer, and its size and position is indicated on the mechanical.

There are two basic types of continuous-tone art: that with squared-up outer contours (square-finish), and that with irregular outer contours (silhouette). To indicate square-finish art, find its reproduction dimensions by the scaling method described below, and accurately draw its outline on the mechanical in red ink. Instead of an inked outline, some designers make a solid panel by placing self-adhesive transparent red film over the pencil outline and cutting it to size. This is not only easier than making an outline with a ruling pen, but most printers prefer it because the resulting transparent window on the negative makes it easier to strip in the halftone. (With an outline, the printer must cut the window out of the negative.)

The reason for using red lines on the mechanical is that they indicate "holding lines" that are not to be printed. If you use black lines, your art will be printed with a black border. You *can* use black lines, however, if you write "holding line" inside the shape, with an arrow pointing to the outline. Red photographs the same as black on lithographer's film, but it must be strong and intense, such as Pelikan 51 Special Red. If such an ink is not available, use black instead.

To insure that a square-finish halftone completely fills the panel provided for it on the mechanical, the original art must be somewhat oversized. This means that crop marks must be drawn in the borders of the original art to indicate to the printer how it is to be positioned in the panel. The distance between crop marks should be in exact ratio to the dimensions of the panel, and it is these measurements that are used when stating reduction or enlargement size.

PROCEDURE FOR CROPPING AND SCALING SQUARE-FINISH HALFTONE ART

If your art must fit a predetermined layout (or mechanical) shape, follow Procedure A. If the composition of your art is more important than its layout shape, follow Procedure B. If both factors are of importance, combine the procedures to find the best compromise. Use mat or illustration board to make the cropping frames. Each arm should be 12″ to 15″ long and 1½″ to 2″ wide.

Procedure A—From Layout to Art.
(1) Tape Frame A to the lower left edge of a sheet of tracing paper that is larger than the original art. (2) On the tracing paper, draw the layout shape at the inside corner of Frame A. Then draw a diagonal line through opposite corners of the shape, extending the line to the edge of the paper (see *Diagonal-line Scaling,* page 60). (3) Place the cropping frames and tracing paper on the original art and move them about to find the best composition, always keeping Frame B parallel with Frame A and its inside corner on the diagonal line. (4) When the best composition is found, tape the frames and paper in position and draw light pencil crop marks on the border of the art, using a T-square and triangle for exact alignment.

Procedure B—From Art to Layout.
(1) Place only the cropping frames on the original art and move them about to find the best composition, always keeping the two frames parallel. When the best composition is found, tape the frames in position and draw light pencil crop marks in the border of the art, using a T-square and triangle for exact alignment. (2) Place the taped-together frames on a sheet of tracing paper, tape Frame A to the paper, and draw the shape delineated by the insides of the frames, with a diagonal line through opposite corners. (3) Place the cropping frames and tracing paper on the layout, detach Frame B from Frame A, and move the frames and paper about

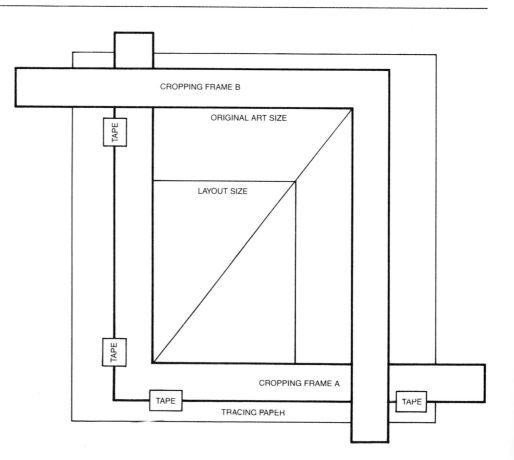

to find the best layout size and position, always keeping Frame B parallel with Frame A and its inside corner on the diagonal line. (4) When the best layout size and position has been found, tape the frames and paper in position, draw the shape delineated by the insides of the frames, detach the frames from the paper, and transfer the shape to the underlying layout.

Photo mounted on stiff board, with inked crop marks, key number and letter, type of halftone (square), and reproduction size in percentage. An illustration would be prepared in same way, but it need not be mounted if it is on illustration board and has borders wide enough for crop marks. Never trim art to its cropped size, and never place crop marks at the exact edge of art. If the art doesn't extend slightly beyond the crop marks, the halftone negative of it may not completely fill the panel provided for it on the mechanical.

Directly below is the square-finish halftone as it would be printed, and at bottom are the three methods of indicating its size and position on the mechanical. Left: Black (or red) holding line. Center: Self-adhesive red film. Right: Black (or red) holding line, with photostat pasted up to show subject matter and cropping. Photostat must not cover holding line.

8A
SQ HT
68 %

PHOTO FROM GEORGE ANCONA'S BOOK, *BANANAS* (SEE PAGE 82).

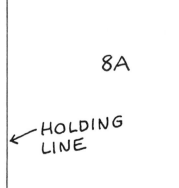

8A

← HOLDING
LINE

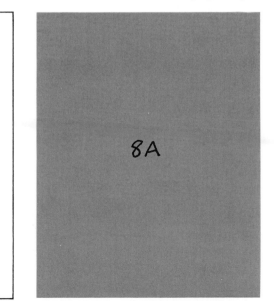

8A

8A
FPO
HOLDING LINE ↓

The easiest way to indicate silhouette art is by pasting a photostat of it on the mechanical and writing "for position only", or "FPO", someplace within its contours. This is to insure that the printer doesn't use the stat for "shooting copy" instead of the original art. The stat doesn't have to be of good quality, but its outer contours must be dark enough to be visible on the negative. In fact, you can even use a xerographic copy if you have access to an office copier that reduces and enlarges by 1% increments.

You can also indicate silhouette art by drawing its outer contours on the mechanical in red ink. To do this, however, you need to use an art projector (page 61) to reduce (or enlarge) the original art to reproduction size. The outline doesn't have to be exact, but it must be good enough to serve as an accurate positioning guide for the printer.

17 B
SIL HT   REDUCE FROM 5⅛" TO 3⅞"

Photo mounted on stiff board, with key number and letter, type of halftone (silhouette), and reproduction size in inches (the height of the foreground figure). The photo was silhouetted with a band of white paint. Silhouette illustrations, of course, are executed as such, and do not require this procedure.

17B FPO

Photostat pasted on the mechanical.

17 B

Red (or black) outline drawn on the mechanical.

and just feeling good.

9

A page from George Ancona's book, *Dancing Is* (1981), which shows the above photo reproduced. The other photos were prepared in the same way.

When art is reproduced in halftone, its white areas will contain a fine dot pattern. While this is not objectionable with most forms of art, it would be with such art as pencil drawings. The printer will drop out these highlight dots (as in the above drawing by Gerry Contreras) if you specify a *dropout* or *highlight* halftone. Don't use tones lighter than 10% in your art because they may drop out as well. It is also possible to drop out highlight dots in photographs.

Specifications for the Printer. Every piece of continuous-tone art must be "keyed" with a letter or number that is written in red or black ink at the bottom of the original art and also inside its contours on the mechanical. Usually, the key is an encircled A,B,C, etc., but if many pieces are involved, the key might include the page number, such as 10A, 10B, 11A, 12A, etc.

The original art must also state how much it is to be reduced (or enlarged). For example, if the width of the original art is 10″, and its width on the mechanical is 6″, write *reduce from 10″ to 6″* under the key letter. The reduction can also be stated in percentage (see *Ordering Photostats*, page 135). For example, the above reduction would be written as *60%*.

Original art that is sent to the printer should be protected with a tracing paper, or "tissue", overlay and a heavy paper cover. Attach the overlay along the top front edge of the board with masking tape, and attach the cover along the top back edge of the board with rubber cement. Be sure that both can be folded back easily so they don't need to be removed when the printer photographs the art.

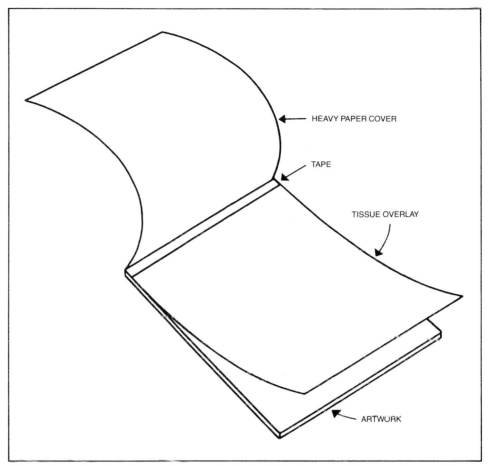

All art to be sent to the printer, such as mechanicals, illustrations, and photographs, should be on sturdy board and flapped with a tissue overlay (tracing or layout paper) and a heavy paper cover.

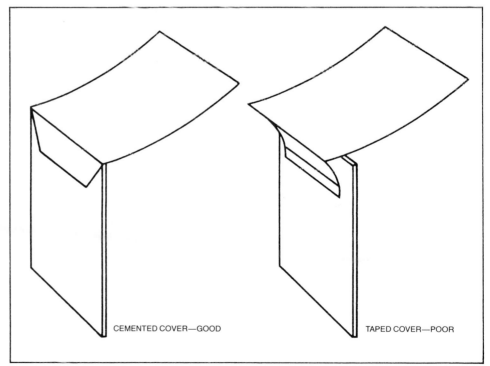

The printer must fold the cover to the back of the artwork in order to photograph it. If the cover is not easy to fold and/or poorly attached, as in the illustration at right, the printer may remove and discard it, thus placing your art at risk of damage.

PHOTOSTATS

Photostats, or stats, are black & white paper photographic prints made directly from opaque original copy. There are two photostat systems in common use: the standard negative-positive system, and the newer direct-positive (DP) system. In the standard system, a negative print (called a *first print*) is made, and from that a positive print (called a *second print*) is made. In the direct-positive system, only a positive print is made, although it is possible to make a negative print if the original copy is to be reversed.

High-contrast paper is used for line copy. It is called *glossy* in the standard system, and *line* in the DP system. DP line stats are sharper than standard glossy stats, and should be used for copy that contains very fine details. If details are lost even when using DP stats, paste the stat on the mechanical, mark it "for position only," and ask the printer to shoot the original copy. Lithographer's film can hold details much better than stat paper.

Regular-contrast paper is used for continuous-tone copy. It is called *matte* in the standard system, and *tone* in the DP system. DP tone stats hold tones better than standard matte stats, but they are not as good as regular photographic prints. Therefore, neither tone nor matte stats are used for reproduction. Rather, their main use is for indicating the position of continuous-tone copy on mechanicals.

Maximum reduction and enlargement sizes vary among brands of stat cameras. The maximum reduction size ranges between 30% and 50%, and the maximum enlargement size ranges between 200% and 330%. When using the standard system, of course, both the negative and the positive prints can be enlarged or reduced. For example, if the negative, or first, print is reduced to 50%, and the positive, or second, print is reduced to 50%, the second print will be 25% of the original size. Similarly, if the first print is enlarged to 200%, and the second print is enlarged to 200%, the second print will be 400% of the original size.

Original copy.

50% first print.

50% second print.

Original copy can be reversed left to right (mirror image) by ordering a *flopped* photostat. Be aware that if your copy contains type or lettering, it will be wrong-reading when flopped.

Ordering Photostats. If the original copy is on paper, it should be taped onto stiff board for protection. Specifications should be written at the bottom of the board, and fragile artwork should be flapped. Following are the specifications that must be provided:

1. Number of prints.

2. Type of print; either first print (negative), second print (positive), or direct-positive.

3. Type of paper; either glossy or matte for standard photostats, or line or tone for direct-positive photostats.

4. Area of copy to be statted. If extra paper is desired around the imagery, indicate the amount with crop marks, and specify "shoot to crop marks."

5. Size of print; either same size (SS or 100%) or the size of reduction or enlargement. The most common method of specifying a reduction or enlargement is to state the size of one dimension of the original copy (usually the overall width or height), followed by the size to which it is to be reduced or enlarged. For example, if the copy is to be reduced from 8″ to 6″, the specification would be written as *8″ to 6″*. If the copy is to be enlarged from 8″ to 10″, the specification would be written as *8″ to 10″*. In order to set the camera, the operator must convert these measurements to a percentage size with a circular proportional scale. For example 8″ to 6″ is 75% (of the original size), and 8″ to 10″ is 125%.

If you have a circular proportional scale, you can make the conversion from inches to percentage yourself, and use only the percentage for specifying size. This not only avoids the risk of operator error, but frequently results in lower stat costs. For example, if you have a number of pieces that are the same or very close in percentage of reduction, group them on one board so they can be shot as one stat.

I GLOSSY 2nd PRINT 68%
SHOOT TO CROP MARKS

A typical example of photostat specifications written on the original copy.

Using the Circular Proportional Scale. To convert an 8″ to 6″ reduction to percentage, for example, align 8″ on the "original" scale with 6″ on the "reproduction" scale, and 75% will appear in the "percentage" window. Similarly, to convert an 8″ to 10″ enlargement to percentage, align 8″ on the "original" scale with 10″ on the "reproduction" scale, and 125% will appear in the "percentage" window.

Another use for the circular proportional scale is to determine the proportions of re-sized shapes. For example, if an illustration is to be reduced in width from 12″ to 9″, align 12″ on the "original" scale with 9″ on the "reproduction" scale. This setting is then used to convert all other measurements in the same ratio. If the original height of the above illustration is 6″, for example, its reduced height would be 4½″.

Circular proportional scale.

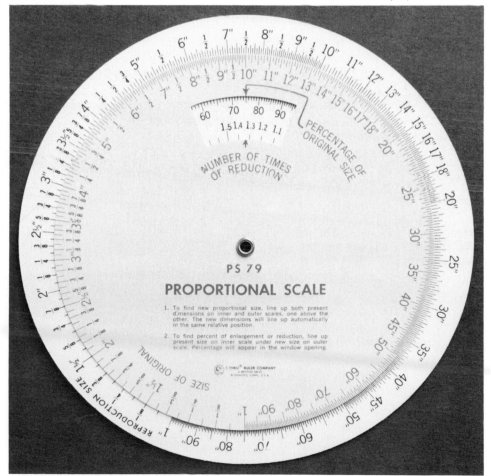

BLEED

If an illustration runs off the edge of a page, extend it about ⅛″ beyond the trim dimensions. This extended portion, called the *bleed*, is necessary to insure that the illustration doesn't end short of the edge in the event of inexact trimming.

A page from *Creative Carousel Coloring Book* (1984), illustrated by Storm.

Mechanical showing bleed. Note that illustration bleeds on trim sides only, not on binding side indicated by dash line.

SCREEN TINTS

Screen tints are flat tints of black or color. They can be applied to the art with shading film (page 69), or they can be applied by the printer. If the printer is to lay the screen tint, its shape and percentage must be indicated on the mechanical. If the tint is totally enclosed within a solid shape, the solid shape serves as a guide for the printer. If the tint is not enclosed, its shape must be indicated in red or black, either outlined or filled-in. A filled-in shape is preferable, but an outlined shape is necessary

Result when printed (50% tint).

Black (or red) holding line on mechanical.

Filled-in black (or red) shape on mechanical. Write "50% tint" within shape in red (or black).

when it abuts another shape on the same board or overlay.

Screen tints are available in 10% increments ranging from 10% (very light) to 90% (very dark). The specified percentage can be written within the shape on the mechanical, or it can be written directly over the shape on the tissue overlay. So that the specification on the mechanical will not reproduce, use light blue to write on a white surface, red to write on a black surface, and black to write on a red surface.

Result when printed (solid and 30% tint).

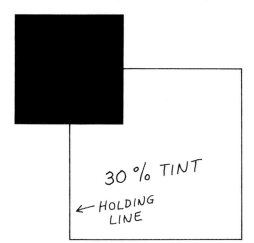

Black (or red) holding line used on mechanical to separate solid and tint areas.

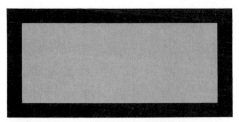

Result when printed (solid and 40% tint).

40% TINT

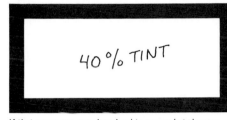

If tint area on mechanical is completely surrounded by a solid shape, no special procedure is required except tint specification.

PANTONE
COLOR/TINT OVERLAY
SELECTOR

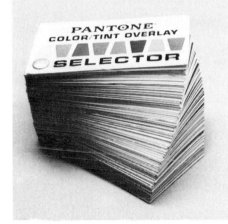

This book contains acetate pages of Pantone colors, both solid and tints (see *Pantone Matching System,* page 140). By overlaying these pages, it is possible to see the effect of overprinted colors in flat color printing.

YELLOW
MAGENTA
CYAN
BLACK
10%
20%
30%
40%
50%
60%
70%
80%
90%
100% (SOLID)

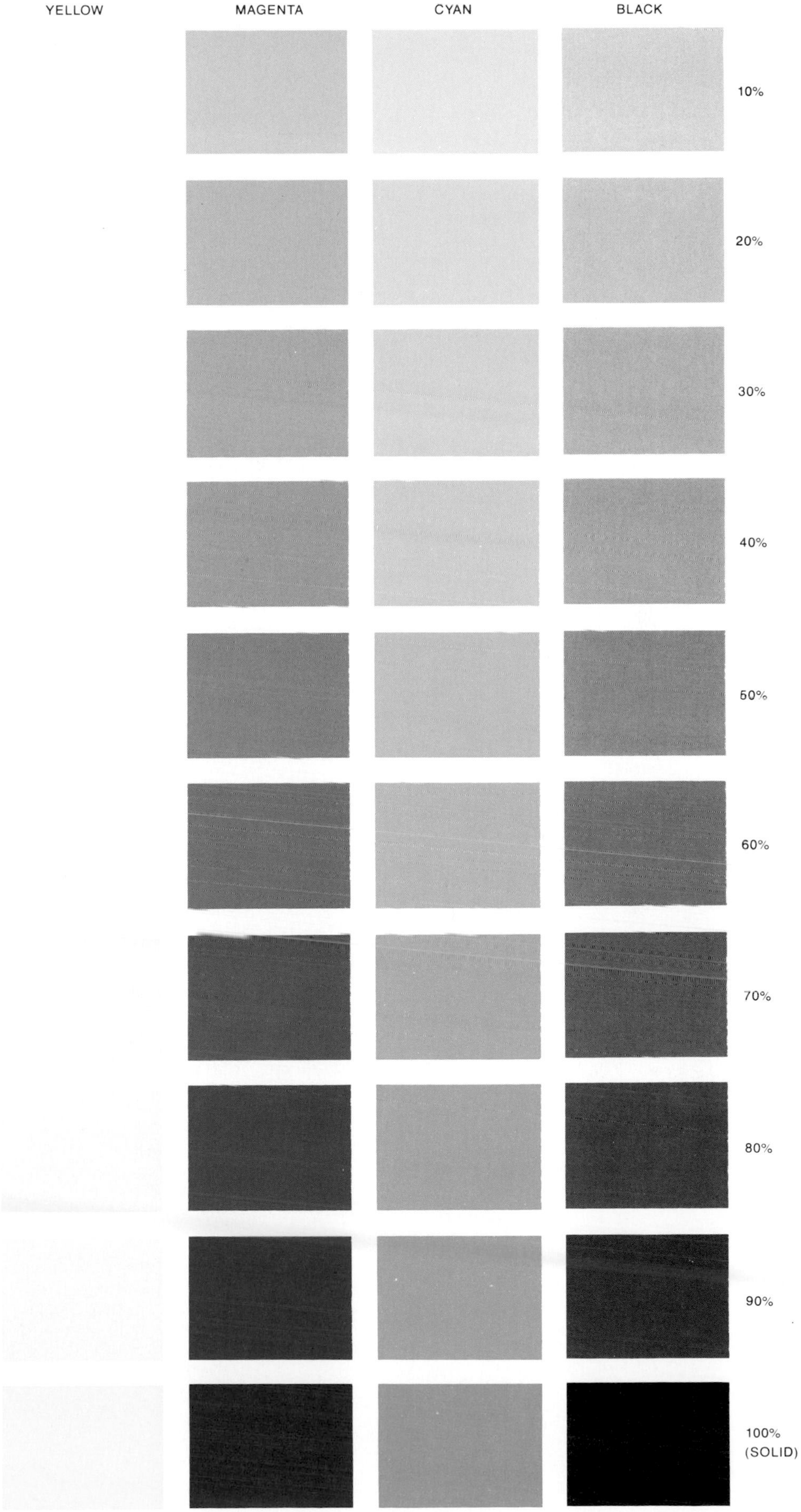

Process color tints and solids. As mentioned on page 87, a color guide is necessary when using overprinted process colors and tints in flat color printing. The *Pantone Color/Tint Overlay Selector* (shown above) can be used for this purpose, but it is not as accurate as a color guide in which the colors are actually overprinted.

Two flat colors: black (solid) and yellow ochre (solid and two flat tints). *Really Ridiculous Rabbit Riddles* (1979), written by Jeanne & Margaret Wallace and Dave Ross, and illustrated by Dave Ross.

Three flat colors: black (halftone); yellow ochre (solid and one flat tint); red ochre (solid and one flat tint). *This Time, Tempe Wick?* (1974), written by Patricia Lee Gauch and illustrated by Margot Tomes.

Three flat colors: black (solid and flat tints); process yellow (solid); process red (solid and flat tints). The green is achieved by printing a black tint over solid yellow. *From Ungskah 1 to Oyaylee 10* (1965), written and illustrated by Lucille Corcos.

Three flat colors: black (solid and one flat tint); process red (solid and three flat tints); process yellow (solid and one flat tint). *Scarlet Monster Lives Here* (1979), written by Marjorie Weinman Sharmat and illustrated by Dennis Kendrick.

Note: These illustrations are reproduced here in four-color process, which imparts a dot pattern to all colors, solid and tint. You must look at the books themselves to see the true effect of flat color printing.

PREPARATION FOR
COLOR PRINTING

Full-color Printing. As explained on page 84, full-color continuous-tone art is printed by four-color process. It is prepared for printing in the same way as black & white continuous-tone art, as described on page 130. For silhouette art, a position stat is pasted on the mechanical, and for square-finish art, a red outline or solid red panel is used to delineate its shape on the mechanical. The square-finish original art must have crop marks that are exactly proportionate to the mechanical shape.

Flat Color Printing. Art for flat color printing, as described on page 85, must be color-separated for the printer. The most common method is to place the art for one color (usually black) on the mechanical board, and the art for the other colors on individual overlays hinged over the "key" art on the board. Use either drafting film, frosted acetate, or prepared acetate for the overlays. Don't use regular acetate, because ink and many other mediums applied to it will crawl and/or chip. Cut the overlays to about 1″ larger on all sides than the trim dimensions, and hinge each one on a different side of the mechanical with masking tape, making sure that any one of them can be brought into direct contact with the key mechanical or with each other.

Register marks are used to insure accurate color registration. These are fine, crossed black lines about ½″ long, placed about ¼″ outside the trim dimensions on all four sides of the key mechanical and the overlays. The register marks on the overlays must align perfectly with those on the key mechanical. In lieu of ruling pen lines, you can use purchased register marks printed on self-adhesive transparent tape. To insure that the overlay doesn't shift while working on it, attach two masking tape tabs to the side of the overlay opposite the hinge. The tabs should extend onto the mechanical board at least ½″.

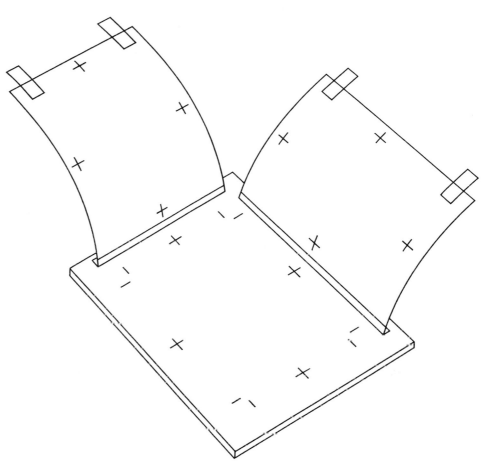

Key mechanical on illustration board. The two acetate overlays are attached with masking or white tape. A third overlay would be attached at the left, and a fourth would be attached at the bottom. Note the trim marks on the key mechanical, and the register marks on the key mechanical and overlays. Also note the masking tape tabs for attaching the overlays to the key mechanical while working on them.

The pencil guidelines for all colors in the illustration should be placed on the key mechanical. To execute the art for a particular overlay, position it in direct contact with the key drawing. When drawing straight lines, the T-square or triangle will press the overlay down tightly, but with freehand drawing you will need to press down the overlay with the handle-end of a brush held in the non-drawing hand.

Overlay art is usually executed in red ink or, for large, simple shapes, red color film with adhesive backing. Black may also be used, but the advantage to red is that, being transparent, it is possible to see how much the colors overlap. To insure against gaps between butted colors in the event of printing misregistration, the colors must overlap .010″ to .015″ (.015″ is 1/64″). Too wide

Register marks printed on clear, self-adhesive cellophane tape.

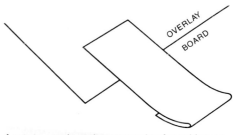

Acetate overlay tabs are made of masking or white tape, about 2″ long. Attach them permanently to the overlays, leaving about 1½″ for attachment to the board. The ends of the tabs should be folded over so that they can easily be lifted from the board.

an overlap, of course, will result in an obvious and unwanted third color in the overlap area. The red must be strong and intense in order to reproduce well. A good ink to use is Pelikan 51 Special Red, which is made specifically for reproduction. Any strong red color film will work, but most brands have a special red film for overlays and masking. Be sure that the film has a wax-paper backing. (There is a masking film available with an acetate backing which serves as a readymade overlay sheet, but the acetate does not accept ink and other mediums.) See *Shading and Pattern Film*, page 69, for the method of applying paper-backed film.

It is important to understand that the only colors used on a mechanical are black, red (which photographs as black), and light blue (which doesn't photograph at all). The printing colors are specified by pasting color swatches (at least ¾″ square) at the bottom of the mechanical board, and indicating the color for each overlay on a label attached to it. After the plates are made and put on the press, the printing inks are mixed to match the color swatches. To insure accurate color matching, most designers use the Pantone Matching System (PMS). In this system, the designer selects the desired colors from a book which contains number-coded swatches of over 500 colors, and pastes these swatches on the mechanical. The printer is able to match the specified colors by referring to the Pantone ink-mixing formulas for them.

Pantone Color Specifier. Printer's Edition in front; Designer's Edition in rear.

Book jacket printed in four flat colors: black, violet, red, and green. Because this chapter is printed in four-color process, mixtures of process colors have been used to simulate the Pantone colors on the actual jacket. The mechanical for the front of this jacket is shown on the facing page. Normally, a book jacket mechanical would also include the front flap, spine, back, and back flap, but space does not permit that here.

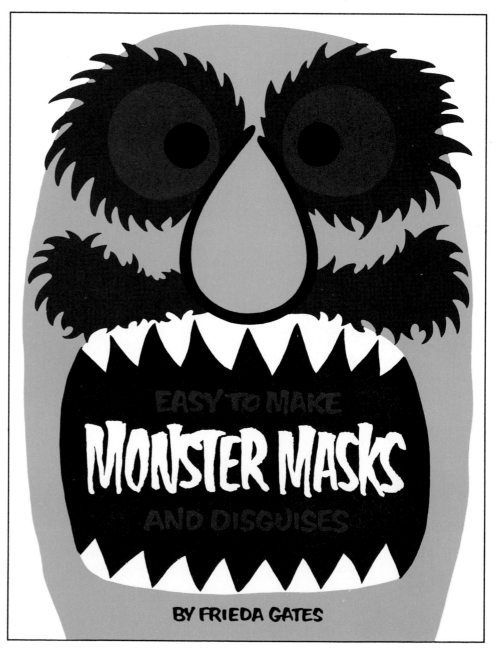

BLACK PLATE

VIOLET PLATE

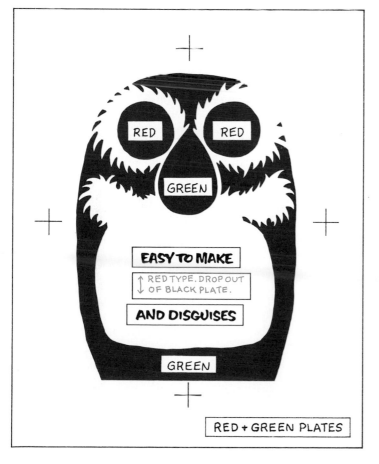

RED + GREEN PLATES

(Above left) Black color separation on illustration board. This is the key mechanical. Art is executed in black ink directly on the board, and type proofs (in this case, photostats of hand lettering) are pasted on. The white edges of the negative stat for "Monster Masks" must be blackened so that they will not reproduce. Paste all the color swatches on the key mechanical, and use a self-adhesive label on each separation to identify its printing color (specifications written directly on transparent overlays would be hard to read).

(Above right) Violet color separation on acetate or drafting film. Art is executed in red ink or red color film. Where a shape on one separation abuts a shape on another separation, be sure to provide a slight overlap, or "trap." If the printing colors of the abutting shapes are different in value, make the darker-colored shape accurate in size, and "spread" the size of the lighter-colored shape.

(Left) Red and green color separations, executed in the same way as described for the violet color separation. Since the red and green shapes do not abut, they can be combined on one overlay. The printer will make two negatives of this overlay and opaque the unwanted shapes to achieve separate red and green negatives. A photostat of the hand lettering is pasted in position on the overlay, with a non-reproducing notation of its color and a reminder to drop it out of the black plate (type and other intricate art cannot be accurately color-separated by the artist; the printer must do it photographically). Black is the only printing ink color that completely masks underlying colors. Thus, the black pupil shapes need not be dropped out of the red eyes; the black simply overprints the red.

Note: The reason for using transparent red on transparent overlays is so that the art elements can be accurately sized and positioned. Since the printer backs the overlays with white and shoots them as opaque copy, type proofs and other opaque art can be pasted on them. Black ink may also be used directly on overlays if hairline overlapping is not involved.

Keyline Color Separation. This method of color separation for flat color printing is more expensive than the overlay method and is generally used only when the overlay method is unsuitable, such as where the sizes or shapes of butted colors are too small or too intricate to be accurately executed and/or overlapped. The art for all colors is placed on the key mechanical, and the printer separates the art for each printing plate through camera and/or stripping techniques.

The art for one color (usually black) is executed in solid black shapes, and the art for the other colors is executed in red or black outlines. The printer makes as many negatives as there are colors, and on each negative he removes and completes imagery as necessary to achieve a separate negative for each color. Since the outlines are common to both abutting colors, their thickness determines the amount of overlap. To achieve a consistent line of the proper thickness, use a technical pen with a .25mm to .35mm point.

Book cover printed in four flat colors: process yellow, process red (magenta), process blue (cyan), and black. By overprinting these four colors in various combinations of tints and solids, eleven colors were achieved.

Portion of keyline mechanical extending to the bleed for the front cover (the non-repro blue outline indicates the actual cover size). Keyline art is executed in red, either directly on the mechanical board, or separately on bristol board and then pasted up. Black keylines may also be used, but the printer must be told that they are holding lines so that they will not be printed as black outlines. Color and tint specifications are indicated on the tissue overlay as shown on page 144.

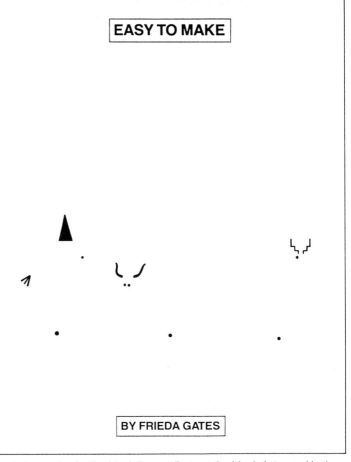

Acetate overlay for the black line art (but not the black tints used in the keyline shapes). This black line art could be executed on the keyline mechanical as solid black shapes, but since it overprints the other colors and registration is therefore not critical, platemaking costs are reduced by separating it from the other art.

Fake Color Process Printing. Full-color, continuous-tone illustrations can be economically reproduced by hand-separating the four process colors, thus eliminating the need for photomechanical color separation, which is quite expensive. The art for each color is executed in continuous tones of black & white on the key mechanical and overlays, using a color guide that shows all possible overprinting combinations of process colors and tints. To make the printing plates, the printer merely photographs the mechanical and overlays in halftone.

Hand-separation of the four process colors is a difficult technique, since the color percentages indicated in the color guide must be converted to comparable gray values on the art. A gray scale with 10 percent gradations is necessary for this conversion.

A simpler variation of this technique is to execute the black art in continuous-tone on the key mechanical, and the color art in flat colors and tints on the overlays. The overlay art is executed in solid red shapes with ink and/or color film. If two shapes abut on the same overlay, however, one of them must be in outline. Use a process color guide to determine tint percentages. See *Screen Tints,* page 136, and *The Tissue Overlay*, page 144, for the methods of specifying tint percentages.

Process colors can also be used for flat color printing where the art is entirely line copy. The use of the four process colors is usually preferable to four colors mixed by the printer because an unlimited range of colors can be achieved by overprinting various combinations of tints and solids. The mechanical preparation is the same as described in the preceding paragraph, the only difference being that the black copy is line rather than continuous-tone. The book cover on the preceding page employs this method.

(Top right) In this illustration, the black is continuous-tone and the colors (yellow and magenta) are flat tints and solids. *The Walking Coat* (1980) by Pauline Watson. Illustrated by Tomie De Paola.

(Right) In this four-color illustration, the tonal modulations were achieved with stippling and thus did not require halftone screening. *Selected Writings of E.T.A. Hoffman* (1969), illustrated by Jacob Landau.

Glossary

Acetate overlay. A transparent plastic sheet hinged over the mechanical for color separation.

Adhesive binding. See *Perfect binding.*

Ampersand. The symbol & used in place of *and.* It is the Latin word *et,* which means *and.*

Ascender. The portion of a lower case letter that extends above the x-height.

Author's Alteration (AA). In proofreading, any alteration which is not a *printer's error (PE).* The *printer* refers to the typesetter.

Backbone. See *Spine.*

Back matter. In books, any information following the main text, such as the index, bibliography, and picture credits.

Bad break. In type, an incorrect or undesirable end-of-line hyphenation. Also, a *widow* (which see).

Baseline. The imaginary line upon which capitals and most lower case letters stand.

Base mechanical. See *Key mechanical.*

Benday process. An obsolete system for applying flat tints to printing plates. Now superseded by *screen tints* (which see).

Binding. The process of joining separate sheets into pamphlet, magazine, or book form. Also, the cover of a book.

Binding board. Stiff cardboard used for the covers of hardcover books.

Bleed. The portion of a printed image that extends beyond the trim edge of a sheet or page.

Blow-up. An enlargement of artwork.

Blues. Pre-press proofs made on blueprint or brownprint paper.

Blurb. Summarized information about a book or author, usually on the jacket. Also, a *caption.* Also, the balloon and enclosed text in a comic strip.

Body type. See *Text type.*

Bold face (BF). A heavy version of a text-weight typeface.

Bristol board. In printing paper, a stiff board in many textures, colors, and weights. In drawing paper, a white kid or plate finish paper in many weights. The different weights in drawing bristol are achieved by laminating sheets together (1 ply to 5 ply).

Bulk. The thickness of paper, usually measured by the number of pages per inch (PPI). To *bulk-up* means to use heavier paper to make a book thicker.

Camera-ready. Finished art or copy that is ready to be photographed for platemaking.

Caps and small caps (C&SC). Two sizes of capitals in the same point size. Small caps are the same height as the x-height of the lower case letters.

Caption. The text accompanying illustrations or photographs.

Casebound. See *Edition binding.*

Casting off. See *Copyfitting.*

Character count. The total number of characters in typewritten or typeset copy.

Chrome. A color transparency, such as Kodachrome.

Cold type. A term used to differentiate between metal keyboard composition (hot type) and photographic keyboard composition (cold type). See *Linotype, Phototypesetting,* and *Hot type.*

Collating. The arranging of sheets or signatures in correct sequence. Also called *gathering.*

Colophon. A publisher's symbol or trademark. Also, an inscription placed usually at the end of a book listing the editor, designer, typographer, printer, paper, etc.

"Color." The overall tone of type or other graphic elements on a page. "Color" refers to the optical mixture of black and white or actual color and white.

Color breaks. Color shapes pre-separated by the artist with overlays or keylines. Also called *mechanical color separation* (which see).

Color correction. In process color printing, modifying the dot sizes on the color separations to improve color rendition.

Color matching system. A method of specifying flat color by using standardized printing ink formulas and coded color swatches.

Color process. See *process color printing.*

Color separation. The separating of full-color art into the four process colors by means of color filters, either photographically or by electronic scanning. Also see *Mechanical color separation.*

Color swatch. A color sample attached to the mechanical, to be matched in printing ink.

Composition. See *Typesetting.*

Compositor. A person who sets type. Also called a *typesetter.*

Comprehensive (comp). A tightly-rendered layout that accurately simulates the printed piece.

Continuous-tone copy. Copy that has a full range of gradated tones, such as wash drawings and photographs.

Copy. In graphic design, reading matter as opposed to art. In printing, anything to be reproduced, including reading matter and art.

Copyfitting. The process of determining the amount of space it will take to set copy in a specific type size and style. Also see *Type specifications.*

Crawling. The contraction of ink or other medium on a slick surface such as acetate.

Crop. To eliminate unwanted portions of copy. Cropping is indicated on the original art with *crop marks* (which see).

Crop marks. Short, fine lines drawn on the copy to indicate the cropped area. Also called *trim marks* when used to indicate the trim size of a printed sheet.

Cyan (Process blue). One of the four *process inks* (which see) used in full-color printing.

Descender. That portion of a letter that extends below the baseline.

Diazoprint. A black & white direct-positive contact photoprint on paper or film. Used for producing positive proofs from film positives, as in phototypesetting.

Display type. Any bold, decorative, or large type generally used for headlines, titles, and other display purposes, as opposed to *text type* (which see).

Double-page spread. Two facing pages. More commonly called a *spread.*

Dropout halftone. In photographs, a halftone in which the small dots in the highlight areas have been removed. In pencil, charcoal, and wash drawings, a halftone in which the small dots in the non-image, or blank paper, areas have been removed.

Dropout type. Type dropped out of a solid or screened background so that it is the color of the paper.

Dummy. A mock-up of a book, package, display, folder, etc. It may be either blank or graphically rendered. In publishing, the unbound page layouts for a book are also called a dummy.

Duotone. A two-color halftone reproduction made from one-color continuous-tone copy, such as a black & white photo or wash drawing. Usually, one plate is printed in black or a dark color, and the other in a light color.

Dye transfer. A full-color photographic paper print made from any transparent or reflective copy.

Edition binding. A hardcover book with sewn signatures and end papers (which see). Also called *hardcover* or *casebound.*

Ellipsis. In type, any intentional omission of one or more words, usually indicated by three dots (. . .). The plural is *ellipses.*

Embossing. Impressing a relief image in paper or other material, either in conjunction with a printed image, or on blank paper (blind embossing).

Em quad. Commonly called an *em*. A unit of space that is the square of the type size being used. For example, in 12 point type an em is 12 points wide, in 10 point type an em is 10 points wide, etc.

End-of-line decisions. In typesetting, decisions regarding hyphenation and justification.

End papers. In hardcover books, the sheets that attach to the insides of the covers and the binding edges of the first and last pages.

En quad. Commonly called an *en*. A unit of space that is one half the width of an *em* (which see).

Fake color process. Full-color printing done from hand-rendered color separations. Usually the separations are executed in continuous tones of black and white, but line techniques may also be employed.

Finished art. Art or copy to be photographed for reproduction, as opposed to layouts, comps, sketches, etc.

First proof. See *Galley proof.*

Flat. The assemblage of film negatives and/or positives on goldenrod paper. It is used to image the sensitized printing plate.

Flat color printing. The method of color printing in which the copy is color-separated on the mechanical, and printing ink colors are mixed to the designer's specifications. This is as opposed to *process color printing* (which see).

Flat-tint halftone. A halftone printed over a screen tint of another color. Also called a *fake duotone.*

Flop. To reverse an image from left to right (mirror image).

Flush cover. A book or booklet cover the same size as the enclosed pages, such as in paperbacks. Also see *Overhang cover.*

Flush left (or right). Type set to line up at the left (or right) of the column.

Folio. The page number. Also, a sheet of paper folded once to make a 4-page signature.

Font. See *Type font.*

Foot. The bottom of a sheet or page. The top is called the *head.*

Foreword. A statement, usually written by someone other than the author, preceding the text of a book.

Format. The size, layout system, and other design factors of a page, book, etc.

Fountain. The ink reservoir on a printing press. Also, in offset lithography, the water reservoir on a press.

Four-color process. See *Process color printing.*

Frisket. A mask or stencil made of paper, film, or other material to block out or protect portions of plates or artwork.

Frontispiece. An illustration or photo on the page preceding the title page.

Front matter. In books, any information preceding the main text, such as the title, table of contents, and preface.

Full color. See *Process color printing.*

Galley Proof. Also called a *rough* or *first* proof. The first proof made after type is set. After it has been proofread and errors have been corrected, a *reproduction proof* (which see) is made.

Gathering. See *Collating.*

Goldenrod. A yellow-orange paper used for assembling film negatives and positives for exposure to the printing plate. The completed assemblage is called the *flat.*

Grain. In paper, the predominant direction of the fibers. Paper tears and folds straighter with the grain than across the grain.

Gray scale. A strip containing gray tones from white to black, usually in 10 percent increments. Used to measure the tone or value of grays and colors to insure proper reproduction.

Gutter. The margin on the binding side of a page. Also, the space between two columns of type.

Hairline. A very thin line or space. The finest line that can be reproduced.

Half-title page. In hardcover books, the first page after the endpaper. In paperback and other types of bindings, usually page 3 but sometimes page 1. The use of a half-title (the title in a small size) is a tradition but not a necessity.

Halftone. Continuous-tone copy that has been photomechanically converted to a pattern of tiny dots of various sizes through the use of a halftone screen.

Hardcover. Usually refers to a sewn-signature book with hardcovers (see *Edition binding*). In some hardcover books, however, the pages are held together with adhesive (see *Perfect binding*).

Head. The top of a sheet or page. The bottom is called the *foot.*

Heading. Words set in a different size and/or style than the text. Also called a *head.* If there are two headings, the second in importance is called a *subhead.* If there are many types of headings in a book, they may be designated as *A heads, B heads, C heads,* etc.

Hickey. A spot or imperfection on a printed piece due to lint, bits of ink skin, etc. on the plate or offset blanket.

Highlight halftone. See *Dropout halftone.*

Holding lines. Outlines drawn on the mechanical to indicate the position of halftones, screen tints, etc. Usually red, but may be black.

Hot type. Typesetting in which the type is cast in molten metal at the time of composition, such as Linotype (which see) and Monotype, as opposed to photographic *cold type* (which see).

Imposition. The arrangement and positioning of pages or other units of a job so that they fit the press sheet properly.

Introduction. A statement that introduces the subject or purpose of a book.

Italic. Slanted type with cursive, or flowing, strokes. Also see *Roman.*

Jacket. The printed wrapper on a hardcover book. Also called a *dust cover.*

Justify. To make lines of type equal in width (flush left and right) by adjusting the space between words.

Kerning. To space certain letter combinations closer than normal for a better fit.

Key. To code original copy and its layout or mechanical position with a number and/or letter.

Keyline. A mechanical in which color and screen tint shapes are drawn in outline on the board rather than on acetate overlays.

Key mechanical, negative, or plate. In color printing, the mechanical, negative, or plate that contains the basic format of the job and is used as a guide for registering the other colors.

Lamination. A transparent plastic liquid or film applied to a printed sheet, such as a book jacket, for appearance and durability.

Lap. Also called *trap.* In color printing, the slight overlap that occurs where colors abut. Also see *Register* and *Spreading or Shrinking.*

Layout. A hand-rendered design for a printed piece. The four types of layouts are (in order of degree of finish): thumbnail sketches, rough layouts, finished layouts, and comprehensive layouts, or comps.

Lead-in. One or more words at the beginning of a block of copy set in a different typeface.

Leading. (Pronounced *ledding.*) The amount of additional space (measured in points) placed between lines of type. Also called *linespacing.*

Ligature. In certain typefaces, two or three characters specially joined or fitted together, such as *ff, fi, ffl,* etc.

Line conversion. Continuous-tone copy that has been converted to line copy through the use of a screen that creates such textures as crosshatching, stippling, and woodgrain. It is similar to a *velox* (which see).

Line copy. Any copy composed of solid blacks and whites with no tonal gradations.

Line gauge. See *Type gauge.*

Line spacing. See *Leading.*

Linotype. The trade name for a keyboard-operated typesetting machine that casts lines of type in hot metal. Now largely superseded by phototypesetting (which see).

Lower case. The small letters of an alphabet, as opposed to capitals.

Magenta (Process red). One of the four *process inks* (which see) used in full-color printing.

Manuscript. The original typewritten copy to be set in type. Also called *copy, typescript,* or *script.* The abbreviation is *Ms.* (Plural is Mss.)

Margins. The blank borders of a page, called *head* (top), *foot* (bottom), *outside* (trim side), and *inside* or *gutter* (binding side).

Mark up. To mark copy with type specifications.

Mask. Paper, film, or other material used to block out selected portions of an image. Also see *Frisket.*

Match color. Another term for *flat color printing* (which see).

Measure. In typesetting, the pica width of a line or column of type.

Mechanical. A camera-ready assembly containing all copy pasted or executed in printing position. Also called a *paste-up* or *keyline.*

Mechanical binding. A binding method employing a mechanical device, such as a metal or plastic coil.

Mechanical color separation. The pre-separation of colors by the designer on the mechanical, either with overlays or by keylining. Also see *Color separation.*

Modern Style type. A style category typified by strong contrast between thick and thin strokes, unbracketed serifs, and symmetrically-balanced swells. Bodoni is a typical Modern Style type.

Negative. In photography, a tone reversal of the original on film, paper, glass, etc., as opposed to a *positive.*

Oblong. A book that is bound on its short dimension. When bound on its long dimension it is called *upright.*

Offset lithography. Commonly called *offset.* A planographic printing process in which the printing and non-printing areas of the plate are on the same level, or plane. The plate is chemically treated to make the printing areas ink-receptive, and the non-printing areas water receptive. The printing plate image is first "offset" onto a rubber blanket, and from there onto the paper. Almost all children's books are printed by this process.

Old Style type. A style category typified by mild contrast between thick and thin strokes, bracketed serifs, and off-center swells. Caslon is a typical Old Style type.

Opaque. Non-transparent. Also, to block out transparent portions of film. Also, the medium used for opaquing film.

Overhang cover. A cover larger than the enclosed pages, as opposed to a *flush cover* (which see).

Overlay. See *Acetate overlay* and *Tissue overlay.*

Overprinting. Printing over an area that has already been printed with another color. Not to be confused with *surprinting* (which see).

Pagination. Numbering the pages of a book.

Pantone Matching System (PMS). The brand name for a *color-matching system* (which see).

Paste-up. An assembly of various elements with adhesive, usually rubber cement. Also, another term for *mechanical* (which see).

Perfect binding. A binding method in which the pages and cover are held together with adhesive only. Also called *adhesive binding.*

Photocopy. A photographic copy of a print or transparency.

Photolettering. Also called *photodisplay.* A photographic method of setting display sizes of type and lettering on paper or film.

Photomechanical. Pertaining to any platemaking process in which the plate is imaged photographically.

Photostat. A photographic reproduction method in which paper prints, both negative and positive, are made directly from original copy.

Phototypesetting. A keyboard composition system that utilizes photographic, electronic, and mechanical components to produce letter images on photosensitive film or paper.

Pica. A typographic measurement, approximately 1/6 of an inch. There are 12 points in a pica.

Point. A typographic measurement, approximately 1/72 of an inch. There are 12 points in a pica. Also, a thickness measure for paper and board. In this use, one point is one mil (.001").

Positive. In photography, a reproduction on film, paper, glass, etc. that matches the tones of the original, as opposed to a *negative.*

Preface. A statement, usually by the author, that precedes the introduction of a book. Also see *Foreword* and *Introduction.*

Pre-press proof. A proof made from the *flat* (which see) on photosensitive paper or film before the plate is made. Also see *Blues.*

Press proof. In color printing, a proof made from the printing plates, either on a proofing press or at the beginning of the run on a production press. Usually, most jobs require only *pre-press proofs* (which see).

Press run. The number of sheets or copies to be printed.

Printer's error (PE). An error made by the typesetter, as opposed to an error or alteration made by the author or editor (AA).

Process color printing. Also called *full-color* or *four-color process printing.* The method of reproducing full-color copy by printing it in process inks (which see). Also see *Color separation.*

Process inks. The four special inks used in process color printing: yellow, magenta (red), cyan (blue), and black.

Progressive proofs (or progs). In process color printing, proofs made from the four color separations or plates, printed separately and progressively overprinted.

Proof. A trial print taken from a printing plate, flat, or type.

Proofreaders' marks. Symbols and abbreviations used to indicate corrections and alterations in copy.

Ragged right (or left). In type, lines of varying length vertically aligned, or flush, on one side and thus unaligned on the other. Usually specified as *flush left/ragged right* or *flush right/ragged left.* Such a column is called *unjustified.*

Recto. The right-hand page of a book, as opposed to *verso,* or the left-hand page.

Register. The correct relative position of two or more negatives, printing plates, impressions, etc., so that they align exactly with each other.

Register marks. Small crosses or other similar marks placed on copy to facilitate the registering of overlays, negatives, printing plates, etc.

Reproduction proof (or repro). In type, a final, high quality proof made following corrections indicated on the rough or galley proof. It is pasted on the mechanical and used for reproduction.

Retouching. The correcting or altering of artwork, photographs, negatives, etc.

Reverse. To reverse tonal values, as with a negative.

Reverse type. See *Dropout type.*

Roman. Upright type of any style, as opposed to *italic* (which see). Less frequently, a typeface based on early Roman letterforms.

Rough layout. See *Layout.*

Rough proof. See *Galley proof.*

Run in. Type to be set without paragraph breaks.

Running head. A title or other heading that runs at the top of every page.

Saddle-wire stitching. A method of binding in which staples are inserted through the spine and clinched in the centerfold.

Sans Serif type. A style category for any type without (sans) serifs. Helvetica is a typical Sans Serif type.

Scaling. Determining the ratio of enlargement or reduction.

Screen. A sheet of glass or film having a dot pattern and used to make halftones (which see).

Screen tint. A flat, unmodulated tint or tone usually achieved by stripping a piece of dot-pattern film on the platemaker's negative. Also called a *Benday tint, halftone tint,* or *flat tint.* Also see *Shading film.*

Separation. See *Color separation* and *Mechanical color separation.*

Serif. The short cross-stroke, or spur, at the end of a letter stroke.

Set solid. Lines of type set with no leading, or additional space, between lines.

Sewed soft cover. A paperback book with sewn signatures.

Shading film. A dot-pattern film applied to artwork to achieve tints. Also see *Screen tint.*

Sheet-fed. A press that prints sheets rather than a *web,* or continuous roll, of paper.

Shooting copy. Copy to be photographed for reproduction. Also, the act of photographing copy.

Side-sewing. A method of binding in which the signatures are sewn adjacent to the binding edge with thread.

Side-wire stitching. A method of binding in which staples are inserted from the front to the back of the book, about ⅛″ in from the binding edge.

Signature. One sheet of paper printed on both sides and folded and trimmed in such a way that it results in four or more consecutively-ordered pages.

Silhouette halftone. A halftone in which the background has been eliminated.

Small capitals (SC). Capitals that are the x-height (which see) of the lower case letters of the same point size.

Smyth-sewing. A method of binding in which the signatures are sewn through the centerfold with thread.

Soft cover. A paperback book.

Solid color. A printed area with 100% ink coverage, as opposed to areas containing screen tints.

Spec (Pronounced *speck*). Short for *specify* or *specification.* For example, to spec type means to write the type specifications on the copy.

Spine. The binding side of a book. Also called *backbone.*

Spiral binding. See *Mechanical binding.*

Spread. Two facing pages. Also called *two-page spread* or *double spread.*

Spreading or shrinking. In color printing, to photographically alter the size of an image slightly to achieve sufficient *lap* (which see).

Square-finish halftone. A halftone having four straight sides and squared corners, either rectangular or square in shape. Usually called a *square halftone.*

Stamping. The imprinting of book covers with a relief-imaged die, and usually in conjunction with ink or metal foil. If no ink or foil is used, it is called *blind stamping.*

Stripping. The assembling of film negatives and/or positives on a *flat* (which see).

Surprinting. Line copy superimposed over screened copy on the same printing plate. Not to be confused with *overprinting,* which involves two printing plates.

Text type. Small sizes of very legible type generally used for the main body of text, as opposed to *display type* (which see).

Thumbnail. A rough, miniature layout sketch.

Tint. A *screen tint* (which see). Also, to add white to a color.

Tissue overlay. A sheet of tracing or layout paper hinged over artwork for protection and marking specifications.

Title page. The page of a book that carries the title, author's name, and publisher's name.

Transfer type. Acetate film backed with typeface alphabets that can be transferred to another surface by rubbing with a stylus.

Trim marks. Short, fine lines drawn on the mechanical to indicate the trim size of the printed sheet. Also called *crop marks.*

Type font. The complete assortment of characters for one size of a typeface, which includes capitals, lower case, figures, and punctuation marks.

Type gauge. A scale containing typographic measurements such as points, picas, and agate lines. Also, a *line gauge,* which contains scales for measuring line depths of columns.

Typesetting. Also called *composition.* The composing of type by any method.

Type specifications. Typesetting information written on the manuscript. Also called *type specs* (pronounced "specks"). Also see *Copyfitting.*

Typo. A typographic error, either on the manuscript or on the type proof.

Typographer. A company that specializes in typesetting. Persons who set type are called *typesetters* or *compositors.*

Upper case. Capital letters, as opposed to lower case, or small, letters.

Upright. A book that is bound on its long dimension. When bound on its short dimension it is called *oblong.*

Value. The lightness or darkness of a color or tone of gray. It is measured with a *gray scale* (which see) and stated by percentage.

Velox. A halftone printed on photographic paper, to be pasted on the mechanical as line copy. Also see *Line conversion.*

Verso. The left-hand page of a book, as opposed to *recto,* or the right-hand page.

Vignette halftone. A halftone in which the edges fade into the white of the paper.

Wash drawing. A drawing done with black ink, dye, or watercolor, diluted to various degrees to produce a complete range of tonal gradations.

Web-fed. A press that prints a continuous roll, or web, or paper, as opposed to a sheet-fed press.

Widow. A single word in the last line of a paragraph; the last line of a paragraph carried over to the next page; the first line of a paragraph at the bottom of a page; or any other situation where a word or line stands alone.

Wrong font (WF). In typesetting, the erroneous inclusion of a letter or letters from another font.

Xerography. A copying process that uses static electricity to form an image, such as a Xerox machine.

x-height. The height of lower case letters without ascenders or descenders.

Bibliography

A number of these titles overlap from one category to another.

HISTORY

Cobwebs To Catch Flies. Illustrated Books for the Nursery and Schoolroom 1700-1900. Joyce Irene Whalley. University of California Press, 1975.

Early Children's Books and Their Illustration. The Pierpont Morgan Library. David R. Godine, 1975.

From Primer to Pleasure in Reading, Mary F. Thwaite. The Horn Book, Inc., 1972.

Pictures and Stories from Forgotten Children's Books. Arnold Arnold. Dover Publications, Inc., 1969.

The Oxford Companion to Children's Literature. Humphrey Carpenter & Marie Prichard. Oxford University Press, 1984.

Three Centuries of Children's Books in Europe. Bettina Hurlimann. World Publishing Co., 1967.

Written For Children. John Rowe Townsend. J.B. Lippincott Company, 1975.

DISCOURSE

American Picturebooks from Noah's Ark to the Beast Within. Barbara Bader. Macmillan Publishing Co., Inc., 1976.

Children & Books. Zena Sutherland, Dianne L. Monson, May Hill Arbuthnot. Scott, Foresman and Company, 1981.

Children And Their Literature. Constantine Georgiou. Prentice-Hall, 1969.

Choosing Books for Children. Betsy Hearne. Laurel Books, Dell Publishing Co., Inc., 1981.

Dick & Jane As Victims. An Analysis. Women on Words & Images, Princeton, NJ, 1975.

Down The Rabbit Hole. Selma G. Lanes. Atheneum, 1976.

The Unreluctant Years. Lillian H. Smith. Viking Compass Book, 1970.

The Uses of Enchantment. Bruno Bettelheim. Vintage Books, Random House, 1975.

WRITING

The Children's Picture Book, How To Write It, How To Sell It. Ellen E.M. Roberts. Writer's Digest Books, 1981.

The Elements of Style. William Strunk, Jr. & E.B. White. Macmillan Publishing Co., 1959.

How To Write A Children's Book & Get It Published. Barbara Seuling. Charles Scribner's Sons, 1984.

How To Write A Story. Bentz Plagemann. Lothrop, Lee & Shepard Co., 1971.

Life Into Language. Eric W. Johnson. Bantam, 1976.

The Way To Write For Children: An Introduction to the Craft. Joan Aiken. St. Martin's Press, 1982.

Writing Books for Children. Jane Yolen. The Writer, Inc., 1983.

Writing For Children & Teenagers. Lee Wyndham, revised by Arnold Madison. Writer's Digest Books, 1980.

Writing For The Juvenile And Teenage Market. Jane Fitz-Randolph. Funk & Wagnalls, 1969.

Writing the Natural Way. Gabriele Lusser Rico. J.P. Tarcher, Inc. Distributed by Houghton Mifflin Company, 1983.

Writing The Story Of Your Life. Ruth Kanin. Hawthorn/Dutton, 1981.

ILLUSTRATION

The Artist's Handbook of Materials & Techniques. Ralph Mayer. The Viking Press, 1940.

The Complete Guide To Illustration And Design. Edited by Terence Dalley. Chartweil Books Inc., 1981.

The Illustrated Book: Its Art and Craft. Diana Klemin. Clarkson N. Potter, Inc. Distributed by Crown, 1970.

Illustrating Children's Books. Henry Clarence Pitz. Watson-Guptill Publications, 1967.

Printmaking, History & Process. Donald Saff. Holt, Rinehart & Winston, 1978.

A Treasury of The Great Children's Book Illustrators. Susan E. Meyer. Harry N. Abrams, Inc., 1983.

The Twentieth Century Book. John Lewis. Reinhold Publishing, 1967.

PRODUCTION AND TYPOGRAPHY

Color Atlas. Harald Kueppers. Barron's Educational Series, Inc., 1982.

Graphic Design Studio Procedures. David Gates. Lloyd-Simone Publishing Company, 1982.

Pocket Pal: A Graphic Arts Production Handbook. International Paper Company, 1983.

Type. A Type Specimen Book. David Gates. Watson-Guptill Publications, 1973.

Type & Typography. A Type Specimen Book. Ben Rosen. Van Nostrand Reinhold, 1963.

PUBLISHING

Alternative Press Publishers of Children's Books. The Cooperative Children's Book Center. Revised periodically.

The Art and Science of Book Publishing. Herbert S. Bailey, Jr. University of Texas Press, 1970.

Book Publishing: What it is, What it does. John P. Dessauer. Bowker, 1981.

The Dictionary of Publishing. David Brownstone and Irene Franck. Van Nostrand Reinhold, 1982.

How to Get Happily Published: A Complete and Candid Guide. Judith Appelbaum and Nancy Evans. Harper & Row and NAL, 1978.

How to Publish Your Own Book. L.W. Mueller. Harlo Press, 1978.

Into Print: A Practical Guide to Writing, Illustrating, and Publishing. Mary Hill and Wendell Cochran. William Kaufman, 1977.

The Publish-it-Yourself Handbook. Bill Henderson. The Pushcart Book Press, 1973.

The Self-publishing Manual: How to Write, Print, & Sell Your Own Book. Dan Poynter. Para Publishing, 1980.

The Writer Publisher. Charles N. Aronson. Charles N. Aronson, 1976.

Writer's Survival Manual: The Complete Guide to Getting Your Book Published Right. Carol Meyer. Crown, 1982.

LEGALITIES

Legal Guide for the Visual Artist. Tad Crawford. Hawthorn Books, Inc., 1977.

The Writer's Legal Guide. Tad Crawford. Hawthorn Books, Inc., 1975.

Illustration Credits

ADDISON-WESLEY PUBLISHING COMPANY Norma Farber: from *Six Impossible Things Before Breakfast*, copyright © 1977. Reprinted with permission.

ERNEST BENN Ed Young: from *The Lion and the Mouse*, adapted by Ed Young. Copyright © 1979 by Ed Young.

BOBBS-MERRILL CO. Frank Bozzo: from *The Beasts of Never*, by Georgess McHargue. Illustrations copyright © 1968 by Frank Bozzo.

BOWMAR Jay Ells: from *Spoiled Tomatoes*, by Bill Martin Jr., copyright © 1970 by Bill Martin Jr.; John Rombola: from *Freedom's Apple Tree*, by Bill Martin Jr., copyright © 1970 by Bill Martin Jr.; Symeon Shimin: from *I am Freedom's Child*, by Bill Martin Jr.; copyright © 1970 by Bill Martin Jr.

ROSEMARY CAPOZZA Susan J. Ghezzi: from *Candy Canes and Dandy Planes*, by Rosemary Capozza. Copyright © 1981 by Rosemary Capozza.

CAROUSEL CREATIONS Storm: from *Creative Carousel Coloring Book*, by Storm, copyright © 1984 by Storm R. Hammond.

THE CHAMBERLAIN PRESS Sarah Chamberlain: from *Stone Soup*, by Kenneth Jones. Illustrations copyright © 1985 by Sarah Chamberlain.

CLARION BOOKS—TICKNOR & FIELDS: A HOUGHTON MIFFLIN COMPANY George Ancona: from *Bananas*, by George Ancona, copyright © 1982 by George Ancona.

COWARD, McCANN & GEOGHEGAN, INC. Fred Brenner: from *Little One Inch*, by Barbara Brenner. Illustrations copyright © 1977 by Fred Brenner; Murray Tinkelman: from *Backyard Bestiary*, by Rhoda Blumberg. Illustrations copyright © 1979 by Murray Tinkelman; Margot Tomes: from *This Time, Tempe Wick?*, by Patricia Lee Gauch. Illustrations copyright © 1974 by Margot Tomes; Jerry Pinkney: from *Femi and Old Grandaddie*, by Adjai Robinson. copyright © 1972 by Jerry Pinkney.

THOMAS Y. CROWELL COMPANY Ed Emberley: from *The Big Dipper*, by Franklyn M. Branley. Illustrations copyright © 1962 by Ed Emberley; Sean Morrison: from *Armor*, by Sean Morrison, copyright © 1963 by Sean Morrison.

THE DIAL PRESS Leo & Diane Dillon: from *Why Mosquitoes Buzz in People's Ears—A West African Tale*, retold by Verna Aardema. Illustrations copyright © 1975 by Leo & Diane Dillon.

DOUBLEDAY & COMPANY, INC. James Barkley: from *Winds*, by Mary O'Neill. Illustrations copyright © 1970 by James Barkley.

DOVER PUBLICATIONS, INC. Arnold Arnold: from *Pictures and Stories from Forgotten Children's Books*, copyright © 1969.

E.P. DUTTON & CO., INC. George Ancona: from *Dancing Is*, by George Ancona. Copyright © 1981 by George Ancona; Leo & Diane Dillon: from *Gassire's Lute*, translated and adapted by Alta Jablow. Illustrations copyright © 1971 by Leo & Diane Dillon.

FOUR WINDS PRESS Fred Brenner: from *The Tremendous Tree Book*, by May Garelick and Barbara Brenner. Illustrations copyright © 1979 by Fred Brenner; Pamela Caroll: from *Strange Creatures*, by Seymour Simon. Illustrations copyright © 1981 by Pamela Carroll; Erik Hilgerdt: from *I, Tut*, by Miriam Schlein. Illustrations copyright © 1979 by Erik Hilgerdt; Arnold Lobel: from *Miss Suzy*, by Miriam Young. Illustrations copyright © 1964 by Arnold Lobel; Bernice Myers: from *Not This Bear*, by Bernice Myers, copyright © 1968 by Bernice Myers.

GALLOPADE PUBLISHING GROUP Carole Marsh: from *The Mystery of the Biltmore House*, by Carole Marsh, copyright © 1982 by Carole Marsh.

GREENWILLOW BOOKS—A DIVISION OF WILLIAM MORROW & CO. Anita Lobel: from *A Treefull of Pigs*, by Arnold Lobel. Illustrations copyright © 1979 by Anita Lobel; Murray Tinkelman: from *Cowgirl*, by Murray Tinkelman, copyright © 1984 by Murray Tinkelman.

GROSSET & DUNLAP, INC. Ray Barber: from *Who Lives Inside?* by Lynda Graham Barber. Illustrations copyright © 1976 by Ray Barber. Reprinted by permission of the publisher.

HARCOURT BRACE JOVANOVICH, INC. Fritz Eichenberg: from *Dancing In The Moon—Counting Rhymes*, by Fritz Eichenberg. Copyright © 1955, 1983. Reproduced by permission; Douglas Gorsline: from *Sky Pioneers*, by Jeanne LeMonnier Gardner, copyright © 1963 by Jeanne Gardner.

HARPER & ROW, PUBLISHERS Dennis Kendrick: from *Scarlet Monster Lives Here*, by Marjorie Weinman Sharmat. Illustrations copyright © 1979 by Dennis Kendrick; Arnold Lobel: from *Frog and Toad Together*, by Arnold Lobel, copyright © 1972 by Arnold Lobel; Ed Young: from *The Mean Mouse and Other Mean Stories*, by Janice May Udry. Illustrations copyright © 1962 by Ed Young.

HARVEY HOUSE Beatrice Darwin: from *Sunflower Garden*, by Janice May Udry, copyright © 1969; Joan E. Drescher: from *Milton The Model A*, by Donald J. Sobol, copyright © 1971; from *Nonna*, by Jennifer Bartoli, copyright © 1975; Seymour Fleishman: from *The Boy Drummer of Vincennes*, by Carl Carmer, copyright © 1972; Frieda Gates: from *Foot and Feet*, by Carolyn Ramirez, copyright © 1973; from *Easy To Make Puppets*, by Frieda Gates, copyright © 1976; from *Easy To Make North American Indian Crafts*, by Frieda Gates, copyright © 1981, from *Easy To Make Monster Masks and Disguises*, by Frieda Gates, copyright © 1979; Marilyn Hirsh: from *The Pirate of New Orleans*, by Carl Carmer, copyright © 1975; Taylor Oughton: from *Whitey and Whiskers and Food*, by Constantine Georgiou, copyright © 1964; Sofia Pelkey: from *Holidays of Legend*, by Mildred H. Arthur, copyright © 1971; Robert Quackenbush: from *"D" Is For Rover*, by Leonore Klein, copyright © 1970; Carl Ramirez: from *Small As A Raisin, Big As The World*, by Carolyn Ramirez, copyright © 1961.

THE HERITAGE PRESS Lucille Corcos: from *The Complete Household Tales of Jakob and Wilhelm Grimm*, edited by Louis and Bryna Untermeyer. Illustrations copyright © 1962 by Lucille Corcos Levy.

HOLIDAY HOUSE Leonard Everett Fisher: from *The Seven Days of Creation*, adapted by Leonard Everett Fisher, copyright © 1981 by Leonard Everett Fisher.

HOLT, RINEHART & WINSTON, INC. Sal Murdocca: from *The Maestro Plays*, by Bill Martin Jr., copyright © 1970 by Bill Martin Jr.

J.B. LIPPINCOTT COMPANY Joel Schick: from *The Remarkable Ride of Israel Bissell, As Related by Molly the Crow*, by Alice Schick & Marjorie N. Allen. Illustrations copyright © 1976 by Joel Schick.

LLOYD-SIMONE PUBLISHING COMPANY David Gates: from *Graphic Design Studio Procedures*, by David Gates, copyright © 1982.

THE MACMILLAN COMPANY Jacob Landau: from *The Gold Bug and Other Tales*, by Edgar Allen Poe. Illustrations copyright © 1953 by Jacob Landau; Arnold Roth: from *The Witch Who Wasn't*, by Jane Yolen. Illustrations copyright © 1964 by Arnold Roth; John Trotta: from *Jinjero, The Scar-Faced Baboon*, by Cliff Jolly. Illustrations copyright © 1975 by John Trotta.

McGRAW-HILL BOOK COMPANY Jessica Ann Levy: from *She Was Nice To Mice*, by Alexandra Elizabeth Sheedy. Illustrations copyright © 1975 by Jessica Ann Levy.

WILLIAM MORROW & COMPANY Pamela Carroll: from *Nature's Light: The Story of Bioluminescence*, by Francine Jacobs. Illustrations copyright © 1974 by Pamela Carroll.

PARENTS MAGAZINE PRESS Leonard Kessler: from *Splish, Splash*, by Ethel and Leonard Kessler. Illustrations copyright © 1973 by Leonard Kessler.

PANTHEON BOOKS Jacob Landau: from *Our Eddie*, by Sulamith Ish-Kishor. Illustrations copyright © 1969 by Jacob Landau; Lucille Corcos: from *From Ungskah 1 to Oyaylee 10: A Counting Book For All Little Indians*, by Lucille Corcos, copyright © 1965 by Lucille Corcos Levy. Pantheon Books—division of Random House.

PHILOMEL BOOKS Ed Young: from *The Emperor and the Kite*, by Jane Yolen. Illustrations copyright © 1967 by Ed Young / World Publishing Company, reprinted by permission of Philomel Books; from *The Terrible Nung Gwama*, adapted by Ed Young, copyright © 1978 by Ed Young, reprinted by permission of Philomel Books.

PRENTICE-HALL, INC. Joan Lesikin: from *Down the Road*, by Joan Lesikin, copyright © 1978 by Joan Lesikin; Lee Lorenz: from *Big Gus and Little Gus*, by Lee Lorenz, copyright © 1983 by Lee Lorenz; Edna Miller: from *Mousekin's ABC*, by Edna Miller, copyright © 1972 by Edna Miller.

G.P. PUTNAM'S SONS Leonard Everett Fisher: from *A Jungle Jumble*, by Anico Surany. Illustrations copyright © 1966 by Leonard Everett Fisher; Trina Schart Hyman: from *On To Widecombe Fair*, by Patricia Lee Gauch. Illustrations copyright © 1978 by Trina Schart Hyman. Reprinted by permission of the publisher.

RAND McNALLY & COMPANY *The Real Mother Goose*, copyright © 1916, 1944 by Rand McNally & Company. Used by permission.

TUFFY BOOKS INC. Tony Tallarico: from *Shapes*, by Tony Tallarico, copyright © 1985 by Tony Tallarico & Tuffy Books, Inc. Used by permission.

UNIVERSITY OF CHICAGO PRESS Jacob Landau: from *Selected Writings of F.T.A. Hoffman*. Illustrations copyright © 1969 by Jacob Landau.

WALKER AND COMPANY Anthony Accardo: from *Bug Scanner and The Computer Mystery*, by Walter Olesky, copyright © 1983; Jan Adkins: from *Inside: seeing beneath the surface*, by Jan Adkins, copyright © 1975; Bernard Colonna: from *Star Ka'at*, by Andre Norton and Dorothy Madlee, copyright © 1976; Barbara Cooney: from *Seven Little Rabbits*, by John Becker, copyright © 1973; from *How The Hibernators Came To Bethlehem*, by Norma Farber, copyright © 1980; Tomie DePaola: from *The Walking Coat*, by Pauline Watson, copyright © 1980; Paul Frame: from *Fly Like An Eagle & Other Stories*, by Elizabeth Van Steenwyk, copyright © 1978; Antonio Frasconi: from *How The Left-Behind Beasts Built Ararat*, by Norma Farber, copyright © 1978; Frieda Gates: from *Monsters and Ghouls: Costume and Lore*, by Frieda Gates, copyright © 1980; from *Glove, Mitten and Sock Puppets*, by Frieda Gates, copyright © 1978; from *North American Indian Masks—Craft and Legend*, by Frieda Gates, copyright © 1982; Jean Jenkins: from *Star Ka'ats And The Plant People*, by Andre Norton and Dorothy Madlee, copyright © 1979; Sonia O. Lisker: from *Captain Hook, That's Me*, by Ada Litchfield, copyright © 1982; Dave Ross: from *Really Ridiculous Rabbit Riddles*, by Jeanne & Margaret Wallace and Dave Ross, copyright © 1978; Stanley Spardinsky: from *The Drought on Ziax II*, by John Morressy, copyright © 1978; Kaethe Zemach: from *The Wine Glass: A Passover Story*, by Norman Rosten, copyright © 1978. All of the preceding were used with the permission of the publisher.

WATSON-GUPTILL PUBLICATIONS David Gates: from *Type*, by David Gates, copyright © 1973.

FRANKLIN WATTS, INC. Eric Carle: from *The Rooster Who Set Out To See The World*, by Eric Carle, copyright © 1972 by Eric Carle.

WILLOW TREE PRESS Judith DeBiase: from *Daniel's Question*, by Elaine Sussman Allinson, copyright © 1981 by Elaine Sussman Allinson.

JOHN C. WINSTON COMPANY Jacob Landau: from *The Wonderful Cat of Cobbie Bean*, by Barbee Oliver Carleton. Illustrations copyright © 1957 by Jacob Landau.

THE WORLD PUBLISHING COMPANY Ed Young: from *The Golden Swans*, told by Kermit Krueger. Illustrations copyright © 1969 by Ed Young.

Index